MARCH ON WASHINGTON:

AUGUST 28, 1963

by

Thomas Gentile

New Day
Publications, Inc.

Published by NEW DAY PUBLICATIONS, INC.,
            P.O. Box 70161
            Washington, D.C.   20088
            202-832-0570
            302-539-0951

10 9 8 7 6 5 4 3 2 1

I.S.B.N.   0-9612328-0-3

Photo credits: Photri International, Lydia
                  Heston, Jessica Davidson,
                  Edward Scurlock, Seymour
                  Posner.

To those who marched

FOREWORD

I have used the term "Negro" throughout much of this narrative, as have most writers and historians in their narratives about this period of the Civil Rights movement, in attempting to place in perspective that particular era and to mesh with the quoted speeches and news accounts, all of which referred to blacks as "Negroes" in 1963. No offense, of course, is intended.

Certain information I wished to obtain for this book was unfortunately not available. The John F. Kennedy Library does not as yet have available for research the transcripts of President Kennedy's meetings with the civil rights leaders on June 22, and after the March on August 28. The transcripts of these critical meetings are important historical documents. The major television networks and the local Washington, D.C. television stations would not permit viewing of their file films of the March for research purposes. Twentieth Century Fox filmed the entire proceedings on August 28, 1963, but similarly declines to make available such important historical films to scholarly researchers. Albert Gollin declined to make available the specifics of his on site survey of the March participants, and thus we are aware only of his conclusions. Several imporatnt participants declined, through their offices, to be interviewed.

I do wish to thank the many persons who wrote to me with their recollections of the March on Washington, and those who spoke with me personally, particularly Bayard Rustin, Alan Raywid, Charlton Heston (whose wife Lydia provided me with an invaluable photographic essay of her own composition), Patrick Cardinal O'Boyle, Seymor Posner, and Mary Travers. I also wish to thank the several students at Northern Virginia Community College who assisted me in researching this book.

Several persons offered to read portions of the manuscript while it was being written, and provided constructive criticism, including Liz Sporkin of U.S.A. Today, Sheila Michaels Kessler, and Professor David Edelstein of Western Connecticut State College. Walter Naegle of the A. Philip Randolph Institute assisted me in going through the files of the March on Washington Committee, and personal papers of A. Philip Randolph and Bayard Rustin. William Johnson assisted me at the John F. Kennedy Library in Boston. Angela Domanico at the Non-Print Media Division of the University of Maryland Library in College Park, and Dr. Elinor Sinette, the oral history librarian at Howard University in Washington, D.C. made available to me the materials in their respective collections, and greatly assisted me in finding the specific information I required.

Jerry Keker of Takoma Park, Maryland ably and professionally edited this entire volume, and I am in his debt. Lisa Peklo of West Friendship, Maryland was a valuable research assistant, and she and her husband Gary, besides providing continuing encouragement, were helpful in uncovering several primary sources. Anne Hummer provided research and writing assistance on the events in Birmingham. George Ware and Milton Viorst gave me valuable tips in getting started on the manuscript. Professor Clayborne Carson shared with me one of his own personal interviews with a participant, and Nita Bolotsky of the Bureau of Social Science Research provided me with two important studies, and I am thankful for their assistance. Geoff Tofield of NBC provided me with Meet The Press transcripts. I am grateful to Natalie Neviasser, and Jacqui Ford for typing the early drafts of the manuscript. Above all, I am truly indebted to Trinie Angeles, Fely Doroteo-Gomez and Marilou Abiera for preparing the final manuscript under severe time constraints.

Thomas Gentile
Washington, D.C.
August, 1983

1

> In the Summer of 1963, the Negroes
> of America wrote an emancipation
> proclamation to themselves. They
> shook off three hundred years of
> psychological slavery and said:
> "We can make ourselves free."
>
>   - Martin Luther King, Jr.

On August 28, 1963, approximately 250,000
persons assembled in Washington, D.C., the
nation's capital, for a march and rally billed
as the "March on Washington for Jobs and
Freedom." The great civil rights march, a
milestone in American black history, was the
brainchild of labor and civil rights leader, A.
Philip Randolph, Jr., the founder and long-time
President of the Brotherhood of Sleeping Car
Porters (AFL-CIO).

It was a beautiful, memorable, and peaceful
day in Washington, unmarred by violence or
arrests. Millions watched the March, and the
rally which followed, live on television.
Indeed press coverage was unprecedented, even
outstripping presidential conventions and
inaugurals. The March was also beamed live
around the world via telestar satellite, which
then was a recent technical innovation.

The March on Washington is often referred
to as the high point of race relations in
America, in contrast to the urban riots that
erupted throughout the nation later in the
1960s. It is also generally credited with being
a major impetus behind passage of the 1964 Civil
Rights Act, the most comprehensive legislation
protecting the rights of Negroes in the 20th
century. The March on Washington is perhaps

best known as the setting for Dr. Martin Luther King, Jr.´s most famous speech, "I Have A Dream."

As one periodical editorialized immediately after the March: "In its dignity and its dream, in its immensity and in its unity, in its composite constituency the March was without example or parallel in American history . There has never been anything like it before; it may never be repeated with the same degree of dignity and restraint." But to others, the March on Washington represented the failure of the non-violent civil rights movement, and an attempted takeover of the movement by moderates and white liberals.

At the time, the March on Washington was by far the largest political demonstration in American history. While peace rallies and demonstrations in later years drawing hundreds of thousands became just short of routine events, in 1963 a march and rally of such proportions as the March on Washington was unthinkable, and an object of much fear in even the world´s most stable democracy. The reasons for such fear had to do with the burgeoning civil rights protest movement in the spring and summer of 1963. Increasingly, violence and arrests were the order of the day. The year 1963 was not the beginning of the civil rights movement, but rather its peak, fitting perhaps for the One Hundredth Anniversary of the Emancipation Proclamation, President Abraham Lincoln´s freeing of the southern slaves in the midst of the Civil War.

The modern era of direct action civil rights protest by Negroes and sympathizers commenced with the legendary Montgomery bus boycott in 1955, which first catapulted the

Reverend Martin Luther King, Jr. to fame. In 1960, the student sit-in movement directed against segregation in private eating places and accommodations began in Greensboro, North Carolina, and spread throughout the South and portions of the North to libraries, hotels, motels, and beaches. Discrimination in interstate transportation was the focus of the Freedom Ride movement which commenced in the spring of 1961. The Congress of Racial Equality (CORE) sent thousands of its members throughout the South to test segregation laws and other forms of discrimination in interstate transportation, and arrests and violence ensued. In the fall of 1962, the court-ordered integration of the University of Mississippi touched off a violent confrontation involving white students, state officials, and federal authorities sent south to ensure James Meredith's admission to the University. Picketing and public demonstrations were numerous throughout the South and border states on smaller scales in 1961 and 1962.

The events of 1963, undoubtedly the most important year of the civil rights movement, are the subject of this book, with particular focus on the background and planning of the historic August 28 March and rally. The cast of characters is familiar to students of the civil rights movement.

Originally, there were six civil rights leaders who organized the March : A. Philip Randolph, Roy Wilkins, Whitney Young, Jr., Dr. Martin Luther King, Jr., James Farmer, and John Lewis. They were referred to by the press and within the movement as the "Big Six". All but Randolph headed major civil rights organizations in 1963, each of which organizations had a focus as diverse as the personality and proclivities of its respective leader. The sponsoring entities ran the gamut of major Negro movements in America except for so-called extreme militant or separatist groups such as the Black Muslims. An understanding of the nature of each of the civil rights organizations, and the personality of its leader is significant to a study of the planning for the March on Washington.

A. Philip Randolph was born in Crescent City, Florida, a small town in the swampy lake country on April 15, 1889. Randolph attended Cookman Institute, a black college in Jacksonville, Florida. After college, he was unable to secure employment in the South, so he moved to New York City in 1911. He took courses at the City College of New York and ideologically drifted into socialism prior to World War I. Randolph, through a small radical newspaper, The Messenger, urged blacks to avoid induction into the Armed Forces during World War I.

After the war, Randolph was approached by Pullman Sleeping Car employees in hopes that he might help them organize a union. After extensive efforts, Randolph organized the Brotherhood of Sleeping Car Porters on August 25, 1925.

The Pullman car was a very popular means of travel at the time and Pullman Car porters were always poorly paid blacks. In the 1920's, the several thousand black porters were paid only $60.00 a month for over 400 hours of work and over 11,000 miles of travel per month. They were known, however, for their meticulous service and cheerful attitudes. It took Randolph twelve years of hard work to obtain an agreement with the Pullman Company for recognition of the porter's union. The Railway Labor Act of 1926, which gave railroad workers the right to organize, excluded the black porters from its provisions. The Brotherhood of Sleeping Car Porters eventually became an affiliate of the AFL-CIO, and Randolph became an important labor leader as well as civil rights leader.

Randolph had urged the AFL-CIO to come out publicly against racial discrimination as far back as 1955, and was its first black vice-president in 1957. In 1941, Randolph had threatened a massive march by blacks on Washington in order to coerce President Franklin Roosevelt to issue a Presidential directive against discrimination in the defense industry on the eve of World War II. In 1948, Randolph had been influential in urging President Harry S. Truman to bar segregation in the military services. Randolph had early adopted a belief in civil disobedience tactics and mass protest, but he was a life-long pacifist and abhorred violence.

Randolph was often described as tall and courtly, a distinguished public speaker, and effective negotiator. Of the "Big Six" civil rights leaders in 1963, Randolph alone did not head a major civil rights organization. But his position as vice-president of the AFL-CIO, and head of the Negro American Labor Council made him a major spokesperson for the civil rights cause. He was also a unifying force, and described as "unique because he accepts everyone in a movement whose members do not always accept one another."

The National Association for the Advancement of Colored People (NAACP) and the National Urban League were considered the more conservative of the civil rights organizations in the early 1960s. The Urban League was founded in 1910 with the stated purpose of easing the transition of southern rural Negroes into northern urban life. The Urban League attempted to deal with white businessmen through rational economic appeals, gathering and publishing facts and figures about conditions under which Negro citizens lived and worked. It was always non-profit, non-partisan, and interracial in its leadership and staff. In 1963, the Urban League had affiliates in 64 cities in 30 states and the District of Columbia. Its national headquarters was in New York, and it had 500 paid employees and over 6,000 regular volunteers. The Urban League regularly published reports and brochures on race relations and conditions of the American Negro. Its involvement in the March on Washington in 1963 was a new field for the Urban League, as direct action politics had not been one of its regular tactics prior to that time. Whitney Young, Jr. was its chairman, and he became one of the major organizers of the March on Washington.

The National Association for the Advancement of Colored People emerged from W.E.B. Dubois's Niagara Movement. It was initially set up in 1909 in New York City and was known initially as a militant group because its views diverged sharply from those of the famous moderate, Booker T. Washington. Over the years the NAACP became the major civil rights organization in the United States. It was well funded and well respected, and the greater respect it seemed to gather the less militant and more conservative appeared its approach. The NAACP, however, did not totally reject direct action politics and was involved in a number of peaceful protests in the late 1950's and early 1960's. With the advent of the newer, more militant civil rights organizations in the late 1960's, the NAACP would lose considerable support, particularly among younger Negroes.

Roy Wilkins was the NAACP's executive director in 1963. Wilkins was born in St. Louis on August 30, 1901, but raised mainly in St. Paul, Minnesota, thereby avoiding much of the overt discrimination faced by Negroes in other areas of the country prior to World War II. He graduated from the University of Minnesota, ironically supporting himself as a Pullman car waiter during his college summers in the period just prior to a A. Philip Randolph's founding of the Brotherhood of Sleeping Car Porters.

Employed initially as a journalist, Wilkins first became involved in the anti-lynching movement in the 1930's and came to New York City to work for the NAACP in 1931, then a rather small organization of 25,000. By the late 1960's, Wilkins had directed its growth to nearly 400,000 members.

Wilkins was an early advocate of direct action protest, despite the widely held view of him as conservative. In 1934, he was arrested for picketing the Justice Department in Washington over the federal government's lack of concern with the 35 or so lynchings of blacks per year in the South.

Wilkins was involved in scores of demonstrations over the years, and was arrested several times. He was known as an effective speaker and writer, and the most diplomatic of the civil leaders. Wilkins spearheaded the NAACP's successful legal attacks on segregated public schools culminating in the United States Supreme Court's historic 1954 decision, Brown v. Board of Education.

In the spring and summer of 1963, Roy Wilkins bristled under the criticism that the NAACP was an organization of the past. In a speech in June of 1963, for example, Wilkins charged that the other, newer civil rights groups, furnished "the noise and get the publicity while the NAACP furnishes the manpower and pays the bills." Wilkins argued that only the NAACP among the civil rights organiations could handle a long sustained legislative battle for civil rights. The other organizations "start a little and then run off somewhere else. They are here today, gone tomorrow." In 1963 the more militant groups were indeed getting more publicity, and draining from the NAACP its hard-earned but limited sources of funds.

Wilkins had been most critical of the Congress of Racial Equality (CORE) whose director in 1963 was the well-known freedom rider and civil rights activist James Farmer. CORE had been founded in Chicago in 1942 by a group of pacifists, many of them members of an organization called the Fellowship of Reconciliation. CORE from the outset was committed to non-violent means of achieving integration including direct pacifist actions such as sit-ins. Farmer himself was a committed pacifist and a former Methodist minister. In terms of militance, CORE was considered close to the Student Non-violent Coordinating Committee (SNCC), in contrast to the NAACP and the Urban League, which groups CORE viewed skeptically. The friction between the two groups was evident as the planning for the March on Washington went forward. When the idea of the March on Washington was first put forth, CORE's steering committee eagerly agreed to act as a co-sponsor. CORE's enthusiasm for the March waned, however, as the focus and style of the March changed from one of confrontation in the early summer of 1963 to one of polite demonstration by August 28.

Farmer himself was an impressive orator and committed activist. He joined local demonstrations and "was approachable - called Jim even by acquaintances - and he identified himself with the hardships and sacrifice of his followers." He went to jail often in the late 50´s and early 60´s and was rarely bailed out quickly.

The Student Non-violent Coordinating Committee (SNCC) was the newest of the civil rights organizations in 1963. It had been organized in 1960 in Raleigh, North Carolina with the intention of coordinating student protests, especially sit-ins, against the lack of access to public accommodations by Negroes in the south. By definition its members were young, were considered impatient, and were unafraid of confrontation with authorities. Many of the major black leaders of the late 1960´s and 1970´s got their start in the protest movement through involvement with SNCC.

SNCC had its headquarters in Atlanta and for a while was closely allied with Martin Luther King, Jr. By the summer of 1962, however, in a series of disputes arising out of protests in Albany, Georgia, SNCC leaders had a falling out with Dr. King. In 1963, SNCC´s new chairman was 23-year old John Lewis, a short, somewhat stocky but fiery leader who even at that young age, by 1963 was a veteran of numerous sit-in campaigns throughout the south. Lewis was one of ten children born and raised on a farm near Montgomery, Alabama.

Martin Luther King, Jr. was born on January 15, 1929 in Atlanta, Georgia. He was ordained a Baptist Minister in 1948, following in his father's footsteps, with whom he shared the leadership of the Ebenezer Baptist Church in Atlanta. King received a doctorate of philosophy from Boston University in 1955 and a doctorate of divinity from the same university in 1959.

He was a disciple of Thoreau and Gandhi. In 1955, soon after he accepted a position at a Baptist Church in Montgomery, Alabama, he became a leader of a year long bus boycott by Negroes protesting the segregated seating policy of the local bus company. After a year of Negroes walking to work, and financial drain on the bus company, desegregation was achieved. Dr. King became a familiar national figure as a result of widely reported weekly mass meetings called to give ongoing encouragement to the boycott.

Thereafter, King returned to Atlanta and set up the Southern Christian Leadership Conference (SCLC), an organization of Negro ministers throughout the south which sponsored direct action protests against all forms of discrimination.

By 1963, King was clearly the superstar of the civil rights movement. His oratory had already become legendary, and his willingness to accept physical abuse, arrest and incarceration at the hands of law enforcement officials, was an example to an entire generation of committed Negro activists.

Although he was not one of the "Big Six", the man who eventually became the chief organizer of the March on Washington was Bayard Rustin. Rustin was 53 years old in 1963, and was probably the most experienced and most

astute organizer of non-violent protest in the
United States. Rustin was described as
"elegant, urbane, with a large, high-cheekboned
face, expressive beneath a bushy shock of
hair." He was born in a Quaker community in
Westchester, Pennsylvania, in 1910, and was a
life-long pacifist. He did not have many of the
bitter, early youthful experience of the other
civil rights leaders growing up in the
segregated south. He attended an integrated
high school, was a sports star and class
valedictorian. Rustin then went to Wilberforce
College in Ohio and Cheney State Teachers
College in Pennsylvania. Afterwards he settled
in New York City and attended City College.
Early in his life Rustin was a talented singer,
both of spirituals and protest songs. He was an
accomplished musician who sang with the famed
black singers, Leadbelly and Josh White, in his
early days in New York City.

Rustin turned to politics, however, in 1938
when he joined the Young Communist League:
"They appeared genuinely interested in peace and
racial justice," Rustin explained in a later
interview. When Russia joined World War II,
however, the communists were no longer pacifists
and Rustin left the League. Rustin attempted to
organize blacks against joining the segregated
armed forces during World War II and himself
refused induction. He served 28 months in
Lewisburg Penitentiary for draft evasion, the
first of a score of arrests over a period of
years for protest activities. Rustin had
volunteered in 1941 to help A. Philip Randolph
in his planned March on Washington and was said
to be severely disappointed when Randolph called
the march off at the last minute after a
compromise was reached with the Roosevelt

Administration regarding Negro hiring in the defense industry.

Rustin was controversial throughout his career. In 1947 he planned and organized the first Freedom Ride, and beginning in 1955 served as a close associate to Martin Luther King, developing many of the tactics used in the Montgomery bus boycott in 1955–56. In 1958 he organized massive ban-the-bomb protests in Britain, and in 1960 led a march across the Sahara Desert in an attempt to stop the first French nuclear test explosion. Throughout, he was a close admirer and associate of A. Philip Randolph and it was natural for Randolph to turn to him in the latter part of 1962 when the time seemed ripe for another attempt at a massive March on Washington.

The time was ripe in 1963 for a variety of reasons, not the least of which was President John F. Kennedy's Administration's lip service to equality. Along with the rhetoric went the expectation of Negroes that things would get better. By 1963, however, the statistics did not match the expectations. For example, one and a half million Negroes were unemployed in 1963. Although Negroes made up 11% of the work force, they comprised 22% of the jobless. In 1963, 25% of the American people lived below the poverty line. In fact, the economic gap between whites and blacks was widening rather than narrowing, as it had immediately after World War II.

To complicate economic matters, the country was gripped by a recession which begun in 1959 and from which slow recovery was not complete until 1963. Manufacturing jobs, where blacks had made the greatest advances in the past, had dried up during this period, due both to automation and the recession. In the building trades, one of the few areas where the workforce was expanding, blacks could find laboring jobs but were generally barred by the apprentice system from the skilled construction jobs.

It was statistics such as these that had prompted many to feel that emergency measures and legislation were needed to recover from this crisis facing blacks in 1963. But to the black worker, the black student, or to the member of the rising black middle class, like most Americans, statistics are sometimes hard to grasp. What was more salient was the lack of freedom of movement and freedom of choice in daily living activities as a result of continuing invidious forms of discrimination, particularly in the south, but throughout the country. Economic freedom and human freedom for Negroes were certainly connected, but it was the latter that set aflame the fires of anger and frustration in 1963. Negro demonstrations had brought small gains commencing with the Montgomery bus boycott in 1955. "Rising expectations coupled with the youthful impatience quickened the number and pace of civil rights demonstrations... Angry, bitter and frustrated by lack of jobs and opportunities in the urban slums of the north, an increasing number of blacks, especially among the young, clamored for more militant, direct, mass action."

In this situation two forces were at work among the Negro civil rights leadership. One, symbolized by A. Philip Randolph, and in a quieter sense by the Urban Leage, was desirous of making an impact on the nation to focus on the plight of the Negroes in an economic sense. The focus of the SCLC, the NAACP, SNCC and CORE appeared to be on the more visual restraints on Negroes, that is, the lack of freedom in the use of accommodations, housing, and treatment by law enforcement officials.

The idea for a 1963 March on Washington, long simmering in Randolph's mind, had its active incarnation at the very end of 1962. Bayard Rustin had dropped by A. Philip Randolph's office at the headquarters of the Brotherhood of Sleeping Car Porters one afternoon in December, 1962. The two men were discussing the civil rights protest movement in the south and their own wish to become active once again in the movement. Rustin had been working on peace activities at the time and Randolph was heavily involved in the struggle within the AFL-CIO, to better the lot of Negro union members. The two men discussed Randolph's life-long dream of an effective mass March on Washington, and at the end of the meeting Randolph asked Rustin to prepare a memo outlining the possibilities and tentative plans for such a march.

Over the next few months Rustin prepared such a memorandum with the assistance of two young followers, Norman Hill and Tom Kahn. Randolph had told Rustin "that while Dr. King's street demonstrations in the south were imperative, a complementary demonstration was needed, in order to embody in one gesture civil rights as well as national economic demands." By the end of February the memorandum had been submitted to Randolph. It called for sponsorship of the March by the Negro American Labor Council. It would be a two-day program, a Friday and Saturday in May. Later, it was decided that to effectively plan and gather support for the March it would be held in October 1963. The first day of the program was to be dedicated to lobbying at the White House and Congress by labor, church and civil rights leaders. The second day would be the mass march and rally. Support of big labor would be sought as well as the support of some of the other civil rights leaders.

Even while the memorandum was being written there was said to be a rumor spreading in Harlem that Randolph was planning another mass March on Washington in the summer of 1963. In Atlanta, Dr. King's SCLC was also said to be making preliminary plans for a mass March on Washington that summer. Events in Birmingham later that spring, however, turned the SCLC's attention temporarily away from such a planned March.

The first public announcement of the March on Washington was probably on March 7, 1963, when Randolph told the Negro-American Labor Council of his plans for a march for jobs in Washington that fall. The idea seemed to generate little excitement. After consulting with Rustin, the two decided to equally stress the freedom aspects of the civil rights struggle in their call for a March.

In preparing their memo, Hill and Kahn relied on their work with Rustin in the second youth march for integrated schools which had been held in Washington in the spring of 1959. Norman Hill himself had organized bus transportation from Chicago to that earlier, smaller Washington march. In 1960, Hill had worked with CORE on a March on Conventions movement, designed to present the Negro plight to the Republican and Democratic presidential nominating conventions that summer.

At the time Hill was an assistant program director of CORE. The original memo included plans for peaceful non-violent direct action, leaving open the possibility of sit-ins in certain Senate or House members' offices. The memo dealt with logistics of the March and called for step-by-step involvement of civil rights, labor and church organizations in the planning and publicity for the March.

The actual planning for a March got underway early in the spring of 1963. However, little publicity was generated about the plans in view of the travails of civil rights demonstrators in Birmingham throughout the spring. How did 250,000 people wind up in Washington, D.C. on August 28, 1963, in the largest demonstration in American history? The story begins in Birmingham in the spring of 1963, the city that became a symbol of resistance by white racists to the freedom of Negro Americans.

Early in 1963, Reverend Martin Luther King, Jr., at the request of Reverend Fred Shuttlesworth, leader of the SCLC affiliate in Birmingham, agreed to lead a direct action campaign in Birmingham. Still reeling from an unsuccessful attempt to desegregate accommodations in Albany, Georgia, after a protracted campaign, King pledged his total commitment to the Birmingham effort saying he would not leave "until Pharaoh lets God's people go."

By 1963, the iron and steel industrial city of Birmingham, Alabama had a population of nearly 350,000, and was over one-third black. But the city was entirely segregated: neighborhoods, parks, libraries, taxicabs, transportation terminals, churches, and of course restaurants and public accommodations. King referred to Birmingham as the most segregated city in the United States.

The Birmingham campaign was carefully planned in advance by King and his associates. It was to commence immediately after an April 2,

1963 election for Mayor, the city's first since it had recently changed its political structure to a council system. Long time City Commissioner of Public Safety Eugene "Bull" Connor was challenging the more moderate Albert Boutwell. Moderates feared that demonstrations and confrontations would tip the election to Connor, and thus King delayed the start of the campaign until after the voters had gone to the polls. The electorate chose Boutwell over Connor, but outgoing Mayor Arthur Hanes, an ardent segregationist and supporter of Connor, challenged the election results and continued in office while the question went to court. At this point, Dr. King decided to begin "Project C – Confrontation Birmingham." The goal of the campaign in Birmingham was to desegregate the city's buses, schools, parks and lunch counters. This was to be achieved by sit-ins and boycotts of targeted local establishments. The plan was to cut into the profits of local businesses and force the community to see the need for change. Planners of the direct action campaign met regularly with Birmingham's black leadership to keep them informed, and advance teams were sent to each store to determine such things as the number of seats at lunch counters and accessibility to the stores. In addition, through the efforts of entertainer Harry Belafonte, a bail fund was established should confrontation lead to mass arrests.

Since Bull Connor had a track record for using force and brutality against demonstrators, Dr. King predicted that confrontations would force Connor into "committing his brutality openly in the light of day -- with the rest of the world looking on." The strategy was to arouse the national conscience, and demonstrate to the federal government the need for legislation that would desegregate accommodations all over the South.

The demonstrations and arrests commenced immediately. On April 6, Rev. Shuttlesworth led a group of demonstrators to City Hall where 45 were arrested. On the next day, Palm Sunday, the Reverend A. D. King, a local minister and brother of Dr. King, led 26 hymn-singing demonstrators downtown, where they were arrested for parading without a permit. It was on Palm Sunday that the police dogs first appeared. To avert further demonstrations, the city obtained a state court injunction on April 10. However, Dr. King immediately announced that he considered it his "duty" to violate the injunction and prepared to do so on Good Friday, April 12, 1963. "I am prepared to go to jail and stay as long as necessary." King left behind his clerical garbs, and dressed in denim trousers and a workshirt, symbolic of the movement's new militancy, King, Rev. Ralph Abernathy, blind singer Al Hibbler and Rev. Shuttlesworth, led 50 demonstrators from Zion Hill Church to City Hall. The demonstrators sang hymns as they walked, and were allowed to march to the downtown sector before being arrested.

Rev. King and Abernathy were placed in solitary confinement. Prompted by calls from Mrs. King, President Kennedy called Birmingham officials to request adequate treatment while King was in jail. It was during this stay in jail that King wrote the famous "Letter from a Birmingham Jail," which actually was a response to Birmingham ministers who had called King "an outside agitator." Appealing to the Christian conscience, King argued that he had the responsibility to disobey unjust laws. He also criticized the ministers´ silence about the conditions that led to the demonstrations.

On April 20, King and Abernathy decided to accept bail in order to revitalize the waning demonstrations. The "massive" non-violent demonstrations, at this point had failed to materialize because of disagreement within the black community about the tactics and timing of the campaign. Desperate to mobilize the black community, King initiated a children´s crusade, at the suggestion of a young associate, Jim Bevel. Six thousand children were recruited from the elementary and high schools to "walk for freedom." When later criticized for using children in the effort, King asked the critics where they´d been "when down through the years Negro infants were born in ghettos, taking their first breath of life in a social atmosphere where the fresh air of freedom was crowded out by the stench of discrimination?"

Tensions mounted on May 2, the first day of the children´s crusade, when 959 children were jailed along with 10 adults. Some of the children had fled as police approached, but most maintained discipline and dropped to their knees in prayer before being arrested. Bull Connor was determined to thwart a repeat performance. As more children jammed into the Sixteenth Street Church the next day preparing to march, Connor barred the exits imprisoning half of the would-be demonstrators. When the rest of the demonstrators attempted to proceed with he planned march, Connor released police dogs and ordered the use of fire hoses to disperse the remainder of the crowd. In response, rocks and bottles were thrown. Several children were severely bitten and others suffered injuries when knocked over by the water spray which spewed from hoses at 50 to 100 pounds of pressure. One boy's shirt was torn from his back from the water pressure. Two fireman and a photographer were also injured.

Scenes from these confrontations with police were shown on the nightly television news across the United States. The New York Times carried on the first page a picture of a Negro woman being attacked by a police dog. The nation responded with shock to the brutal police response to the demonstrations. President Kennedy, worried that the Birmingham conflict "was seriously damaging the reputation of the country," sent Assistant Attorney General Burke Marshall to Birmingham to negotiate with business leaders and demonstration leaders to attempt to reach an agreement. National industry leaders were asked to contact Birmingham associates to urge a settlement.

The momentum was building as demonstrators continued crowding into the streets and packing the jails. By May 4, there were over 2,000 protestors in jail, and while trying to calm an angry crowd, Rev. Shuttlesworth was knocked against a building by the force of the water spray and hospitalized for bruises and abrasions. As police continued to use dogs, clubs and fire hoses to keep blacks in the black section of the city, blacks retaliated by throwing rocks, jeering and taunting. Periods of peace were precarious, and each day the situation on the streets became more volatile. Behind the scenes negotiations between Rev. King and the business community intensified. Meanwhile, Bull Connor requested the assistance of state troopers from Governor George Wallace, who obligingly sent over 500 highway patrolmen under the direction of Commander Albert J. Lingo, who was said to favor the use of electric cattle prods on demonstrators.

In an attempt to avoid further violence, Burke Marshall contiued to urge a truce. He argued with white business leaders that black demands were not unreasonable -- to sit at a lunch counter, to have jobs, and amnesty for the demonstrators. Marshall also urged King to cease demonstrations in order to aid settlement negotiatons and King agreed to a brief truce. By May 9, the only unresolved issue was amnesty for the jailed demonstrators. Until this could be resolved King and his associates decided to resume demonstrations. But just before the demonstrations were to start the next day, King announced that a settlement had been reached.

Terms of the agreement included desegregation of public facilities, hiring and promotion of blacks in local businesses, and the establishment of a permanent bi-racial committee to deal with ongoing problems. The issue of the jailed demonstrators was resolved through the efforts of the Kennedy administration and the AFL-CIO who raised the $160,000 needed for bail for those still incarcerated.

In announcing the settlement King said "it was the most significant victory for justice we've ever seen in the Deep South," and called on the demonstrators to "move from protest to reconciliation." Bull Connor reacted by calling for a white boycott of desegregated businesses and outgoing Mayor Hanes said the white negotiators were "quisling gutless traitors." But less than 24 hours after the agreement was reached, violence erupted in Birmingham again. The home of A. D. King was bombed as well as the motel that had been the headquarters for the demonstrations. This incident set off rioting in Birmingham's black community as irate blacks looted stores, set fires and skirmished with police. It took most of the night for state troopers to restore order. President Kennedy alerted military units in the area, trained in riot control, and threatened to send them to Birmingham if order was not restored. Mayor-elect Boutwell (who had been ruled the winner by a state appeals court), the business community, and the Birmingham newspapers came out in support of the settlement and promised to implement it. For Birmingham that promise was in itself a major change.

The Birmingham conflict was a factor in President Kennedy's realization of the need for federal laws to ensure "equal rights and equal opportunity." When introducing Civil Rights legislation in June, Kennedy said, "The events in Birmingham and elsewhere have so increased the cries for equality that no city or state can prudently choose to ignore them." It also gave a new impetus to A. Philip Randolph's dream for a mass March on Washington. Now the country was alive with the cry for civil rights. Bayard Rustin would say later that the real organizers of the March on Washington "were Bull Connor, his police dogs and his fire hoses."

2

> "In the space of a few months, President Kennedy had made the Negroes' troubles his troubles and their problems his priority."
>
> — Theodore Sorenson

> "When Administrations start playing such games and seeing themselves as directors, as puppeteers, as orchestrators of history, history itself may suffer. Or they trivialize their talent and waste energies. The Kennedy whiz kinds were no exception. The March on Washington was a case in point."
>
> — Victor Navasky

The NAACP had developed a feeling of near jealousy at the attention and support now being given to King and the more activist civil rights organizations throughout the country. These newer, younger organizations were grabbing all the headlines, while the NAACP was responsible for true progress, they argued. But progress in the summer of 1963 would not come via the courtroom. Recognizing the trend and correctly sensing the movement's mood, the NAACP decided to shift tactics, and at least publicly appear to break from its relatively conservative methods. On the last day of May 1963, the NAACP announced a shift in its methods to direct political action. As if to demonstrate the NAACP's resolve, Roy Wilkins got himself arrested in Jackson, Mississippi the next day. The thought of the conservatively dress, mild-mannered Wilkins getting arrested was perhaps unsettling to the more moderate supporters of civil rights. Jackson, Mississippi officials had taken the tact of simply rounding up all pickets or peaceful demonstrators. On the day before Wilkins´ arrest, 531 demonstrators were arrested and held. The next day, June 1, Mississippi NAACP Field Secretary Medgar Evers, Wilkins and several others walked a picket line in front of a downtown Woolworth store and were thereupon taken into custody. The Jackson police were able to avoid the use of fire hoses and the like, in combatting the NAACP´s campaign against discrimination in serving and hiring Negroes by white merchants.

The demonstrations in Jackson, Mississippi continued for several days. On June 5, some organizers began using a technique that King had employed successfully in Birmingham, the use of school children as demonstrators. Thirty-two children were arrested on the 5th, and over the next few days, a total of 600 juveniles were arrested for protest activities.

The week commencing June 7, 1963, saw some of the most widespread demonstrations that the country had ever experienced. In Los Angeles, California, CORE picketed the Beverly Hilton Hotel over hiring bias. On the same day, Sarasota, Florida Negroes picketed downtown theatres, and in Florida´s capital, Tallahassee, a demonstration occurred in the State Office Building cafeteria. More than one thousand Negroes demonstrated on Friday night, June 7 in Greensboro, North Carolina demanding desegregation of accommodations in that town. In Lexington, North Carolina on the same day, the Mayor declared a state of emergency as 500 whites battled 50 Negroes who had been demonstrating. One man was killed and a newspaper photographer was seriously wounded in rioting. On the same day, police arrested twelve demonstrators at a grocery store in Nashville, Tennessee, who were demonstrating against hiring bias by the grocery store chain.

The next day, Saturday, saw a fight erupt in a cafeteria in Atlanta, Georgia where a group of Negroes were protesting discrimination. Police in Bradenton, Florida closed the beach there after Negro demonstrators were threatened by milling crowds of whites. In St. Louis, Missouri, on the 7th, thirty Negro parents blocked school buses in a protest against segregation of the schools there. On Sunday the ninth, a group of CORE demonstrators conducted sit-ins at restaurants in Ocean City, Maryland. On Monday, the 10th some 700 prisoners at the Rahway, New Jersey prison farm reported on sick call in what officials declared was a demonstration stemming from racial tensions. On the same day, 100 Negro demonstrators were arrested in Beauford, South Carolina while attempting to get service at a restaurant. More than 300 had been arrested in one week of demonstrations there.

Meanwhile, in Texarkana, Texas 200 whites demonstrated against desegregation of Texarkana Junior College. The same week saw demonstrations at the State Legislature in Columbus, Ohio in favor of a fair housing bill. Similar demonstrations took place at the Rhode Island legislature in Providence with 250 Negroes and whites jamming the house gallery in support of a fair housing bill. In Charleston, South Carolina, 33 Negroes were arrested on June 13 for trespassing after seeking services and at a hotel and at a drug store lunch counter. In New York City at the construction site of a Harlem hospital, police battled demonstrators protesting alleged job discrimination. In Savannah, Georgia about 300 Negroes on June 13 marched with placards into the downtown area demanding immediate desegregation. Arrests in the first two weeks of June in Savannah numbered 500. Three hundred demonstrators marched on June 12 in Gadsden, Alabama, and hundreds of District of Columbia activists marched from the White House to the Justice Department in an action sponsored jointly by CORE and the SCLC.

More serious demonstrations were taking place in Danville, Virginia where on June 10, Major Julian Stimson, turned fire hoses on demonstrators and threatened to fill "every available stockade." Thirty-seven were arrested in Danville on the 10th and many more in the days that followed. In Cambridge, Maryland, violence erupted and a form of martial law had to be declared by Governor Tawes on June 14.

While all these local demonstrations were occurring, the focus of the Federal Government was on the impending showdown at the University of Alabama in Tuscaloosa. The University was under a Federal Court order to desegregate on June 11, and admit two black students for summer school studies. A third black student was to be admitted to the Huntsville Campus of the university. The University of Alabama had had one previous black student in February of 1956 named Autherine Lucy. Ms. Lucy, however, was expelled from school after a campus riot and the University returned to segregation. Alabama's governor was now George Wallace, who had been elected on a pro-segregation platform and whose inaugural address in January 1962 had carried the promise "segregation now, segregation tomorrow, segregation forever".

This showdown between Federal officials and the University of Alabma proved to be last of the great campus showdowns. It also proved to be a re-run of the University of Mississippi showdown which had occurred the previous fall when James Meredith was admitted pursuant to a Federal Court order. Wallace had promised, unlike Governor Barnett, to personally stand in the school house door to prevent students from entering. On Attorney General Robert Kennedy´s advice, President John F. Kennedy at 11:30 a.m. on June 11, issued a proclamation ordering the Alabama Governor and all other state officials to cease and desist from obstructing the Court ordered desegregation of the University. Attorney-General Kennedy, meanwhile, had sent Deputy Attorney-General Nicholas Katzenbach and a team of Justice Department officials to Tuscaloosa to enforce the Court order. Two thousand army troops were on standby alert 70 miles from the campus.

When Katzenbach and two other Justice Department attorneys arrived on campus with the two black students, Wallace kept his promise and stood in the doorway preventing them from entering. Katzenbach then read to Wallace the President´s cease and desist order to which the Governor responded by reading a proclamation of his own, calling the Federal presence, and the presence of the black students an unwelcome, unwanted and unwarranted intrusion upon the campus of the University of Alabama. Outnumbered, Katzenbach retreated and called Washington. President Kennedy thereupon federalized the Alabama National Guard, which was under the command of General Henry C. Graham of Birmingham. At 5:30 in the afternoon, General Graham returned to the campus with Katzenbach and the students and informed the

Governor: "It is my sad duty to ask you to step aside on an order of the President of the United States." Now Wallace was the one who was outnumbered, and he stepped aside permitting the students to enter the campus and register. On June 13, the third student registered at the Huntsville Campus without incident.

Buoyed with the success of the desegregation effort at the University of Alabama campus and pleased that none of the violence that occurred at the University of Missippippi had reoccurred in Tuscaloosa, President Kennedy went on national television on the evening of June 11. It was one of the most memorable speeches of his career, and marked a major turn in the Kennedy Administration's attitude towards civil rights which had been building for some time.

Birmingham and the other demonstrations were influencing those in high places. Ramsey Clark, then an assistant attorney-general in the lands division of Justice, complained in a memo to Robert Kennedy that the sporadic city by city battles could not continue without intolerable risks, and that broad civil rights legislation was needed immediately. Assistant Secretary of State and Kennedy confidant G. Mennen Williams wrote to the President in June suggesting "hard-hitting administrative actions" - presumably executive orders - be issued every 10 days "to take the edge off demonstrations." Meanwhile, a city-by-city score sheet of civil rights progress was being kept weekly by Louis Oberdorfer, an assistant to the Attorney-General. Secretary of Defense Robert McNamara was also in the camp stressing stronger action on civil rights. On June 7, he had issued a strong directive to all armed forces bases that discrimination be actively· opposed by the military. This went far beyond any previous orders designed to prevent discrimination within the military, and seemed to encourage anti-discrimination protests, picketings and even sit-ins at segregated facilities in communities near military bases:

> "Discriminatory practices directed against Armed Forces members ... are harmful to military effectiveness, therefore, all members of the Department of Defense should oppose such practices on every occasion while fostering equal opportunity for servicemen and their families on and off base ... Every military commander has the responsibility to oppose discriminatory practices affecting his men and their dependents and to foster equal opportunity for them, not only in areas under his immediate control, but also in nearby communities where they may live or gather in off-duty hours."

Above all, Vice President Lyndon Johnson was emerging as the administration's biggest advocate of a strong Civil Rights Bill, to the amazement of liberals like Joe Rauh, who in 1960 had objected to Johnson being placed on the Democratic ticket. If the Kennedy administration was to preach moderation and then drag out passage of a Civil Rights Act to save the southern vote, no one got the word out to Vice President Johnson, the administration's main bridge to that southern vote. The former Texas senator and Senate Majority Leader spoke at Gettysburg, Pennsylvania in late May of those who had died there for freedom: "One hundred years ago this land was free. One hundred years later, the Negro remains in bondage to the color of his skin. The Negro today asks justice. We do not answer him--we do not answer those who lie beneath the soil--when we reply to the Negro by asking patience."

The Kennedy Administration's commitment to the civil rights struggle was a long time coming. Candidate John Kennedy had made a famous phone call to Martin Luther King's wife while King was imprisoned in Georgia in October 1960 during the campaign for the Presidency against Richard Nixon. The symbolic gesture was considered somewhat courageous on Kennedy's part at the time, and was helpful to him in rolling up large majorities among Negro voters in the November election, insuring that he carried several large industrial states in the northeast. Negro leaders were hopeful that Kennedy's election would mean a dramatic change in the federal government's involvement in the civil rights area. The President's brother Robert, the new Attorney-General, worked behind the scenes in the spring of 1961 to aid freedom riders whose safety was endangered in Alabama. Eventually, Robert Kennedy sent 500 marshals to Montgomery to protect the freedom riders. At the same time, however, Kennedy was urging the freedom riders to desist in their actions, citing the threat of violence. Meanwhile, the Kennedy Administration was appointing segregationists to the federal bench in the South, and refusing to intervene in less dramatic, but equally threatening situations as the freedom rides. This was particularly true during the unrest in Albany, Georgia in the summer of 1962. More importantly perhaps, there was a dearth of legislative proposals in the civil rights area during the first two years of the Kennedy Administration.

After the upheaval at the University of Mississippi in October of 1962, when James Meredith was admitted with the backing of federal marshals dispatched by the Attorney General, the Administration began to shift toward activism in the area of civil rights, initially with a relatively weak legislative proposal to Congress in February, 1963. Birmingham, and a meeting the Attorney General had with black artists and entertainers in May, accelerated his own desire for action which he was successful in impressing upon his brother the President. The stormy May 24 meeting between Robert Kennedy and a group of Negro activists assembled by writer James Baldwin, Harry Belafonte, and Professor Kenneth Clarke, took place in Kennedy's Manhattan apartment. For nearly three hours the group upbraided Kennedy for his insensitivity to the Negro's struggle. The New York Times' Anthony Lewis described the scene:

> "It was a disaster. Early in the meeting one of the Negroes made a sarcastic reference to 'the Kennedys'. Another said he would not fight for the United States if the tension with Cuba came to arms. Kennedy bristled, and tempers rose....When Baldwin and the others talked about how Negroes felt, Kennedy kept saying: 'What is it you want me to do.'"

Although Kennedy was angry when he left the meeting, particularly at Belafonte and Clarke for not sticking up for him, the message of the face to face meeting apparently had gotten through to him. Up until that point, the Attorney-General had not felt the overriding sense of importance attached to federal intervention that was being demanded by these civil rights activists.

In February, the President had sent to Congress his first civil rights message, which was attacked by many civil rights supporters as being too moderate. Nonetheless, it was a significant step in the Administration's evolution. That message called for an expansion of the role of the Civil Rights Commission and for technical and economic assistance to school districts in the process of desegregation. It also called for some reforms designed to insure voting rights. The bill received little press attention, and no response at all from Congress. But by June 11, civil rights was on the front page, the events in Birmingham and elsewhere having assured that fact. Two weeks prior to his speech on June 11, President Kennedy had made his final decision to introduce strong civil rights legislation over the protests of some of his advisors who were concerned about him losing electoral support in the South. "Recognizing the call of history, Kennedy had made an abrupt turn and accepted the mantel of world leadership...(becoming) the first American President to take the official position that segregation was morally wrong". The President's June 11 speech, hastily prepared and delivered in part extemporaneously, contained a plea to take the demonstrations out of the streets and place the battle for civil rights in the halls of Congress:

> "One hundred years of delay have passed since President Lincoln freed the slaves, yet their heirs, their grandsons are not fully free. They are not yet freed from the bonds of

injustice; they are not yet freed from social and economic oppression. And this nation, for all its hopes and its boasts will not be fully free until all its citizens are free...We preach freedom around the world, and we mean it. And we cherish our freedom here at home. But are we to say to the world – and much more importantly to each other – that this is the land of the free, except for the Negroes; that we have no class or caste system, no ghettoes, no master race, except with respect to Negroes?

"Now the time has come for this nation to fulfill its promise. The events in Birmingham and elsewhere have so increased the cries for equality that no city or state or legislative body can prudently choose to ignore them.

"The fires of frustration and discord are burning in every city, North and South....We face , therefore, a moral crisis as a country and a people. It cannot be met by repressive police action. It cannot be left to increased demonstrations in the streets. It cannot be quieted by token moves or talk. It is time to act in the Congress, in your state and local legislative body, and, above all, in all of our daily lives...

"Those who do nothing are inviting shame as well as violence. Those who act boldly are recognizing right as well as reality..."

The following day Southern senators met on Capitol Hill, and vowed to fight the President's proposals to the bitter end, Senator James Eastland of Mississippi calling them a "complete blueprint for a totalitarian state." But the President's frank message, if not the specifics of his legislative proposals, were elsewhere well received. One columnist observed: "Seldom has a chief executive of any nation ever discussed in public so frankly the failings of a great nation. Seldom has a President put in such simple and compelling terms the case for righting ancient wrongs".

The peaceful resolution of the University of Alabama desegregation battle, and the promise of the President's civil rights message to the nation were marred by the assassination shortly after midnight on June 12, only hours after the President's speech, of Mississippi NAACP leader Medgar Evers. Shot in the back as he was entering his Jackson, Mississippi home, Evers' death represented a great loss to Mississippi Negroes and the civil rights movement. A white racist gun dealer, Byron de la Beckwith, fired the shots which killed Evers as Evers got out of his car in his driveway. Within days, the FBI had arrested de la Beckwith in connection with the shooting.

A World War II infantryman, Evers had returned home to Mississippi determined to better the lot of Negroes, violently if necessary. But he decided instead to assist in organizing NAACP chapters in the Mississippi Delta. He left his job with an insurance agency in 1954 to work full time for the NAACP. He had graduated from a small black college, Alcorn A & M in Mississippi in 1952, and was a star halfback on the football team. Greater opportunity lay in the North for a man of Evers' background and intelligence, but he felt he was needed in the South: "One day, you know, whites and Negroes will live here in Mississippi side by side in love and brotherhood. And we know each other better in the South. That's why it should work better here than anyplace else." Evers' assassination was a rallying cry for Negroes throughout the country for the remainder of the summer.

A week later, President Kennedy sent his Civil Rights Bill to Capitol Hill along with a message repeating themes emphasized in his June 11 speech. The February proposals were now amended to include a ban on discrimination in places of public accomodations, including hotels, restaurants, places of amusement, and retail stores that had a substantial effect on interstate commerce. Such discrimination which prevailed throughout the South in 1963 was the most visible badge of slavery remaining for American Negroes. This was the sort of discrimination that had given rise to the freedom rides, picketing, and demonstrations over the prior decade. The second important amendment to the February legislation was a provision which gave authority to the Attorney-General to seek desegregation of public education on his own initiative, rather than leaving the job to local parents and organizations to file law suits in unfriendly courts and in an unfriendly atmosphere. The President was relying upon bipartisan support for passage of the Bill and hoped that demonstrations would subside, lest there be a backlash favoring the Bill's opponents: "While peaceful communication, deliberation and petitions of protest continue, I want to caution against demonstrations which can lead to violence...the problem is now before

Congress...the Congress should have an opportunity to freely work its will". The President would probably have preferred that all demonstrations cease, not just violent ones, even though one of Kennedy's closest advisors had observed that all the warnings about violence in 1963 " had been directed at Negroes, yet almost all the victims had been Negroes."

About the time of the President's submission of the Civil Rights Bill to Congress on June 19, serious talk of a mass march on Washington began appearing in the press. On June 11 at a press conference in New York City, even before the President made his speech to the nation, the Reverend George Lawrence and Clarence Jones, associates of Martin Luther King, announced plans for demonstrations in Washington, D.C. No date was set at that point, for it was unknown exactly when Congress would take up civil rights legislation, and when the expected southern filibuster against it would begin. King's deputies stated that there would be "massive, militant, monumental sit-ins on Congress" with 50,000 Negroes from the New York area alone participating: "There will be massive acts of civil disobedience all over this nation. We will tie up public transportation by laying our bodies prostrate on runways of airports, across railroad tracks, and in bus depots."

That initial announcement of the tactics to be employed stuck in the minds of those who opposed the March throughout the summer. While such tactics were discussed among King's associates, and probably among CORE and SNCC leaders, there were never any concrete plans to implement them, although the possibility of civil disobedience had been raised in Rustin's initial memo to Randolph. But the latter wanted the March on Washington to be a mass, broad-based movement, and that meant a peaceful, lawful scenario. Otherwise, the NAACP, still the largest and most influential civil rights organization, would not have gotten involved. Randolph had already obtained King's support for a March on Washington, and James Farmer and John Lewis were enthusiastic about what they considered a militant action. Wilkins and Whitney Young were predictably cool to the idea at first, but events were happening too fast for the moderates to control.

Word of the proposed March on Washington reached the White House about the time the Civil Rights Bill was being sent up to Capitol Hill. "Everyone started getting panicky," recalled Robert Kennedy's aide, Burke Marshall. The President asked his advisors who was leading the March. No one seemed to know, and indeed the organization had not been set up. "Well, if we can't stop it, we'll run the damn thing," the President is said to have told his intimates. Stop it is what the President tried to do at first. The occasion was a June 22 meeting at the White House between administration officials, including the President, his brother, and the Vice President, and the major civil rights leaders.

Kennedy had been holding a series of meetings over a two week period in mid-June in which he brought business, labor, religious, educational leaders, lawyers, and finally the civil rights leaders to the White House. The purpose of these meetings was to establish a united front in support of the President's legislative package. Given the hysteria that was beginning to develop over the call for a March on Washington, the President took the opportunity to explain his views on the subject. In fact, the President went into the meeting

almost believing he could get the civil rights
leaders to call off the planned March, just as
President Franklin Roosevelt had done in 1941 –
that time in return for an executive order
regarding discrimination – when A. Philip
Randolph had planned a mass march on Washington.
"We want success in Congress, not just a big
show at the Capitol", Kennedy told those
assembled. Referring to Republican moderates and
conservatives, Kennedy further told them: "Some
of these people are looking for an excuse to be
against us; and I don´t want to give any of them
a chance to say "Yes, I´m for the Bill, but I am
damned if I will vote for it at the point of a
gun...(It may) create an atmosphere of
intimidation – and this may give some members of
Congress an out." Appropriately, Randolph spoke
first for the group. He had been to the White
House 22 years earlier to hear President
Roosevelt ask him to call off a march on
Washington. This time things were different, and
there would be no capitulation: "Mr. President,
the Negroes are already in the streets. It is
very likely impossible to get them off. If they
are bound to be in the streets in any case, is
it not better that they be led by organizations
dedicated to civil rights and disciplined by
struggle rather than to leave them to other
leaders who care neither about civil rights nor
about non-violence?"

James Farmer pondered aloud what would
happen if the demonstrations, including the
March on Washington were called off, and the
legislative battle should fail. "It may seem
ill-timed," Dr. King spoke next. "Frankly, I
have never engaged in any direct action protest
which did not seem ill-timed. Some people
thought Birmingham ill-timed." The President
then joked: "Including the Attorney-General."

The President knew by then the March was inevitable, and he ended his participation in the meeting on a conciliatory note: "I have my problems with the Congress, you have yours with your own groups. We will undoubtedly disagree from time to time on tactics. But the important thing is to keep in touch." King and the others came away from the meeting enthusiastic about the March, but Wilkins was still undecided about supporting it. "That little baby does not belong to me," he told reporters outside the White House. The consensus on the meeting was said to be an agreement to disagree on the demonstrations. Kennedy never directly asked the leaders to cease demonstrating, which would have been fruitless anyhow.

Unable to dissuade the civil rights leaders from going ahead with the March, the Administration fell back on its next line of strategy, running the "damn thing." That track was felt to be necessary because of the March's apparent lack of organization in June, an undeniable fact, but this was before the leaders had gotten together to select a chief organizer and even set down in writing their plans. Nonetheless, the Attorney-General began putting together a task force at the Justice Department to monitor plans for the March, and give assistance wherever appropriate.

The day after the June 22 meeting at the White House, the Attorney-General appeared on NBC's Meet the Press. He was evidently still hopeful that the March on Washington would never come to fruition, calling the announcement of such a march "premature." He felt Congress should be given a chance to act on the Civil Rights Bill first. But the Attorney-General refused to condemn street demonstrations in general:

"They go to the local authorities, to
the local merchants and they are not
able to get anywhere, and so the only
way in which they can air their
injustices and try to obtain remedies
is to picket, to have a parade, to
have a demonstration. I think this is
in the oldest tradition of the United
States, so I have great sympathy for
that kind of effort."

Dr. King left the White House meeting along
with the United Auto Workers´ Walter Reuther to
fly to Detroit for a mass march and rally
through the city´s streets the following day,
Sunday. What occurred was living proof to the
Kennedy Administration that the Negroes were
indeed in the streets and that there was little
the leaders could do to prevent it, even if they
wanted to. An incredibly large turnout of
125,000 persons, by police estimates, rallied
and then marched through the city´s streets to
protest segregation and police brutality.
Thousands more were said to have cheered the
marchers on from the sidewalk. There was no
violence or arrests. The parade had had
relatively little advance publicity, and was
only loosely organized by a newly formed group
called the Detroit Council on Human Rights. It
was the largest civil rights demonstration in
history at that point, and enough to make those
worried about a March on Washington very
nervous. Planned as a 20th anniversary
commemoration of Detroit´s 1943 race riot, the
Detroit Freedom Walk had official support from
Detroit´s mayor and Michigan´s governor, as well
as Dr. King and Reuther. Some of the crowd
squeezed into COBO Arena to hear Dr. King call
for "Freedom Now." The crowd was diversified,
and included church, social, civic, religious

and labor groups, and good weather helped swell the numbers.

Although the Detroit Freedom Walk received little attention in the white press, perhaps because no violence or arrests resulted, it buoyed the spirits of those civil rights leaders supporting the March on Washington, and perhaps was a factor in getting the uncommitted into the pro-March on Washington camp. Those efforts continued throughout the end of June. The August 28, 1963 date was first announced at a night rally in New York City on June 25. At that point Cleveland Robinson of Randolph's Negro American Labor Council and the SCLC's George Lawrence were co-chairman of the planned March, a position they would only hold for about a week. In Washington, the SCLC's Walter Fauntroy, CORE's Julius Hobson, and the NAACP's Edward Hailes were making preliminary plans for the March. Randolph and the others recognized however, that the support of Roy Wilkins was important. A meeting was called to be attended by all of the Big Six: Randolph, King, Wilkins, Farmer, Young and John Lewis. Wilkins was ready to accept the inevitable by then, but he wanted assurances that the March would be above reproach, a peaceful, impressive affair. Gone was the talk of sitting-in the galleries of Congress, and laying down on runways. Wilkins would have his way on many points. Randolph wanted Bayard Rustin to be chairman of the March, as he was the most qualified organizer in their ranks, and was also Randolph's close friend and associate. Rustin, unlike the other leaders, was also free to dedicate himself totally for the eight-week period that was available before August 28. He did not head one of the major civil rights organizations, and was free of other concerns. King, for whom Rustin had worked in Montgomery and elsewhere in the late 1950's, agreed with Randolph. But Wilkins was opposed to Rustin's participation, arguing that Rustin was too controversial, too radical, that some had the idea that he was a "draft dodger", and a homosexual. "I just think he would be too much of a liability." A compromise was reached whereby Randolph himself would be Chairman, although everyone knew that Rustin, who carried the title of Deputy Chairman, would be doing the actual work. That decided, Wilkins totally committed the NAACP to the success of the March.

Initial negative reaction to the proposed March did not come from the Kennedy Administration alone. Wilkins' associate at the NAACP, President Arthur B. Springarn opposed it, as did liberal Congressman Emanuel Cellar, a New York Democrat who was fearful that it might cause uncommitted legislators to oppose the Civil Rights Bill. Senator George Aiken (R-Vt.) was more direct: "I guarantee that there will be no legislation this year if any effort is made to intimidate Congress by bringing 300,000 people up there to sit on the Capitol lawn." Ultimately, a Gallup Poll found 63% of Americans had an "unfavorable" attitude toward the March. That attitude no doubt grew out of the almost universal condemnation of the plans for the March by the establishment press. The New York Herald-Tribune headlined its editorial with "The March Should Be Stopped." The Washington Star acknowledged that it would be a summer of mounting bitterness and turmoil in cities across the land, but warned "if this misguided pressure is to be capped by some climatic idiocy, like the proposed March on Washington of one hundred thousand demonstrators, then it will have no happy ending." The liberal Agnes Meyer, whose

family owned the Washington Post and Newsweek
magazine, called plans for a proposed March on
Washington disastrous, and predicted,
"catastrophic outbreaks of violence, blooshed,
and property damage."

On the other hand, The Nation could not see
why everyone was so upset by the supposed
pressure for action being placed on Congress:
"The average Congressman is being pressured all
the time, and he rarely succumbs to nervous
prostration."

By the end of June the stage was set for an
interesting summer. There would be no vacation
from the issues of the day, no putting off to
fall the great debate. Congress would remain in
session through Labor Day, and its committees at
least would debate the Civil Rights Bill. Also
by the end of June a rumor was already rampant
that the Administration had made a deal to
scuttle the most controversial part of the Bill,
the public accommodations section. The story
went that if the Southerners let the
Administration have the rest of the Civil Rights
Bill, the Administration could claim that they
had fought for the public accommodations section
only to have lost out to Republican indifference
and Southern opposition. For their part,
Republicans in Congress had introduced a public
accommodations section of their own which was
much milder than the Administration's all
pervasive measure. Liberal Republicans like
John Lindsay of New York were angry about the
Administration's supposed deal on the public
accommodations section. They did not want the
onus to fall upon them for the failure of
Congress to pass any public accommodations
section.

Years later critics of the Kennedy Administration, Victor Navasky and Gary Wills in particular, would point to the civil rights struggle and the Administration's handling of the March on Washington as evidence of the duplicity of the Kennedy men, a group concerned only with votes, with public relations, with maintaining the image of the forward looking Presidency. The argument makes little sense, at least when it is applied to this aspect of Kennedy's tenure. Kennedy's critics cannot have it both ways. If he was really cool toward the civil rights struggle, why the public posturing in favor of it - the Bill, the March, the speeches? He would have lost votes to Goldwater in 1964 as a result of the foregoing, not saved them because the white voter would have somehow seen through all this supposed posturing to discover that the Kennedys, like the white voter, held private racist attitudes.

As far as the original coolness toward the March and the decision to monitor its planning, it must be remembered that the executive branch did have the duty to uphold and enforce laws. The Attorney-General was in no position for example, to officially condone civil disobedience. Further, the feared backlash President Kennedy spoke of at the June 22 meeting was not a bluff. Surveys taken throughout the summer of 1963 showed that Kennedy was rapidly losing support among white voters who had backed him in 1960, in states such as such as Illinois, New Jersey, Missouri and Michigan. Indeed the popular notion at the time was that Robert Kennedy was hurting his brother politically by being a "militant spearhead of the Negro drive, the man out in front of the Negro leaders."

The Kennedy brothers came around on civil rights because it was to them the morally correct position, not the politically expedient one. True, they had not realized the depth of the plight of the American Negro prior to 1963, but nor had very many other white Americans. When they did discover what they had been shamefully overlooking, they acted as no prior administration had dared. King would say later that President Kennedy acted as he did in the summer of 1963, not out of political expediency but "because he thought it was right to do so. This is the secret of the deep affection he evoked. He was responsive, sensitive, humble before the people, and bold on their behalf."

3

"Congress shall make no law...
abridging ... the right of the
people to assemble and petition
the government for a redress of
grievances."

　　　　　　　　　　- 1st Amendment
　　　　　　　　　　　U.S. Constitution

It is forbidden to parade, stand,
or move in processions or
assemblages in said United States
Capitol Grounds, or to display
therein any flag, banner, or
device designed or adapted to
bring into public notice any
party, organization, or
movement...

　　　　　　　　　40 United States Code
　　　　　　　　　Section 193g (1882)

　　　Eight weeks was a relatively short period
of time to organize the largest political
demonstration in American history. One
important factor that the Big Six had going for
them was momentum - civil rights demonstrations
were the order of the day that summer.
Thousands of Negroes and their committed white
counterparts had thrown themselves into the
struggle at great personal, and in some cases
professional risk. The nation's press was
critical of demonstrations, but criticism was
relatively mild, and support for the Negroes'
goals was always attached to such criticism.
Scare tactics by journalists about violence at
demonstrations, and at the upcoming March on
Washington in particular would not in the summer
of 1963 keep the crowds away, such was the
country's mood. Indeed, political

demonstrations were more "acceptable" that summer than at any other time in the nation's history.

Bayard Rustin's first tasks as Deputy Director of the March on Washington were to assemble a staff and to find headquarters. For office space, Rustin turned to an old friend, the Reverend Tom Kilgore, a minister in Harlem. Kilgore offered the use of a small four-story stucco-fronted tenement next to his church at 130th Street and Seventh Avenue. The building had housed the Utopia Neighborhood Clubhouse, the recreation and welfare center of Kilgore's Friendship Baptist Church. Rustin moved into the quarters in late June and worked feverishly, "a lithe bundle of energy, smoking far too many cigarettes."

From below the third story window a huge banner was hung, advertising the "March on Washington for Jobs and Freedom – August 28." Rent was $350.00 per month for the two months that the committee occupied the building. "Visitors found it hard to believe that an enterprise of such proportions was being planned amid such humble appointments, in an office furnished with nothing more than a water cooler, a few scabrous and creaky old desks and chairs, and a small bank of temporary telephones."

Recognizing the short period of time allotted to organizing, Rustin sought a staff that he had worked with before, and who had experience organizing mass demonstrations. School integration and youth marches held in Washington in the late 1950's were the models, and much of his New York staff had worked with Rustin on those earlier marches.

Rustin's top aide proved to be Tom Kahn, a white graduate of Howard University who had been active in the civil rights movement in Washington. Kahn was paid $100.00 a week for his 16 to 18 hour days at committee headquarters. Rustin was paid $135.00 per week.

Rustin also solicited Courtland Cox, Edward Brown, Bill Mahoney and Cleveland Sellers, all members of the SNCC affiliated group at Howard University in Washington. Brown, Sellers and Mahoney worked with the Washington office of the March while Cox went to New York to work directly under Rustin. Mahoney was assigned to strategy while transportation became the purview of Brown. The latter often clashed with Walter Fauntroy, King's representative at the Washington office, Sterling Tucker, Executive Director of the Washington Urban League, and CORE's man in Washington, Julius Hobson. With so many organizations involved, there was often a question as to who had authority to make decisions. Rustin handled day-to-day decisions and the Big Six, which became the Big Ten when chruch and labor leaders were joined in July, had the overall power to set policy.

The Washington office was intended only to implement the New York office's decision. At one point Rustin had to send a letter of reprimand to Brown. It was sent at Fauntroy and Tucker's request and stated clearly that no single member of the Washington committee was free to make any unilateral decisions. The periodic bickering between the younger, more progressive SNCC workers and the representatives of the more established civil rights organizations was perhaps to be expected.

One SNCC leader who probably foresaw such problems and steered clear of the March and its planning altogether was Stokely Carmichael, at that time also a student at Howard. Rustin and Kahn had tried to persuade the talented Carmichael at the beginning of the summer to work on the March but Carmichael flatly refused. He felt that the struggle for voting rights in Mississippi was more important than a showy display in Washington: "Demonstrations were mobilizing without organizing." Carmichael spent a fruitful summer in Mississippi and missed the March altogether. Rustin had argued that coalition politics would be most advantageous, joining together labor, the churches, and progressive activists in one cause. Carmichael eschewed coalition politics. He felt direct action community organization was essential to SNCC's goals. This difference was the opening of a schism between Carmichael and Rustin which would greatly widen over the next few years.

Carmichael's fellow students at Howard stuck with Rustin that summer because the planned March had been described to them as mass direct action to secure jobs, freedom and voting. "It was to be a confrontation between black people and the federal bureaucracy. Rustin told us that some people were talking about disrupting Congress, picketing the White House, stopping service at bus and train stations and lying down on the runways at the airports."

Rustin's request for assistance from the Howard students was in June, at the time the previously indifferent Kennedy Administration introduced its new civil rights bill which became a rallying point. This was before the focus of the March was turned away from direct, on-site, congressional lobbying. The students claimed to be disappointed with the ten March demands published in August, shortly before the

March. The demands were termed "vague" and "basically unrelated to the dominant thrust of the movement."

In fact, this observation was of questionable validity, and SNCC leader John Lewis' speech at the March stressed those very demands, although in more strident terms.

The SNCC students also claimed later that they were never consulted, given prior notice, or provided a satisfactory explanation as to why the direct action of lobbying Congress was dropped from the March's plans, even though Lewis, Kahn, and Cox were involved daily in planning decisions. Some felt that Stokely Carmichael had been right all along. Yet, caught up in the excitement of the massive preparations for the March that summer, and with the anticipation that the March would be a major historical event, the SNCC students diligently labored on.

Rustin also drafted for his New York staff, the young but experienced Norman Hill from CORE. Rustin persuaded CORE Director James Farmer to release Hill from his duties to work on the March. It proved to be one of national CORE's few contributions to the organization. CORE, which tended to be in the more progressive camp with SNCC, began to lose interest in the March as the summer wore on, and it concentrated its efforts on local protests.

Hill's primary responsibility was to mobilize support in the large cities of the mid-west, like Cincinnati, Louisville, Minneapolis, St. Paul and Chicago. Local leaders were urged to set up March committees in their cities and, of course, to drum up local interest. Prior to arriving at each city, Hill saw to it that communications had gone out to the local leaders from the national organizaton with which they were affiliated, be it the NAACP, CORE, or a labor union. Hill was thus "going in there to try and pull together an operating vehicle that already had the support of their national offices, which made it a lot easier to get involvement."

When Walter Reuther and the United Auto Workers got involved in July, Hill increasingly would turn to Reuther's top aide, Jack Conway, for labor contacts in the field. Conway would make a prior introduction of Hill, by mail or phone, to local UAW presidents or staff representatives. Conway would advise the local leader of the national union's support, and personally urge cooperation. This greatly eased Hill's task.

At headquarters, Rustin and Kahn had their office on the first floor, which they shared with a tiny kitchen and with a small conference or press room, described by a reporter as "opening on a littered back yard lined with fire escapes, and crowded with the usual clutter of cartons of booklets, rows of coat racks, an upright piano holding little vases with roses, and undertakers' folding chairs." In that unassuming room Rustin and others met the press, and the Big Ten, who that summer had more power to move waves of humanity than the heads of large corporations, held their formal meetings.

Walking into 170-130th Street from the sidewalk, a visitor was directed up a flight of steps by a sign reading "March Office One Flight Up" to a cluttered reception area on the second floor. Needless to say perhaps, there were no elevators. Patty Morris, the receptionist, presided over this scene, constantly answering ringing telephones and referring the calls to the various staffers and volunteers. The office was "littered with piled papers and campaign pamphlets. Specially installed ten-line phone connection boxes are attached every few feet along office walls, with circuits so rigged that each incoming call rings every phone in the place - and the ten-point phones flash and ring incessantly."

Blyden Jackson, a young CORE worker, handled from his second floor desk, assignments for the growing numbers of volunteers who found their way into headquarters. Another youth, Pete Graham, had his desk on the second floor and was assigned to supplies, mailings, and physical plant. Graham was responsible for handling literature printing, envelope stuffing and distribution. He had the assistance of numerous volunteers. Graham also handled requests for March buttons, thousands of which were sold at 25 cents a piece.

When someone wrote to the March committee with a contribution or for information, they received a prompt, individualized reply. There were no form responses, and this was before the age of computer letters. Thank you notes for contributions were individually stylized and signed by Rustin himself. This was true even of individuals who purchased $1.00 or $2.00 worth of March buttons through the mail.

The entire emphasis was on making individuals across the country believe they were part of a nation-wide mass movement, that their local actions were encouraged, and that the leaders of the civil rights movement were behind them. This was evident, for example, in the instance of Edgar Vickery, a CORE worker in Clinton, Louisiana, who sent in $2.00 cash for 8 March buttons. "Hope the small contribution helps. Sorry I can't sent more. CORE's Task Force South hopes to send up about 50 people if we are all out of jail by the 28th. We shall overcome." Rustin replied promptly, thanking him for the $2.00. "I very much hope that jail will not prevent you from being with us on the 28th. If there is any way in which I can be of further assistance, please don't hesitate to call upon me."

The March was resolutely non-partisan. No funds were accepted from political parties, local or national. Nor were parties permitted to be listed as sponsors. All summer commercial proposals poured into March committee headequarters. Some were tantalizing, given the committee's budget problems, but all were summarily rejected. T-shirt makers were the most numerous inquirers. Rustin replied to them all, thanking them, but pointing out the firm policy of no commercial activity.

The March headquarters on 130th Street was no sedate think tank. At times over one hundred volunteers crowded into the cramped headquarters to perform various tasks: "Open virtually round the clock, the headquarters was a hive in which the crescendo of activity rose as the day drew closer."

Rachelle Horowitz, a permanent staffer at the Worker's Defense League, took leave to work with the New York March Committee on transportation planning. From her third floor office Horowitz kept abreast of developments on the complicated transportation front: bus and train charters, which would become bus and train shortages as the March day approached, plane charters, prices and tariffs, group estimates, and so forth.

Seymour Posner was selected by Rustin to be director of public relations. He worked from the fourth and top floor of the March Headquarters, along with staffer Evelyn Broidy, whose area was fund raising. Posner had worked with Rustin previously on two Youth Marches held in Washington, and he fulfilled Rustin´s requirements of experience, commitment and loyalty. Posner was not as experienced a reporter as were some of the public relations men who offered their services to the March committee, free of charge, that summer. Rustin felt, however, that he did not want an individual handling press relations who was there to make a name for himself, but rather someone he knew and who thought exactly like Rustin. Posner was thus tapped to fill the important position as director of public relations for the March. A short, dynamic, 38 year old man, Posner was on loan from the staff of the American Jewish Congress in the summer of 1963. His background included involvement in political campaigns, work as a housing specialist for the New York City Housing Authority, and public relations director of the New York Urban League, as well as his experience with earlier, smaller marches in Washington. Posner´s commitment to the civil rights movement was also clear. He had been on freedom rides in the south and on numerous CORE picket lines in the Bronx, where he was on CORE´s Executive Committee. By August, Posner, like most of the other staffers, was putting in 16-hour days, and began sleeping on an army cot next to his fourth floor desk.

It was not easy to work for Bayard Rustin, most staffers agreed. He was brilliant, a genius at problem-solving, but a most difficult taskmaster. He considered no quantity of work too excessive, and would not entertain complaints about an overload. As one staffer said, "Bayard buried us with work." Rustin was a master at planning such demonstrations, but this was to be the biggest in American history. All eyes were on the civil rights movement and its leaders that summer. The fate of the Civil Rights Bill and of future gains for blacks rested in large part on how the March would be perceived. The well-defined limits which the federal government would place on the format of the March as well as the expected large crowd made Rustin's job no easier:

"We wanted to get everybody, from the whole country, into Washington by nine o'clock in the morning and out of Washington by sundown. This required all kinds of things that you had to think through. You had to think how many toilets you needed. Where they should be? Where is your line of march? We had to consult doctors on exactly what people should bring to eat so that they wouldn't get sick. We even told people what to bring in their lunches. We had to arrange for drinking water. We had to arange what we would do if there was a terrible thunderstorm that day. We had to think of the sound system. There were just a million things."

The first tangible product coming out of the March headquarters was an eight-page brochure entitle "Organizing Manual No. 1." It was sent out in mid-July to numerous organizations, churches and individuals across the nation. Rustin had always been insistent that any demonstration in which he was involved have specific objectives. The organizing manual initially set forth seven: passage of the civil rights bill; desegregation of schools, an end to police brutality; massive federal public works programs; federal legislation to expand the economy; a new fair employment practices act covering state, municipal, and private employers; and a $2.00 minimum wage. In 1963, $1.00 per hour was the minimum wage. The initial organizing manual also suggested that unions seek to have August 28 declared a day off by their employers so that there would be substantial involvement in the March itself by union men and women.

Participation by organized labor was a major issue in the planning of the March. Unfortunately, the key endorsement for any such activity, that of the AFL-CIO Executive Council, was never obtained. AFL-CIO President George Meany opposed the idea of the March on Washington from the very start. Meany and A. Philip Randolph had argued bitterly in the past, in public and in private, over Meany's supposed "gradualism" in desegregating union affiliates. Meany had been irked by Randolph's creation of the Negro American Labor Council in 1959, and its criticism of the AFL-CIO: "Who the hell appointed you guardian of all the Negroes in America?"

Nonetheless, Randolph's pressure on Meany in the early 1960's had brought the AFL-CIO President around to a much more aggressive stance on civil rights, and the leaders of the movement were hopeful Meany would throw his support behind the March.

Meany was, in fact, a strong supporter of the Civil Rights Bill, and beyond that had clashed with the administration in June 1963

over the failure of Kennedy's bill to include a
fair employment practices commission. President
Kennedy thought such a provision would destroy
any chance of the Bill's passage by driving away
support of moderates in Congress.

On June 17, 1963, Meany had aired his views
before the House Judiciary Committee:

> "The plain fact is that Negro workers
> as a whole, North or South, do not
> enjoy anything approaching equal
> employment opportunity.
>
> "We ask you now, as we have asked the
> Congress for many years, for effective
> enforceable legislation to correct
> this glaring injustice, which must be
> corrected in order to make the other
> aspects of a civil rights program
> effective."

Ultimately, the Democratic administration
would come around to Meany's view. On the other
hand, Meany consistently fought against hiring
preferences for Negroes, in defending unionism's
seniority system. Preferring more traditional
methods of persuasion, mass marches were
definitely not George Meany's style. Despite
Walter Reuther's pleas and the support and
participation of many affiliates, there would be
no AFL-CIO endorsement. Some laid the blame on
Randolph for not seeking AFL-CIO endorsement at
the very outset, a tactic which Rustin had
outlined in his initial memo to Randolph the
previous winter. But there is no evidence that
the support Randolph needed would have been
offered, even had it been requested much
earlier.

In the vote on August 13, only Walter Reuther and James Carey of the Executive Council went along with Randolph in calling for the AFL-CIO to endorse the March. The debate was bitter. Other members of the Executive Council were said to be in favor but were unwilling to embarrass Meany. As a conciliatory gesture the Executive Council did issue a statement endorsing the goals of the civil rights movement, the right of affiliated unions to participate, "the right of any American peacefully to protest for a redress of grievances," and invoking "the hope that the March will be helpful and peaceful."

Reuther called the statement "anemic." The Executive Council's gratuitous support of the First Amendment hardly placated Randolph, who called it a "masterpiece of noncommittal noncommitment."

Meany himself told Randolph's biographer: "While we did not object to any of our affiliates participating, we were worried that the March might touch off a situation which might set us back legislatively. I was fearful that there would be disorder, that people would get hurt, and that it would build up resentment in Congress."

The Executive Council of the AFL-CIO, a federation of nearly autonomouos unions, indeed had no control over its affiliates, and many supported and contributed to the March on Washington, including the Auto Workers, Electrical Workers, AFSCME, IIGWU, the Hotel and Restaurant Employees and Bartenders International, and of course Randolph's Sleeping Car Porters. But the AFL-CIO's financial contribution and prestige was missing.

The AFL-CIO Executive Council decisin was subjected to continuing harsh criticism. One radio station editorial wondered "whether big labor would exist at all if its early organizers had followed the kind of leaning back tactics now recommended to the American Negro in his struggle for basic human rights." It went on to point out that mass demonstrations were not invented by the Negro civil rights movement, but by organized labor.

Later in the ´60s, Meany was outspoken in condemning anti-war demonstrations. It was not until September, 1981, after Meany´s death, that the AFL-CIO, under Lane Kirkland, would sponsor a mass march on Washington, the Solidarity Day demonstration in opposition to President Ronald Reagan´s economic policies.

Meany´s views on the direction, if not the tactics of the Civil Rights movement, were not far from the economic-oriented views of Randolph and Rustin. In the summer of 1964, after passage of the Civil Rights Act, Meany was instrumental in the creation of the AFL-CIO´s A. Philip Randolph Institute, which, among other things, funded apprenticeship programs. Despite the receipt of critical dossiers, perhaps directly from J. Edgar Hoover, recounting Bayard Rustin´s prior communist affiliations, Meany selected Rustin as director of the institute.

If support for the March by organized labor was incomplete due to the AFL-CIO´s decision, the slack was more than made up by the unanticipated and enthusiastic support by various church denominations. "Almost overnight America´s religious forces ... switched from mere verbal condemnation of racial discrimination to active, personal participation in the fight against it."

Leadership in race relations by the churches was mixed prior to the summer of 1963, particularly in the South. For every courageous minister who urged acceptance and compliance with the Supreme Court's school desegregation decision, there was another who would refuse to be "a stooge for the Supreme Court." Inspired by the moral leadership of Dr. King in Birmingham in 1963, church groups and individual clergymen began coming out in droves to actively support the cause in the summer of 1963.

The new activism of the churches commenced on June 7, 1963 at a meeting of the general board of the National Council of Churches of Christ in the USA. The Protestant group issued a stinging statement about past neglect by the church of the cause of desegregation coupled with a call for dramatic action.

At the group's urging, the National Council of Churches formed a commission on religion and race, made up of leaders of the Protestant, Catholic and Jewish faiths. Dr. Robert W. Spike, of the United Church of Christ, was named the Director of the commission. Dr. Spike appointed Anna Arnold Hedgeman, who was already on the administrative committee of the March on Washington, to coordinate church participation in the August 28 March. At about the same time, in early July, "the Big Six" became "the Big Ten," when the civil rights leaders added Auto Workers President Walter Reuther and Dr. Eugene Carson Blake of the United Presbyterian Church, Rabbi Joachim Prinz, President of the American Jewish Congress, and Matthew Ahmann, Executive Director, National Catholic Conference for Interracial Justice, to the March on Washington Committee.

Letters were sent to every church in the nation urging them to participate in the March on Washington. Ministers, priests and rabbis were urged to speak from the pulpit about the importance of protesting actively against segregation, and involvement in the March on Washington in particular.

There was said to be some jealousy on the part of civil rights leaders about the late involvement of the church leaders. For example, it was suggested that one of the church leaders speak at the August 28 demonstration rather than all three. As Hedgeman observed: "Civil rights leaders were not always as considerate of these allies as they should have been. There was a new undercurrent among Negroes generally that this was to be their protest to the nation and the world and that allies were, after a fashion, appendages rather than equal participants ... There was no suggestion that one of the six Negro civil rights leaders or perhaps two be asked to speak for the six civil rights organizations."

Bickering and jealousies, however, were very minor, and the churches were of enormous assistance in drumming up support for the march. There were dissenting voices, in particular, from southern congregations of the Presbyterian Church, who officially disassociated themselves from the March on Washington. Nonetheless, individual Presbyterian clergymen from both north and south were active participants in the March, 107 of them having attended on August 28.

While Rustin was getting his organizaion in New York going in early July, Robert Kennedy had set the wheels rolling for Administration involvement at precisely the same time.

For the task of coordinating the efforts of the March organizers with the Administration, the Attorney General chose, on Deputy Attorney General Nicholas Katzenbach´s recommendation, a young Justice Department lawyer named John W. Douglas, who had been with the Department only since January of 1963. Prior to that, Douglas had been with the prominent Washington law firm of Covington & Burling, where he returned after his government service terminated in 1966. Douglas was assisted by Alan Raywid, another young Justice Department lawyer. Their task was essentially to provide government assistance in terms of planning logistics, permits, and physical facilities. This was a new area without substantial precedents or rules since at that time massive political demonstrations on the scale anticipated were practically unheard of.

The administration´s interest was, in one sense, a selfish one – if the March was a failure in terms of poor turnout, in terms of bloodshed or violence, or in terms of mismanagement, it would reflect adversely on the administration.

A task force Douglas assembled to coordinate the Administration´s efforts to assist the March met every day from mid-July up until August 27, the day before the March. Besides Douglas and Raywid, this group included John Reilly, an attorney at the Justice Department, and former Kennedy advance man Jerry Bruno, considered a specialist in logistics and the handling of crowds. Bruno had worked on the President´s 1960 campaign. Raywid had been at Justice since 1957, when he was fresh out of law school. He had toiled as a trial attorney in the Admiralty section of the Justice

Department's Civil Division, before Douglas involved him in the March planning that summer.

Raywid's first assignment from Douglas was to draw up a list of things that could possibly go wrong. Raywid was a bit mystified by the assignment at first. Why didn't Douglas call in an expert to make up such a list? Douglas, reflecting a Kennedy administration bias, was skeptical of experts. Raywid compiled over 70 different negative scenarios, for each of which Douglas' committee developed a contingency plan.

The first meeting which Douglas called with those involved in the March was with District of Columbia police officials in July. This included not only the Metropolitan Police Department but also the Park Police, White House Police, and Capitol Hill Police, each of whom had authority in certain areas of the city.

The Metropolitan Police Department's representative was Deputy Chief Howard Covell, whom the Justice Department officials considered a "hardliner," a true law and order man. The March organizers, he told Douglas and Raywid at the initial meeting, were making demands he didn't like. If they were going to have their March, they would do it his way. The Justice officials were quick to assert their unwritten authority. The position of the government would be cooperation, not resistance. All police officials were to go out of their way to appease the demonstrators.

This was difficult for police officials to stomach, and an early battle took place between Douglas' staff and the police over the use of police dogs. The pictures of Bull Conner's forces in Birmingham were still very fresh in everyone's minds, and Douglas wanted no such confrontations, or even such symbols of confrontation, as police dogs on August 28.

The police position was a simple one: every policeman was to be on duty on the day of the March. The D.C. Police Department had a K-9 corps of 100 policemen with dogs, and they would be on duty on August 28 with their dogs. As a fall-back position, the police argued that the lives and safety of officers was paramount, and that they could not be worried about symbols of police brutality. The Justice officials rejected the idea that a few dogs could protect police lives in the face of thousands of demonstrators. Confrontation was to be avoided at all costs.

The issue became an emotional one for police officials, and a stalemate threatened to destroy federal/local cooperation in planning for the March. Finally Douglas went directly to the Attorney General with the problem. It was a measure of Robert Kennedy's concern about these details that he immediately called District Commissioner Walter Trobiner and told him: "No dogs." Tobriner called D.C. Police Chief Robert Murray, and the District's dogs remained out of sight on the day of the March.

Douglas' group next coordinated the jurisdictional lines of authority of the various police forces. There would be necessarily some overlapping of jurisdiction, and communication between the forces would be critical. The police brought in their traffic control plans for the March day, including elaborate charts. The Justice officials hacked up the plans and the police brought back several revisions.

Standard police procedure for dealing with demonstrations was that to the extent possible, no event or parade should disrupt the rest of the city. In this case, that meant the District of Columbia's workday of August 28 was not to be disrupted by the planned demonstration. From the very start, however, Douglas instructed the police otherwise, and turned the standard routine around: The March on Washington was not to be disrupted by the normal Washington workday.

Rustin was adept in dealing with police and government officials. "One of the reasons the March on Washington went so smoothly was that Rustin planned it, step by step, with the Washington police, who were too surprised to do anything but follow his instructions." On several occasions Rustin came down from New York to meet with Douglas and his associates and the District police. The meetings were generally amiable, at least after the dispute over where the March was to take place was resolved.

The Kennedy Administration's first task upon getting involved in the March on Washington was to convert the organizers' plans from a mass demonstration and possible civil disobedience on Capitol Hill to a peaceful rally at some other site in Washington. The Federal Statute banning demonstrations at or near the Capitol had been selectively enforced over the years but a demonstration of the magnitude that the civil rights groups were planning would clearly have not been permitted by Congress.

Attorney General Robert Kennedy personally took charge of the efforts to persuade the March Committee not to have the demonstration at the Capitol. Kennedy, for example, summoned UAW's Conway to the Justice Department in late June and asked him to use his "good offices" to turn the demonstration away from the Capitol to some other part of the city. Conway was also close to A. Philip Randolph and discussed the matter with Randolph, Rustin and the other leaders on several occasions in the latter part of June. "This took quite a bit of doing. It was not achieved in a single meeting."

Justice Department officials would have preferred merely a rally at the Washington Monument grounds without any march at all. However, a compromise was reached. It was decided that the demonstrators would mass at the Washington Monument in the morning and march the short distance - less than a mile - to the Lincoln Memorial where the rally and speeches would be held.

Even Congressional supporters of the civil rights bill were uncomfortable at the thought of having a mass demonstration within the earshot of Congress. Congressman Emanuel Celler of New York, Chairman of the House Judiciary Committee, warned organizers that he knew of Congressmen and Senators leaning toward support of the Civil Rights Bill, but who would turn against it if the demonstration on Capitol Hill was held.

The compromise was thus reached at an early date, and the decision announced to the press by Bayard Rustin on July 2, 1963. The selection of August 28, a weekday, requires some explanation. Most mass demonstrations were thereafter held on Saturdays, where large groups could be brought to town without conflicting with work schedules or school schedules.

The date selected was also in the last week of August, a traditional vacation time when potential demonstrators might be expected to be away visiting relatives or at a summer resort.

Randolph, Rustin, King and the other leaders wanted to be certain that Congress would be in session the day they marched. They did not want a demonstration without the objects of their plaints to be nearby, even if the demonstrators would be two miles from Capitol Hill. They wanted a media event that Congress could not ignore. Congress would remain in session through August, not adjourning for the Labor Day recess until the 30th, two days after the March. There would be a confrontation with the system while at work, although a peaceful one.

To the civil rights leaders the Lincoln Memorial was the perfect symbolic setting for the March. Workmen had broken ground at the memorial site on Lincoln's birthday, February 12, 1914, and the cornerstone was laid a year later. The completed memorial was dedicated on Memorial Day, May 30, 1922. Ironically, the proceedings were segregated, as were most events and facilities except Griffith Stadium and public libraries in the city of Washington at the time. Even Dr. Robert Moten, President of Tuskegee Institute, one of the principal speakers at the unveiling of Lincoln's statue, was not permitted on the speakers' platform during the ceremonies, but was told to sit in the all-Negro section to the far left of the Memorial, divided from the rest of the crowd by a roadway. So much for the spirit of the Great Emancipator.

Negroes were subsequently barred from bathing at the public beach around the nearby Tidal Basin by the Commissioner of Public Parks. However, the Lincoln Memorial was to figure prominently in what one historian has called the "turning point" in race relations in the District of Columbia in the spring of 1939.

Marian Anderson was a famous Negro contralto who had performed throughout Europe and the United States to great acclaim. In early 1939, her manager, Sol Hurok, booked her into Washington's premier concert auditorium, Constitution Hall. A few weeks before the scheduled concert, however, the Hall's owner, the Daughters of the American Revolution, decided to have the concert shelved because Miss Anderson was Negro. An uproar ensued. The President's wife, Eleanor Roosevelt, resigned from the DAR in protest.

Curiously, Negroes were permitted into Constitution Hall audiences but not allowed to perform. It was part of the patchwork segregation of the period. Across town at the National Theatre blacks could perform on stage but were not permitted to be in the audience.

As the controversy grew over the cancellation of the DAR concert, Secretary of the Interior Harold Ickes invited Miss Anderson to perform at the Lincoln Memorial on Easter Sunday, April 9, 1939. The concert was open to the public, and free of charge. Miss Anderson, who normally shunned publicity, agreed to appear. When she arrived in Washington, she stayed in the home of Gifford Pinchot, former Governor of Pennsylvania, since the city's major hotels were not then open to Negroes.

On Easter Sunday, 75,000 Washingtonians, white and Negro, came to hear Miss Anderson sing The National Anthem, O Mio Fernando, Schubert's Ave Maria, and three Negro spirituals. The crowd was not segregated as it had been for the Memorial's dedication 16 years earlier.

Miss Anderson's appearance was both a personal triumph and a triumph for the city's Negroes. The crowd of 75,000 spectators stretched in a great semi-circle almost back to the Washington Monument. It had been the largest crowd assembled in Wasington since Charles Lindbergh's triumphant return from Paris earlier in the decade.

Soon thereafter, the Daughters of the American Revolution changed their racial policy and Miss Anderson performed there many times, never expressing bitterness over her initial rejection. In later years Miss Anderson lent her hand to the civil rights struggle and accepted an invitation from the March on Washington committee to perform on August 28.

The Lincoln Memorial then was a symbol to black Americans in several ways and natural choice for the great rally. The structure has 36 columns surrounding the walls representing the 36 States in the Union at the time of Lincoln's death. The names of these States are cut into the frieze above the collonade. The Memorial is nearly 10 stories high, and its classic architectural lines are similar in plan to those of the Greek Parthenon, the temple to the goddess Athena on the Acropolis in Athens.

Inside, at the center of the open air Memorial, is the huge sculpture of Abraham Lincoln, seated. It stands 19 feet high and 19 feet wide. The marble statue of Lincoln sits at the back of the Memorial and faces the Reflecting Pool and Washington Monument. The Memorial chamber contains two other attractions other than the colossal seated statue of Lincoln – two huge inscribed stone tablets. On the north wall, inscribed in stone, is Lincoln's Second Inaugural Address; on the south wall, similarly inscribed, is the Gettysburg Address.

The Memorial, Washington Monument and Capitol all appear in a direct line with each other with the Monument in the middle. The Memorial and Monument are separated by the long, narrow reflecting pool, and the Capitol and Monument are separated by the long flat Mall. The distance between the Capitol and the Lincoln Memorial is over two miles - 11,470 feet.

Curiously, the March on Washington was one of the last demonstrations of any magnitude at the Lincoln Memorial. The site lines are not that good if a crowd of more than several thousand is present, since the reflecting pool lies directly in front of the steps of the Memorial, and stretches out the length of the Mall. The crowd is forced almost off to the side into a group of trees, and those in the rear could have a difficult time seeing the podium on the Memorial's steps. This was particularly true before the removal of some temporary office buildings which were a bare 50 feet from the reflecting pool itself, along the side of the Mall beyond the row of elms. These government office buildings, erected in wartime, remained until President Nixon had them torn down in 1969.

The lines of sight are much better at the Monument and Capitol where future mass peace demonstrations were held. However, the symbolism of the Memorial site in the 100th anniversary year of Lincoln's Emancipation Proclamation was apparent. It further answered the Administration's criticisms about a threatening March on Congress creating a backlash against the Civil Rights Bill on Capitol Hill. It was also legal to hold a demonstration there which could not be said for the Capitol.

An examination of the layout of the area demonstrates why the government was much more comfortable with the Lincoln Memorial as the site for the March: First, there was nothing for a crowd to destroy in the area, least of all the seemingly indestructible Memorial itself; second, strategically, with water on three sides, the demonstrators could easily be contained; third, it was distant from any concentrations of people and residences.

The adjacent roads and Constitution Avenue could be sealed off quickly and the demonstrators surrounded. To the west of the Memorial was a semi-circular roadway and Memorial Bridge. To the north beyond the raggedy temporary buidings was an ill kempt pasture and a few baseball diamonds behind the temporaries´ parking lot up to Constitution Avenue, now the site of the Vietnam Memorial and Constitution Gardens. To the east beyond the reflecting pool lay 17th Street and the Monument grounds. To the south a park road and the Tidal Basin, no significant symbols to attack, no passersby to interfere with, and no place for out-of-hand demonstrators themselves to escape or hide. To skittish law enforcement officials it was the perfect place in Washington for a demonstration to be contained.

The threat of violence was perhaps overplayed all summer, but in retrospect, that fact assured such caution and concern by officials and demonstrators that there would be no trouble. Nonetheless, there was planned opposition to the August 28th March. It came in the form of a call for a counter-demonstration by American Nazi Party leader George Lincoln Rockwell.

Rockwell, an outspoken racist, had his headquarters close to Washington, in suburban Arlington, Virginia. He was an avowed white supremacist, and claimed thousands of followers, although he never mustered more than a few hundred at any one time. The party's rhetoric was always stronger than their actions. When Rockwell first heard of the August 28 March, he went through the proper channels to seek a permit for a counter-demonstration.

The decision to grant one was up to D.C. police officials, who with Justice's John Douglas' blessing, promptly turned Rockwell down. Rockwell kept trying, however, and went on a speaking tour of Virginia and other areas of the south to collect followers for his August 28 campaign. The idea of this counter-demonstration was a major worry for administration and police officials throughout July and August, although as the summer wore on it became obvious that Rockwell's planned counter-demonstration would be inconsequential, if it resulted at all.

In order to be apprised of the possibility of violence at the August 28 March, the Justice Department turned, of course, to its own in-house investigative body, the Federal Bureau of Investigation. Unfortunately, J. Edgar Hoover and his Bureau had other concerns that summer which severely limited the ability of Justice to get a handle on possible violence on the day of the March. Rustin's comment to Justice Department officials at a July meeting was enough to warrant close surveillance of opposition groups: "If Negroes coming by buses from Mississippi were attacked and the buses burned, as has happened in our recent history, let us say the night before, then we are faced with a totally new psychological situation." Yet J. Edgar Hoover was less concerned about violence directed at Negroes then was he frightened by the involvement in the March of what he had historically seen as America's true enemies.

In November of 1960, shortly after John F. Kennedy's narrow victory over Richard Nixon in the presidential election, one of the President-elect's first announcements of appointments to his new administration was that of the Director of the Federal Bureau of Investigation. To no one's surprise, Kennedy announced that he would reappoint J. Edgar Hoover as Director, then in his third decade as head of the FBI.

Unfortunately, as the Kennedy Administration's stance on civil rights for Negroes became more progressive, Hoover's own preferences and proclivities suffered. The FBI Chief's racism has been widely documented, as has been his hatred for civil rights leaders, particularly Martin Luther King, Jr.

Thus Hoover was horrified at the Administration's tacit support for the March on Washington. Hoover was determined to discredit the March and its leaders. To do so, presidential speechwriter and historian, Arthur Schlesinger, reports "the Director fell back on the cry that had never failed him in the past: the ineluctable threat, evidently undiminished despite all his effort, of Communist infiltration..."

All summer long Hoover solicited from his agents in the field reports on Communist involvement in the March on Washington. When the initial reports correctly showed little or no involvement, Hoover became angry, and castigated his underlings for not doing their job.

The reports "improved," Assistant Director William Sullivan later saying, "We had to engage in a lot of nonsense which we ourselves really did not believe in. We either had to do that or we would be finished."

The Bureau redoubled its efforts to discredit King, seeking to link him to known or suspected members of the Communist party. One of King's friends was a wealthy New York lawyer named Stanley Levison, who had guided and counseled the SCLC since the mid-50's. Levison, whose affiliation with the Communist Party, U.S.A. has never been proven, was the subject of ongoing surveillance and wiretapping by the FBI. By the spring of 1963 reports reached the highest levels of the Administration concerning King's association with Levison. Harry Belafonte, Harris Wofford, a Kennedy aide, Burke Marshall and finally the Attorney General spoke to King about Levison. Finally at the June 22 White House meeting, the President himself took King into the Rose Garden to warn him about his association with Levison and another suspected Communist, Jack O'Dell. King eventually put distance between himself and Levison, at Levison's own suggestion.

By fall, after the March, the FBI had begun regularly tapping Dr. King's telephone. In the meantime, that summer the Bureau flooded the White House and, in some instances, leaked to the press alleged evidence of Communist affiliation with King and the civil rights movement itself. While the Administration was interested in knowing the possibilities of violence of August 28, they were instead getting from Hoover's Bureau innuendo about disloyalty and in some cases reports on Dr. King's sex life.

The memos and accusations of the FBI had no effect on the Kennedy brothers, at least outwardly. In his July 17 press conference the President would tell reporters that there was no evidence of any Communist involvement in civil rights demonstrations. "I think it is a convenient scapegoat to suggest that all the difficulties are Communist and if the Communist movement would only disappear that we would end this." Robert Kennedy would write to several Senators: "Based on all available information from the FBI ... we have no evidence that any of the top leaders ... are Communists or Communist controlled. This is true as to Dr. Martin Luther King, Jr., about whom particular accusations were made, as well as other leaders."

Hoover called King the "burrhead" in some of his memos - a racist term popular among Washington area whites at the time. An FBI report on the August 28 March would call King's "I Have A Dream Speech" demagogic and term King "the most dangerous Negro in the future of the Nation ..." Meanwhile the FBI dragged its feet all summer, both in investigating police abuses against civil rights workers in the south and in providing adequate intelligence about the prospects of violence at the March on Washington.

4

"The general feeling is that the
Vandals are coming to sack Rome."

- Washington Daily News

The Washington to which Randolph's marchers
would come was no longer, by 1963, the sleepy
southern town which a generation of commentators
had tried to dub it. The New Deal and World War
II had changed that. But neither was it the
cultural and business center to which it aspired
in the 1970's and 1980's. It retained much of
its old characteristics, including lingering
forms of segreation and paternalism, not the
least of which was manifested in the lack of
"Home Rule" for the city. Congress was the
"Mayor" of Washington in 1963, and citizens did
not have the right to vote. Cries for home rule
had fallen on deaf ears for years, and there was
no sign of change.

The most remarkable statistic about the
city of Washington in 1963 was that it had
become the first predominantly Negro large city
in the country. About 800,000 people lived in
Washington, D.C. in 1963, about 55% of them
black, with that percentage increasing rapidly
because of white suburban migration.

These surrounding Maryland and Virginia
suburbs were then overwhelmingly white. During
the workday there was a "population exchange" as
suburban whites poured into the city to work,
and thousands of negro women went to the suburbs
to work at domestic jobs for $5.00 or $10.00 per
day. The white migration to the Maryland and
Virginia suburbs had proceeded dramatically
throughout the 1950's, and white newcomers to
the area typically headed for Montgomery County,
Maryland, or Arlington, Virginia, or at least

were directed there by eager real estate agents. The Southeast and Northeast sections of the city became black enclaves, and in most instances, slums. With the construction of the Capitol Beltway around Washington in the early 1960's, white suburbanites could avoid these slums entirely in traversing the metropolitan area by automobile. This pattern of segregated housing in the city had been formalized in 1926 when the United States Supreme Court upheld the validity of restrictive racial covenants in residential deeds in the District of Columbia. This meant that the Courts would continue to enforce statements in old deeds that said a residential plot of land could never be conveyed to or occupied by Negroes, a typical 19th century restriction. An adjoining homeowner could thus enforce such covenants against neighbors who sought to sell their home to Negroes, or even rent to them.

In the thirties and forties, when the first Maryland and Virginia suburbs began to be settled, racial segregation became the rule. Clarendon, Virginia, and Bethesda and Greenbelt, Maryland simply barred blacks. The latter town was one of the highly touted New Deal planned communities. Up until 1960, Washington's daily newspapers included racial classifications in their classified housing ads. That practice had ended, however, as well as enforcement of racial covenants, and by 1963 neighborhoods were slowly integrating, at least until the white families in the neighborhood made their moves to the suburbs.

Integration of employment, like housing, had been a slow process. In 1956-1957 some modest gains were made with the phone company, transit company and the large department stores, after CORE organized boycotts. When integration in employment stalled thereafter, CORE renewed its boycotts in 1962, again with some limited success. While the D.C. Metropolitan Police Department, for example, was only 10% black by 1957 in a city that was more than 50% black, progress was being made by the time of the March on Washington, with blacks being actively recruited.

Washington's public schools had been desegregated peacefully in the mid-1950's after the Supreme Court's decision in Bolling v. Sharpe, a companion case to the nationwide desegregation case, Brown v. Board of Education. The district's numerous parochial schools had been desegregated even several years before Brown.

Public accommodations in Washington were desegregated in the early 1950's, following peaceful sit-ins and favorable court decisions. Movie theatres were integrated in 1953, and parks and most recreation facilities in 1954, the latter after a bitter struggle. By 1960, much had been accomplished in terms of transforming Washington from a segregated Southern city.

But Washington, D.C. was by no means a model city for race relations in 1963. The official aspects of race discrimination had largely been eliminated, but the fight to open people's minds to equality was hardly getting off the ground. Nor was economic equality anywhere in sight.

In the early 60's, few blacks in Washington had professional jobs, and the disparity in income between blacks and whites was enormous. The social structure and subsistence living of many of the city's poorer blacks was the subject of Elliott Liebow's famous work, Tally's Corner,

which was based on his observations of a
Washington, D.C. neighborhood in 1962.

Even as the legal position of blacks
improved, social relationships between blacks and
whites in Washington, as elsewhere, seemed to be
deteriorating. Crime was epidemic in black
areas and increasingly spilling over into white
neighborhoods, a situation which played on the
fears of the Washington area's white populace.
As late as August of 1963 the Washington Star
and the Washington Daily News continued to
faithfully report the race of crime victims and
their assailants, or at least when a white
victim was involved.

Blacks and whites lived in separate
neighborhoods, generally attended separate
schools, with the prevalence of white private
schools in the area, and had different
employment experiences. In sum, there was
growing mistrust between the races of
"unofficial" Washington, the native residents of
the city whose existence was generally obscured
by the national media's focus on the federal
government in the city.

This underlying tension in race relations
among Washingtonians had exploded to the surface
violently on Thanksgiving Day, November 22,
1962. It was the occasion of the annual city
championship football game at the new District
of Columbia (now Robert F. Kennedy) Stadium,
played before a sell-out crowd of 51,000. At
that time it was the biggest crowd ever for a
sporting event in the District of Columbia.

The city championship game was played every
year between the winner of the Interhigh (D.C.
Public School) League Championship and the
Catholic League Champion. By 1962, all of the
Interhigh Schools in the city except Western and

Wilson in the extreme western portion of the city were almost entirely black. The Catholic schools were predominantly white. In 1962, for the second year in a row, Eastern of the Interhigh was facing St. John's of the Catholic League.

A fight on the field erupted in the 4th quarter between an Eastern player and a St. Johns' player resulting in the Eastern player being ejected and two 15 yard penalties, which effectively eliminated Eastern from the game. St. Johns won, 20-7. As the game ended thousands of black youths poured across the field from the Eastern side. As the crowds attempted to exit the stadium, fights broke out on the concourse and on the exit ramps, in the parking lots and in a 5-block area surrounding the stadium. It took 100 policemen assigned to the stadium area to restore order. There were no major injuries, but many minor injuries. Thirty-three persons were treated at area hospitals and nine people arrested.

While the police and press downplayed the racial aspects of the fighting, it was clear to observers that the fights were racially motivated. Black youths attacked whites and white youths attacked blacks.

Most newpapers called for the termination of the city championship games, and the games were halted for several years. President Kennedy himself referred to the riot on Thanksgiving Day at a press conference in January, decrying what he saw as growing racial tension in America, and in the District of Columbia in particular.

It was with this background that the city of Washington, D.C. faced the prospect of thousands of mostly Negro demonstrators pouring into town to demand civil rights in the summer of 1963, a summer marked by violence throughout the country wherever civil rights demonstrations occurred. That violence, in fairness, was rarely initiated by the civil rights advocates themselves. More often, it was the local police, as in Birmingham, or white counter demonstrators who objected to "parades" or "public singing" or the "carrying of signs."

Washington, D.C. had absorbed crowds before and had handled them well. Every four years hundreds of thousands arrived in town in January for a presidential inauguration. The Fourth of July firewords celebration also brought hundreds of thousands to the Washington Monument area each year without any major incidents. But the March on Washington for Jobs and Freedom was to be different. First, those coming would not be spectators, as inauguration day and independence day revelers were. They would be participants in a political demonstration, petitioning for justice, making demands, and confronting what many saw as the enemy in a recalcitrant Congress. Secondly, the demonstrators would be coming to town in the middle of the work week, not on a holiday, and presumably not in a holiday mood. On a Wednesday such as August 28, 1963, the city would already be crowded with government workes, private industry workers, shoppers and tourists.

Lastly, a factor that went unmentioned by most commentators lest they be labelled racists, these thousands of demonstrators coming to town would be mostly Negro. To nervous whites and to government officials, this meant additional wariness. It did not matter that the violence of the early 1960´s was generally white-induced or police-induced. The week before the March on Washington, Business Week, commented on the large Negro involvement: "One small distrubance could set off a wave of mob violence." It was clear from the precautions taken by federal and District of Columbia officials in the weeks prior to the March that they felt the same way. In reality, relatively affluent Negroes were the typical participants of the March on Washington. In fact, the explosion of the nation's ghettoes was at least a year or two away, and in the case of Washington's ghetto, five years away.

Whatever its background, the city of Washington was not foreign to large-scale demonstrations. There was a mixed record of success in handling demonstrators in Washington, however, and that record was itself a factor to be examined in approaching the 1963 March.

The earliest recorded march to the Nation's Capitol to petition the national government to redress grievances was in 1783, when unpaid soldiers marched to Philadelphia, at that time, the Capitol, to demand the funds due them from the fledgling--and broke--government. In those simpler times the infant Congress had a simple solution to deflect the demonstrators: they packed their bags and held their legislative meetings temporarily in Princeton, New Jersey.

The right of the people peaceably to assemble was severely tested by "Coxey's Army" in 1894. The group of about 400 had come to Washington from Massillon, Ohio, at a time of high unemployment amidst an economic depression, seeking public works programs and a "legal tender" bill designed to put unbacked paper money in circulation. For those radical ideas Jocob S. Coxey and his associates were driven from the Capitol area by mounted police and Coxey was jailed. His "Army of the Commonwealth of Christ" dissipated within weeks.

After the turn of the century, suffragettes began holding springtime parades in New York City, and their numbers gradually increased. In 1913 they decided to stage a demonstration in Washington to coincide with the eve of President Woodrow Wilson's inauguration. Five thousand women marched down Pennsylvania Avenue and over a half million people, many in town for inaugural activities, watched from the sidewalks. Wilson wondered where the crowd was to greet him when he pulled into Union Station while the March proceeded half a mile away. "General" Rosalie Jones' army was orderly, but many of the male spectators were not. The women were jostled and heckled, and a unit of cavalry had to be called from Fort Myer, across the river in Arlington, to clear the parade route.

In the 1920's a revived, out of the closet Ku Klux Klan was gaining a foothold in the North. By 1924, it was purported to have over 4 million members, with its rhetoric heavily anti-Catholic as well as anti-Negro. On August 8, 1925, the Klan boldly staged a march in Washington and obtained a permit for a "formal ceremony" at the Washington Monument. Forty-five special trains carrying 600 "Kleagles" came through Union Station, and auto caravans arrived from as far away as Texas. Officials set aside miles of then barren land in Bethesda, Maryland, outside Washington, for the Klan to set up a camp.

On the big day 25,000 white-robed marchers turned out, with a reported 16,000 family members watching the parade from the sidelines. The Klan had stressed it was to be a non-violent display, although they were said to fear violence by Catholic counter-demonstrators. No trouble occurred, and only one anti-Klan demonstrator was arrested. The Washington Star was said to have played up the event "as if it were a national celebration". Federal officials were certainly cooperative in providing permits and the camp sites, and the Klan was also permitted to erect and burn an 80 foot cross on the Virginia shore of the Potomac.

"Communist inspired" or "communist led" were perjoratives used to describe, by one opponent or another, most subsequent 20th century marches on Washington. Only the December 7, 1931, "hunger march" on Washington of 1,500 unemployed persons probably came anywhere close to being so inspired. Unemployment was well over 20 per cent, with at least 12 million persons out of work, and the New Deal relief programs several years away. In those darkest of economic times for America, the demonstrators were said to have sung the dreaded "International", and to have given three cheers for the Communist Party. The less than revolutionary Salvation Army fed and housed them however, and no major ruckus ensued, despite the fact that the marchers were turned away from the Capitol and White House area.

The following month, in January 1932, a more respectable unemployment march led by a Catholic priest from Pittsburgh, James Cox, brought to Washington a phenomenal 20,000 marchers. Most came from depressed areas of western Pennsylvania in a cavalcade of 2,000 cars. Presumably because of their religious backing, Cox's group was permitted to march up to the foot of the Capitol, unlike their "red" brothers in December. They waited peacefully while Father Cox himself presented a useless "Resolution of the Jobless" to Congress and to President Herbert Hoover, asking for a five billion dollar jobs program. The marchers then staged a quiet, patriotic walk to Arlington

Cemetery to lay a wreath at the Tomb of the Unknown Soldier.

The real trouble took place later in the spring and summer of that year, 1932, when up to 20,000 marchers converged on the District of Columbia in support of Texan Congressman Wright Patman's bill for immediate payment of bonuses to World War I veterans. The bonuses were authorized by Congress in 1924, but not payable until 1945. The veterans, who became known as the Bonus Expeditionary Force, or simply the Bonus Army, felt they would starve to death long before 1945 given the state of the economic depression gripping the nation. Initially from Portland, Oregon, but soon from all over the country came thousands who, indeed, had little else to do with their time, President Hoover's prosperity still lurking around some unknown corner.

At first the Bonus Army appeared to have a benefactor in D.C. Police Chief Pelham D. Glassford, a veteran himself and a World War I General. The first group arrived at the end of May. Glassford put them up in some old abandoned buidings on Pennsylvania Avenue. Evelyn Walsh McLean, the wealthy owner of the Hope Diamond, and others, purchased some food for the marchers but when their numbers swelled in early June, Glassford had to set them up in camps in the forsaken Anacostia flats. It became a disaster.

The shanty city must have resembled a modern day Latin America "suburb" of lean-tos, shacks and tents. One Walter W. Waters from Ohio emerged as a leader of the increasingly ragged band, now approaching 20,000. They were, in fact, not doctrinaire revolutionaries as the December 1931 group were alleged to have been, but then the bonus marchers stayed a lot longer, quickly wearing out their welcome. The city was not taken by the flies, mosquitoes and poor sanitation of the camps.

A week after a June 7 march down Pennsylvania Avenue, the House actually passed the Patman Bill, but it ran into trouble in the more consevative Senate. Hoover, with questionable political wisdom, announced that he would have vetoed the Bill anyway.

The Bonus Army refused to leave town, even after Congress, before adjourning for the summer, authorized $100,000 for free transportation home for the demonstrators. Hoover quickly signed that bill.

Glassford used his influence at first to prevent a contingent of Marines from sweeping through the camps, but the District Commissioners ordered immediate clearance of the Pennsylvania Avenue buildings. The squatters refused Glassford's plea to vacate and the eviction turned bloody, two marchers dying from police gunfire.

The local police were clearly unable to do anything about Anacostia Flats, so Hoover called on the regular army and General Douglas MacArthur, who was ably assisted by Majors Dwight D. Eisenhower and George S. Patton, Jr. Six tanks, cavalry, 600 infantrymen and machine gun crews rolled across the Potomac River bridges from Fort Myer and from Fort Washington in Maryland. The removal of the demonstrators and the sacking of their camp was swift but controversial.

For the next year, into 1933, smaller marches of the unemployed and the hungry were staged in Washington: a "Child Misery march" of 150 in November, 3,000 hunger marchers and 300 dirt farmers in December, and in May 1933, a group of unemployed college graduates.

The second Bonus Army also arrived in May 1933, and the new Roosevelt Administration received them more warmly. The demonstrators were housed rather pleasantly at Fort Hunt near Mount Vernon. They were fed copiously, according to newspaper accounts, and visited by First Lady Eleanor Roosevelt, who led them in songfests. More importantly, most found jobs in the government forestry service and left town without incident. The bonus payment was not authorized until 1936, ironically over President Roosevelt's veto. Later during FDR's tenure three thousand farmers came to Washington, peacefully, in 1935 to support the President's Agricultural Adjustment Act. But it was on the eve of World War II, in the summer of 1941, that trouble brewed for the Roosevelt Admnistration when the cries of March on Washington were heard again, this time from a new source.

The New Deal had made economic conditions better for Negroes in relative terms, but the gap between whites and Negroes was still immense. While there was talk in the 1930's among white liberals and progressive forces about comprehensive reform to assist Negroes, the growing war clouds in Europe tended to "distract," according to one historian, interest in such reform.

War production and preparation put a lot of previously unemployed Negroes and whites to work, but invidious forms of discrimination faced Negroes in the defense factories, military, and federal government. In 1940, the Marines and Army Air Corps simply refused Negroes, and all-Negro army platoons were commanded by white officers. Negro typists and stenographers were placed in segregated pools in federal government offices in Washington, and promotion was illusory. The most severe discrimination occurred, however, in the private defense plants in hiring, and in the pay and promotion of the few Negroes able to land jobs.

A. Philip Randolph had risen to the head of the Brotherhood of Sleeping Car Porters, and was interested in joining forces with Negro leaders in developing strategies for improving the Negro economic plight. In January of 1941, Randolph met with NAACP leaders and announced plans for a mass march on Washington by 50,000 to 100,000 blacks on July 1 to protest discrimination in the defense industry, government, and military:

> "Only power can effect the enforcement and adoption of a given policy... Power and pressure do not reside in a few, an intelligentsia. They lie in and flow from the masses. Power does not even rest with the masses, as such. Power is the active principle of only the organized masses. The masses united for a definite purpose."

The call for the March received immediate support from the supposedly conservative National Association for the Advancement of Colored People and the Urban League, and also from the Negro churches.

Randolph traveled around the country drumming up grass roots support for the March, particularly in Baltimore, New York, St. Louis, Chicago, Detroit and Washington itself. In New York City, Randolph personally invaded the Negro barber shops, saloons, and poolrooms, talking to the unemployed and underemployed, urging them to support the March on Washington. Randolph´s fellow porters used their contacts and and their traveling potential to further publicize the March.

There was no official reaction at first but when Randolph staged a spring rally at Madison Square Garden attended by 30,000 Negroes in support of the March, the White House and the city of Washington began to get worried. The prospect of a segregated city accommodating a group of Negro demonstrators larger than the Bonus Army was discouraging. The attempt to superimpose a picture of the Negroes' plight on American foreign policy was worrisome, as Negro leaders cited the hypocrisy of the posturing of moral outrage at Hitler's policies.

First Lady Eleanor Roosevelt was dispatched to New York City and a meeting arranged by Mayor Fiorello LaGuardia with Randolph and NAACP Executive Secretary Walter White. The white officials urged Randolph to call off the March. They told Randolph there would be bloodshed and death, and that he was going to "get Negroes slaughtered."

Even the usually sympathetic Eleanor Roosevelt suggested the March would be counterproductive. Randolph told the group he would call off the March only if President Roosevelt issued an executive order guaranteeing non-discrimination in the defense industry and government offices. This was a unique, non-legislative proposal, a presidential order to aid civil rights for Negroes. When John Kennedy became President 20 years later, Dr. Martin Luther King, Jr. and others would chide him about his failure to live up to his campaign promises to end much discrimination "with a stroke of a pen." At the New York meeting, Mrs. Roosevelt immediately announced her support for the Presidential Order, and went home to lobby her husband.

The President was still convinced, however, that he could get "Phil" to call off the March in exchange for some vague promises to investigate matters and to persuade private industry to do better by Negroes. He called a meeting at the White House the following week, on June 18, inviting Randolph, who was accompanied by Walter White. Mayor LaGuardia was present as well to witness the expected capitulation of the March planners.

But Randolph never came close to throwing in the towel in exchange for something like a government study commission, as FDR proposed. LaGuardia is said to have spoken up: "Let´s get practical. Phil won´t call off the March."

The President agreed to have an executive order drafted for consideration, but Randolph and his associates could not immediately agree with administration officials on the language, and so they went back to New York and continued their planning for the March. Preparations were nowhere near those of 1963, but there were buses being chartered, and Negro marchers being enlisted.

On the morning of June 24, 1941, one week before the proposed March, Randolph was back at the White House. LaGuardia detailed the proposed executive order, which had been drafted by Joseph Rauh, then a young government lawyer (and in the 1960´s, a principal in the civil rights movement). Randolph and his aides took copies of the plan and mulled over it at lunch. It did not go far enough in Randolph´s view, and did not adequately cover government employment itself.

The While House was said to be "outwardly incredulous" when Randolph and his associates announced this after lunch. Randolph would later tell an interviewer that he figured that he had the administration "on the run" and he was not about to back down.

By four o'clock that afternoon, June 24, all had agreed on Executive Order 8802, which laid down rules of nondiscrimination for all plants with defense contracts and all federal offices and agencies. When the President signed the next day, it was the first time since Lincoln's Emancipation Proclamation in 1863 that a President of the United States had issued an official order protecting Negro rights.

Randolph's decision to call off the March in light of Executive Order 8802 caused a furor in the ranks of the organizers of the March, particularly among the younger activists, including Bayard Rustin. Randolph criticized these younger radicals, but as a consolation, as well as to monitor the effect of the non-discrimination order, he sought to maintain a permanent March on Washington Committee. There were discussions of later marches but nothing was organized until the late 1950's.

The proposed 1941 March received very little press attention, as was characteristic of reporting in those days on civil rights issues. The Washington Star devoted only a few paragraphs to the executive order on an inside page, without even mentioning Randolph's name or the proposed March. Would it have been a success? In later years, Randolph would tell Rustin privately: "Bayard, its a good thing President Roosevelt signed that Executive Order, because I don't know if we would have gotten 500 people to Washington for that March."

"The March on Washington Committee" published a series of demands in 1942 calling for laws against lynching, the poll tax, and discrimination in education, housing, transportation, and "especially we demand, in the capital of the nation, an end to all segregation in public places and in public institutions." The list also called for better Negro representation in the armed forces and federal administrative departments, agencies and missions. During wartime, however, there was apparently little public interest in expanding the modest advances of June 1941, and organized mass political demonstrations of any type were rare in Washington throughout the forties.

In 1953, seven to ten thousand marchers paraded in front of the White House to protest the impending executions of convicted atomic bomb spies, Julius and Ethel Rosenberg. But the most obvious precursor of the 1963 march was the May 17, 1957, march and rally to commemorate the third anniversary of the Supreme Court's historic school desegregation decision, Brown v. Board of Education. It was A. Phillip Randolph's and Roy Wilkins' idea for what was termed the Prayer Pilgrimage for Freedom in deference, it was said, to Martin Luther King's Christian orientation. The young Martin Luther King became the third leader of the Pilgrimage after a meeting with Wilkins' and King's idol, Randolph, in New York City on March 25, 1957. The three met again in Washington on April 5 with 70 associates. Rustin, Ella Baker, Thomas Kilgore, and Ralph David Abernathy did the bulk of the organization over the next six weeks, drumming up support chiefly among Negro church groups. The NAACP, with some help from the SCLC, financed the events.

The cast of participants indeed made the 1957 Pilgrimage a dry run for the 1963 march: speeches by Randolph, Wilkins and others; a song by Mahalia Jackson; appearances by celebrities like baseball star Jackie Robinson, and entertainers Harry Belafonte, Sammy Davis, Jr., and Sidney Poitier; and participation by a few thousand whites. Dr. King gave a rousing speech aimed at voting rights, a speech which climaxed the day's program and which brought the crowd of about 30,000 to life:

"Give us the ballot...and we'll transform the salient misdeeds of bloodthirsty mobs into the abiding good deeds of orderly citizens.

"Give us the ballot...and we will fill our legislative halls with men of goodwill, and send to the sacred halls of Congress men who will not sign a southern manifesto because of their devotion to the manifesto of justice.

"Give us the ballot...and we will place judges on the benches of the South who will do justly and love mercy, and we will place at the head of the southern states governors who have felt not only the tang of the human but the flow of the Divine..."

A year later Randolph and his associates were back in Washington marching down Constitution Avenue to the Lincoln Memorial, as they would in August of 1963. This time about 10,000 black and white "youth" marchers had a narrower stated purpose, school desegregation. Again in 1959, the "third annual" integration march was held, this bringing 25,000 to

Washington. There were no more annual marchers for integration in Washington, perhaps because the focus of the growing civil rights movement switched to the deep south in 1960 with the student sit-in demonstrations.

The final instance of attempted direct political action in Washington, before the 1963 March, was that of about 3,000 college students in February 1962, who had come to urge President Kennedy not to resume nuclear testing. This was some eight months before the Cuban Missile crisis. The peaceful demonstrators were said to have been treated courteously by members of the President's staff who met with them.

By the following year this courtesy had evolved, although slowly, into complete cooperation, or as some critics have said, co-option. These marches and rallies in the several years before 1963 attracted only minimal attention in the mass media, and were not accompanied by threats or expectations of violence. However, in the early 1960's, many civil rights demonstrations had turned violent, with most of the violence fired by white counter-demonstrators or recalcitrant police and city officials. Thus, when the August 1963 March on Washington confronted federal and local officials, they went out of their way to welcome the demonstrators, as much out of a sense of sympathy to their aims as out of a desire to avoid the violence that had taken place in the south.

5

The summer of 1963 was a
revolution because it changed the
face of America. Freedom was
contagious. It boiled in nearly
1000 cities.

— Martin Luther King, Jr.

As July 1963 opened it was evident that the
so-called Negro revolution was in full stride.
A political scientist observed then that
gradualism and tokenism in civil rights would no
longer pass for progress among Negroes, and that
the protest movement had been "suffused with a
new militancy, a new sense of urgency. This is
evident in the widespread use of deliberate mass
jailings, open sneering and jeering at white
policemen, a disposition to meet violence with
violence, a tendency to package several demands
together — to demand total integration rather
than to work for one reform at a time — and the
involvement of greater numbers of people from
all strata of the Negro community. Freedon Now!
has become the new slogan."

In Boston during the last week of June,
three thousand singing and chanting
demonstrators gathered on Boston Common to
eulogize Medgar Evers. Massachhusetts Governor
Endicott Peabody bowed to demands and gave Bay
state employees two hours off to attend the
rally. In Raleigh, N.C., Negro leaders rejected
moderate Governor Terry Standord´s plea to halt
their demonstrations. In Philadelphia, one
thousand civil rights demonstrators marched on
City Hall for four hours to demand an end to
discrimination by unions and contractors on
public building projects. A score of the
demonstrators remained to sit-in at city
offices, and also announced a hunger strike. In

Denver three thousand Negroes staged a three-mile-long parade to a City Council meeting where they demonstrated against discrimination in public and private employment and in housing. In Savannah, there were violent demonstrations and hundreds of arrests as police battled protesting Negroes. Discrimination protests even came to Hollywood during the first week of July. Negro leaders there threatened to picket movie studios and theatres to protest the lack of Negro actors in major films. They pointed to the fact that not one Negro was seen among the thousands of actors in the movie about D-Day, The Longest Day, even though thousands of Negro soldiers landed with allied troops on Normandy in June of 1944.

As the demonstrations continued, so did the successes of the civil rights movement. More than 50 Atlanta restaurants agreed to desegregate on a trial basis starting in July. Under siege, the Catholic Bishop of Savannah, agreed to desegregate diocesan schools in September. New York Governor Nelson Rockefeller announced a speed-up of state construction projects in order to create more jobs, particularly for Negroes. In Washington, the Pentagon announced an end to all forms of discrimination in the Armed Forces Reserves, and tougher enforcement of such regulations. Governor Bert T. Combs of Kentucky issued a number of executive orders designed to end discrimination in that state. Each victory brought renewed hope and renewed protest by increasingly confident, and increasingly militant demonstrators.

In early July, Time observed: "Week by week, the U.S. Civil rights revolution burns more deeply in its intensity, shifts into bewildering new directions, expands fiercely in

its dimensions. Leaders follow and followers
lead. Congressional time tables are upset.
Negro organization officials find themselves
riding a crest they cannot control. Negro
moderates suffer vilification, or the threat of
physical harm, for their moderation. White
politicians who have achieved power through
their championship of civil rights find
themselves hooted by audiences who think they
have not been civil righteous enough."

In July, the white churches climbed aboard
the bandwagon. This was nowhere more evident
than in the National Commission on Religion and
Race's involvement at Gwynn Oak Amusement Park
in Maryland. Gwynn Oak was a private amusement
park in Baltimore Country, Maryland, and had
always barred Negroes from admission. A
carefully planned demonstration on the Fourth of
July resulted in arrest of 300 demonstrators
from CORE and the church group. Among the list
of the incarcerated was the Reverend Dr. Eugene
Carson Blake, executive head of the United
Presbyterian Church, and one of the most
respected clergymen in the United States. Time,
which had placed Dr. Blake on one of its covers
two years previously, reported that Blake had
told fellow clergymen prior to the Gwynn Oak
protest: "Some time or other we are all going
to have to stand and be on the receiving end of
the fire hose." It was a measure of the
clergymen's commitment that they publicly
aligned themselves with one of the most militant
of the civil rights organizations, CORE, for
their first involvement in direct action
protest.

The Fourth of July demonstration began at
Baltimore's Metropolitan Methodist Church where
the demonstrators prayed and sang hymns. They
then marched in groups to Gwynn Oak Park which

had been the scene of CORE protests for eight
years. County police and amusement park owners
were ready for the demonstrators, quickly read
them the trespass law, and began making
arrests. Many demonstrators had to be dragged
away and some were clubbed by police. Many
whites inside the park taunted the demonstrators
but police kept the two groups apart. Some of
the clergymen refused to post bond and remained
in jail for several days.

Eight weeks later after lengthy mediation
efforts undertaken by the Baltimore County Human
Relations Commission, the amusement park's
owners capitulated and agreed to admit blacks,
despite delaying tactics and protests by
Baltimore County Chief Executive Spiro T. Agnew,
who reportedly thought too many concessions had
been given to the demonstrators.

Gwynn Oak Park was not the only site for
demonstrations on the Fourth of July weekend.
On Long Island, demonstrators blocked the road
leading to Jones Beach to protest the State Park
Commission's refusal to hire more Negroes and
Puerto Ricans. There were 123 arrents in
Charleston, South Carolina, after a parade, when
police claimed that the demonstrators had
blocked traffic and refused to obey orders to
move on. Construction workers and demonstrators
battled each other at a school construction site
in Newark, New Jersey. Protesters were
complaining about the lack of jobs for Negroes
and Puerto Ricans in construction jobs. There
were also demonstrations in Gadsden, Alabama and
Chicago, Illinois.

The NAACP held a stormy convention over the
Fourth of July weekend in Chicago. Mayor
Richard Daley was booed when he told the
delegates that there were no ghettoes in

Chicago. The next day Daley was heckled as he marched in the NAACP Fourth of July parade. But the Reverend J. H. Jackson, President of the National Baptist Convention, received even rougher treatment from the delegates. Jackson announced that he opposed any mass Negro march on Washington and was physically as well as verbally abused by some of the delegates. The University of Mississippi's first black student, James Meredith, took up the same theme in opposing the March on Washington at the NAACP Youth Convention, and members roundly booed him.

Some observers felt that this new impoliteness was a result of the "infiltration" of the movement by menial lower class Negroes who had therefore not been active. The Negro Revolution was no longer a black middle class and white liberal movement. Events of that summer and the summers which would follow would give proof to that fact.

The new militancy was in full swing by mid-July. Savannah, Georgia Negroes went on what Time called a window-smashing, tire-slashing rampage that lasted for 48 hours. Police used tear gas and fire hoses to quell the rioters. The following night, as Negroes laid down in the streets to stop traffic, the police began making arrests. A pitched battle began, and the demonstrators threw rocks and bottles at the police.

In Cambridge, Maryland where a truce had been arranged between black demonstrators and city officials, violence erupted when militant blacks allegedly pressured moderates into breaking the truce. The National Guard returned to the riot-torn city. A 9:00 p.m. curfew was invoked, and a form of martial law declared.

The white liberal press reacted adversely to the new Negro militancy, as even the New York Times, complaining about sit-down demonstrations outside Mayor Robert Wagner's office, stated demonstrators should not be allowed to interfere with the functioning of government. But even as the press highlighted increasingly militant Negro protests, it downplayed white violence directed at Negroes throughout the country and daily evidence of police brutality against demonstrators.

On Capitol Hill through mid-July, the Senate Commerce Committee conducted hearings on the administration's civil rights bill. Many of those called to testify were ardent segregationists like Mississippi Governor Ross Barnett, who complained that the Kennedy brothers had encouraged demonstrations, freedom rides, sit-ins, and picketing in violation of the law. "Gentlemen, if you pass this civil rights legislation, you are passing it under the threat of mob action and violence on the part of Negro groups and under various types of intimidation from the executive branch of this government." Barnett went on to accuse the Kennedy brothers of aiding the world-wide communist conspiracy. Barnett displayed a poster allegedly linking Dr. Martin Luther King to a communist training school.

A few days after Barnett's testimony, Alabama Governor George Wallace came to Washington to give his views to the Senate Committee. Wallace saw the real purpose of the civil rights movement as being to disarm the country for the benefit of the Soviet Union. "As a loyal American and as a loyal southern Governor who has nver belonged to or associated with any subversive element, I resent the fawning and pawing over such people as Martin

Luther King and his pro-communist friends and associates." Wallace went on to attack a U.S. Air Force order which permitted Air Force personnel to engage in civil rights demonstrations as long as they did so while in civilian clothes and off duty. Wallace remarked on Defense Secretary McNamara's order: "we will now see Purple Hearts awarded for street brawling.

Secretary of State Dean Rusk and Attorney General Robert Kennedy took their turns in defending the administration's bill. Rusk, a Georgian, noted the connection between foreign policy and civil rights: "We must try to eliminate discrimination not to make others think better of us, but because it is incompatible with the great ideals to which our democratic society is dedicated." Rusk added that if he was a Negro he would be demonstrating on the streets that summer as well. The Attorney General repeatedly clashed with North Carolina Senator Sam Ervin, a former Associate Justice of the North Carolina Supreme Court and a respected constitutional lawyer.

Next to testify was Roy Wilkins who calmly and logically defended the public accomodations section of the civil rights bill. "For millions of Americans this is vacation time. Families load their automobiles and trek across the country. I invite the members of this committee to imagine themselves darker in color and to plan an auto trip from Norfolk, Virginia to the Gulf Coast of Mississippi. How far do you drive each day? Where and under what conditions can you and your family eat? Where can they use a rest room? Can you stop after a reasonable day behind the wheel, or must you drive until you reach a city where relatives or friends will accomodate you for the night? Will your children be denied a soft drink or an ice cream cone because they are not white? ... The Negro American has been waiting upon voluntary action since 1876. He has found what other Americans have discovered: Voluntary action has to be sparked by something stronger than prayers, patience and lamentations. If the thirteen colonies had waited for voluntary action by England, this land today would be part of the British Commonwealth."

President Kennedy, as he heard and read about the sometimes violent July demonstrations, decided to express his concern to the nation. He told a July 17 news conference that the more violent demonstrations were counterproductive. The President, however, made his first public defense of the March on Washington at the July 17 news conference. He called the March a peaceful assembly for the redress of grievances, and indicated that he might even attend himself: "They are going to express their strong views. I think it is in the great tradition. I look forward to being there."

Almost on cue violent demonstrations did indeed diminish as July came to a close, at least temporarily. Many of the civil rights leaders on both local and national levels were now actively involved in the planning for the March on Washington. It had become the focus, with the Presidential seal of approval, for the events of the historic summer of 1963.

At his next press conference, two weeks later on August 2, the President conceded what some public opinion polls were showing: that his stance in favor of civil rights for Negroes was costing him heavily in political prestige and popularity. He stated, however, that he would not retreat from his stand. He remarked that it was a good thing that "extreme form" of demonstrations had recently subsided because he believed in some cases they were becoming "self-defeating." He stated that he believed that responsible Negro leaders realize that they face a long drawn-out task "which requires education and all of the rest, and a quick demonstration in the street is not the immediate answer." Meanwhile some of the demonstrations Kennedy was critical of were bearing fruit.

In Charleston, South Carolima on August 2, 87 white merchants gave into six demands of Negro picketers including the desegregation of the stores' fitting rooms, rest rooms, lounges, and drinking fountains. The store owners further agreed to permit Negroes to try on hats and other articles of clothing; to extend courtesy titles to Negro customers; and to grant equal pay and equal employment opportunities for Negro workers in the stores.

NAACP pickets were out in Farmville, Prince Edward County, Virginia, which had closed its public schools in 1959 rather than integrate. The Mayor of Farmville continued to enforce a week-long ban on all "parades." That Saturday twelve demonstrators, nine of them juveniles, were arrested when they paraded in Farmville despite the ban.

Also, on the 2nd, in Chicago, nearly 100 CORE demonstrators, most of them white, were arrested during a sit-down strike protesting de facto school desegregation. On Chicago's south side, 49 white demonstrators of a different view were arrested when they protested a black family moving into their neighborhood.

Demonstrations and racial unrest went on in Chicago all summer. Initially, there were several neighborhood battles over the moving of

black families into white neighborhoods. After
the publicity of Birmingham, demonstrations
mushroomed in Chicago, most led by CORE or the
NAACP, but some by unaffiliated local groups.
The protests centered around job opportunities
and de facto school desegregation. Only 10
percent of the city's elementary schools were
integrated: 65 percent were all white, and 25
percent all black. White migration to the
suburbs had swelled Chicago's black population
to 23 percent by 1960. Police broke up
picketing on several occasions in August, and
made mass arrests amidst charges of police
brutality. Whites, meanwhile, had formed
neighborhood "improvement associations" designed
to prevent desegregation of housing. SNCC
executive secretary James Forman, a former
Chicago school teacher (not to be confused with
CORE's James Farmer) remarked on the unrest:
"The tradition of non-violence is weaker in the
northern cities than in the south."

In New York City, Jackie Robinson, the
former baseball star and the first black in the
major leagues, marched with pickets demanding
more jobs for Negroes and Puerto Ricans on
publicly financed building projects. Thirty-
four persons, but not Robinson, were arrested
when they sat in at one of the sites. Across
town at the United Nations, U.S. Ambassador
Adlai Stevenson announced an embargo on the sale
of military weapons to South Africa, in a
somewhat mild stand against that country's
racist apartheid policies. Soviet Delegate
Platon D. Moroyov, however, scoffed at what he
saw as hypocrisy on Stevenson's part, alleging
that America's "unbridled racism" proves there
is "no moral basis to claims that the United
States is the defender of human rights in the
free world."

On that Friday, August 2, the Senate Commerce Committee ended hearings on the Civil Rights Bill amid signs that the public accomodations section would be amended to exempt small neighborhood establishments which had little or no impact on interstate travel. The bill's opponents were fond of referring to a fictitious "Mrs. Murphy" who owned a small rooming house and for whom the public accomodations section would be oppressive. "She" became the darling of southern obstructionists. At that time it was thought that the Civil Rights Bill was headed for the Senate flour - and an expected filibuster by the Southern block - in mid-September, after consideration of the Nuclear Test Ban Treaty.

Meanwhile, several miles from Capitol Hill, in Bowie, Maryland that Friday, August 2, the Prince George's County CORE picketed a Levitt subdivision office and model home because of the company's refusal to sell homes to blacks. The company issued a statement: "Our policy, as stated previously, is to obey the law and follow local custom. This policy at Belair is the same as that of every other builder in the area."

Friday, August 2, 1963 was also the day on which Arthur Ashe became the first black named to the U.S. Davis Cup Tennis Team. Ashe was then a 20-year old junior at U.C.L.A. The Davis Cup Chairman told reporters that Ashe was selected on merit, not because he was black, adding that "the boy had a fine year."

On Saturday, August 3, the Big Ten met at March headquarters in Harlem with Rustin and his staff to assess their progress. Walter Fauntroy amd Julius Hobson from the Washington office also attended. Things were going better than anyone had expected. The leaders were now willing to publicly make a crowd estimate of 150,000, based on information received from local organizers. It was decided that there would be no demonstrations in front of the White House on the 28th, with the President himself now behind the March. Nor would there be any individual delegations sent to Capitol Hill other than the 10 leaders themselves for "lobbying." Special seats would be set aside at the Lincoln Memorial, however, for Congressmen who wished to attend the March and rally. The Lincoln Memorial program after the March was to be kept as short as possible so the demonstrators could start filing out of Washington by 5:00 p.m. With the crowd expected now at 150,000, it was decided that there would be two lines of March from the Washington Monument to the Lincoln Memorial, one down Constitution Avenue and a parallel one down Independence Avenue. The March committee's budget was upped to $75,000.00 from $65,000. The extra funds at that point on August 3 were earmarked for bringing poor Negroes up from the south for the demonstration. The extra funds were being derived from sales of the official March button which was a runaway best seller that summer. By August 3, 42,000 of the 25-cent buttons had been sold, and the Big Ten decided to order 50,000 more to augment the remaining supply of 8,000.

A. Philip Randolph beamed with confidence after the meeting as he told reporters of the revised crowd estimate. He also carefully pointed out that no "communists" or "lunatic fringe" would infiltrate the demonstration. This evidently somewhat appeased Arizona Senator and 1964 Republican Presidential Candidate Barry Goldwater, who told reporters that day he thought the August 28 March is "perfectly proper." and that it was alright with him, "as long as it stays peaceful."

But all was not peaceful the weekend of August 3rd and 4th. There were more demonstrations, more arrests, and some white initiated violence. Seven pickets were arrested outside a segregated White Castle diner in Newark, New Jersey, for "singing too loud." Twenty-five CORE pickets in Torrance, California, and 10 NAACP pickets in Athens, Georgia, were jailed. In Huntington, West Virginia, the owner of the White Pantry restaurant was reported to have threatened Negro sit-in demonstrators with a knife, and then to have thrown a cake of sulphur at them. The picketing continued that Saturday at the Levitt project in Bowie, Maryland, and four white segregationists from the "Federation of American Nationalists" arrived to picket the pickets. Despite all the activity at his new housing project, William J. Levitt, President of Levitt and Sons, Inc., one of the area's major home builders, was determined to hold the line against desegregation.

Segregationists in the Washington, D.C. metropolitan area, and there were many of them in 1963, had the unenviable position of having the eyes of national leaders and the national media constantly trained on them. The counties of Montgomery and Prince Georges (where Bowie was located) are the two Maryland jurisdictions bordering directly on the District of Columbia. It was to these two counties that many white District residents had moved in the "white flight" of the fifties, leaving the District as the north's only predominantly black large city. Facilities in Montgomery and Prince Georges' were generally desegregated by 1963, although as a practical matter segregated neighborhoods were the rule, as the Bowie dispute indicated.

There was some fear or at least talk among these white Maryland suburbanites about an "overflow" of violence into their neighborhoods if the March on Washington got "out of hand." With these thoughts floating around, and perhaps not wanting to be left out of the action, the Montgomery and Prince Georges' County police chiefs prepared their forces for the worst. Both announced three weeks before the March that all leave for police officers had been cancelled for August 27-29. In addition, special training in civil disturbance was provided to many of these suburban policemen. There were no plans to use suburban police officers as back-up units for the District policemen or National Guard, and the Lincoln Memorial was at least five miles from the Montgomery or Prince Georges' County line.

All of Maryland's democratic congressmen had gone on record in favor of the Administration's civil rights bill. The lone Republican Congressman, Rogers C. B. Morton, who represented the conservative Eastern Shore, was cool toward the bill and toward civil rights demonstrations. Embattled Cambridge was within Morton's district. Maryland's Governor Tawes and Baltimore's Mayor McKeldin supported the March on Washington and encouraged participation by Marylanders. But Maryland was one state where Alabama Governor Wallace was musing aloud about running in the Democratic Primary for President in 1964.

Virginia, where American Nazi Party leader George Lincoln Rockwell had his headquarters in Arlington, was much closer to downtown Washington than Maryland's border. Virginia was

even officially more hostile. Virginia Governor
Harrison, on August 8, turned down a request of
Virginia Negro leaders to proclaim August 28
"Freedom Day." He noted that to grant the
request would be "entirely inconsistent and at
variance with my views in opposition to Federal
'civil rights' legislation and mass
demonstrations."... He went on to say:

> In Virginia there is great opportunity
> for men and women of all races with
> ability, skills and ambitions and
> possessed of a sense of
> responsibility. My efforts as
> Governor have been, and shall
> continue, along these lines. I am
> convinced that only from that
> direction will come ultimate
> resolution of the problems, real and
> imaginary, that confront the nation,
> and which have brought about racial
> unrest."

In 1963, Virginia remained staunchly within
the southern bloc, like all its sister states of
the former confederacy. Its elected Congressmen
and Senators, almost to a man, were segregationists who staunchly opposed the Civil Rights
Bill. Virginia jurisdictions had been in the
forefront of the "massive resistance" to the
Supreme Court's 1954 Brown vs. Board of
Education decision. There were some exceptions,
such as Manassas, near Washington, D.C. whose
business leaders in August voluntarily announced
desegregation of restaurants and theatres.

On the same day Governor Harrison was
issuing his statement, New York lawyers William
Kuntsler and Arthur Kinoy were in a federal

appeals court in Virginia trying to get an injunction against Danville, Virginia's outright ban on all civil rights demonstrations. It had been a bloody summer in Danville, as demonstrators had repeatedly battled with police, and in that sense Danville was a typical segregated southern town in the summer of 1963.

Danville, in southwestern Virginia, was and is a textile manufacturing town, dominated by the presence of the Dan River Mills, a massive textile mill employing 12,000 people, 10 percent of whom were very low paid Negroes. Danville was nearly completely segregated, including theatres, restaurants, housing, and medical facilities. Only the public library had been desegregated in 1960, after sit-in demonstrations.

Now three years later, Negroes in Danville, stirred by events in Birmingham and elsewhere, and by the call for the March on Washington, were active again. In early June there were several marches to demand segregation of employment in municipal agencies, including police and fire departments. The police scuffled with demonstrators at City Hall and beat and jailed Negro leaders for inciting to riot.

Danville civil rights leaders then called in SNCC field workers for assistance, and the real battle began against Mayor Julian Stimson's obstructionist forces.

A peaceful, prayerful March on June 10 to protest the high bail set for Danville rights leaders ended in a bloody police riot, when demonstrators were suddenly set upon by police with night sticks. Following the example of Birmingham, high pressure fire hoses were also employed to knock demonstrators down, leaving them as easier targets for the police clubs. Forty demonstrators required medical treatment, and 37 were arrested. Mayor Stimson threatened to "fill every available stockade."

The demonstrations continued, however, and SNCC executive secretary James Forman was called in to help. Simultaneously, Danville police increased their armaments by rolling out an anti-riot tank, and machine guns. Forman and thirteen other persons were promptly indicted under an old Virginia law which forbade "inciting the colored population to acts of violence and war against the white population." All except Forman, who managed to leave town before being arrested, were jailed with high bail. The law was ultimately ruled unconstitutional. The police actions in Danville undoubtedly aroused activist feelings in many of the town's previously uninvolved Negroes. A large contingent would make the four-hour bus drive to Washington for the March.

On the evening of August 7th the local District of Columbia march organizers had a meeting at the Shiloh Baptist Church to drum up support among D.C. residents. Four hundred people reportedly attended. Three D.C. residents, Henry Dixon, Richard Lyon and Belford Lawson were appointed to a committee to mobilize District residents.

On the housing front it was urged that people open up their homes to demonstrators, with housing registration booths to be set up on the Monument grounds the day of the March. Walter Fauntroy announced that Georgetown University, at the urging of Archbishop O'Boyle, and several parochial schools, had offered facilities to house demonstrators. Fauntroy, when asked what would make the demonstration successful, cited peaceful demonstrators, effective police, and responsible government officials to hear grievances.

The Civil Service Commission had been encouraging the various federal agencies to freely allow annual leave on August 28. However, it decided against allowing administrative leave, that is, leave with pay. Federal officials were said to feel that the tremendously congested traffic, parking, eating facilities and other problems facing the city would be alleviated this way. There were 260,000 government workers in the D.C. area then, nearly all of them located in the downtown area.

Sterling Tucker, executive director of the Washington Urban League and chairman of the March's housing bureau, predicted that only 40,000 District of Columbia residents would march, noting a tendency for District people to stay at home "because they feel this is somebody else's march."

On the same day, Wednesday, August 7, A. Phillip Randolph met on Capitol Hill with 75 congressmen to discuss plans for the March. All members of Congress had been invited to the meeting. Randolph said the meeting, called by Senators Paul Douglas, Jacob Javits and Phillip Hart, and Congressmen John Lindsay and Emanuel Celler was "to keep Congress fully informed of the purposes and objectives of the March as well as to answer questions and receive suggestions."

Randolph himself had urged Senator Douglas to call the meeting a week earlier, noting his disappointment in a letter to Douglas that prominent Americans, including members of

Congress, "have an altogether mistaken concept of the purpose and character of the March."

After meeting with the Senators and Congressmen, Randolph had a cordial meeting with D.C. Police Chief Murray to discuss organizational details.

The same day Murray also met with American Nazi party leader George Lincoln Rockwell in an effort to dissuade him from carrying out a planned counter-demonstration on the 29th. The police department had earlier denied Rockwell a parade permit for the 28th, and had advised him that this meant he and his followers, if they appeared, would have to remain on the sidewalks and obey all pedestrian traffic signals.

Rockwell, undaunted, told Murray he was seeking a permit from the Interior Department for a rally on the 28th. The Justice Department officials would, of course, see to it that such a permit would never be issued. Rockwell also told Murray that he expected 10,000 supporters to appear for his counter-demonstration. He said he had been traveling and speaking throughout neighboring Virginia recruiting those willing to come to Washington on the 28th. Nazi uniforms would not be worn, but the Nazis would assemble at the Monument on the morning of the March, and "stroll in small groups" to the Capitol to see their Senators and Congressmen.

Nazi recruiting literature was a good deal more strident than Rockwell's comments to the press. A flier that had been obtained by the New York March headquarters stated that August 28 will be the day that the "White Man will sweep away the black revolution. Washington, D.C. will be the battleground."

This threat of trouble between rival groups of demonstrators was being considered in Indiantown Gap, Pennsylvania, where District of Columbia guardsmen were at their annual summer camp that week. Their training there was geared toward riot duty at the March on August 28. Prior to that time, the D.C. guard had not had such experience, at least not in anyone's memory. In the years of the late 1960's it would become their specialty. Murray dispatched Deputy Police Chief Howard Covell to the guard camp to discuss tactics with the guard officers.

The March organizers had decided in July to have their own police force of sorts, so as to better avoid the possibility of a clash between demonstrators and the Washington police. Thus a plan for training 2,000 unarmed marshals was implemented. About half came from a New York City group called the Guardian, an established fraternal organization of New York City policemen. William H. Johnson, the Guardian's President, was named chief parade marshal by A. Philip Randolph. The 45-year-old Johnson had been a patrolman for 22 years, and was assigned to the New York Police Department's Youth Division. Johnson's troops included black officers from New York City suburbs and Hartford, Jersey City, Newark, Atlantic City and Philadelphia, as well as members of Guardian. Johnson spent much of his vacation time in August in the Harlem headquaters recruiting marshals and developing strategy. He also attempted to work with the Washington police department, but on his first trip to Washington in late July he encountered a roadblock in the form of Washington's CORE leader, Julius Hobson, who had independent ideas of his own about a force of marshals.

Hobson was a dedicated activist, but not very easy to get along with in the opinion of most of those involved in planning for the March, both on the government side and within the March committee. Hobson clashed repeatedly with the relatively mild mannered Fauntroy in the D.C. March office, and with Justice and police officials at their frequent meetings. When Johnson returned from his first trip to Washington, he wrote a report to Rustin and Randolph, saying that "Mr. Hobson is going to be a problem throughout."

Hobson was known in the D.C. area for leading a number of successful boycotts and demonstrations aimed at local merchants and utilities. He was able to recruit 1,000 men and women to act as marshals in a short period of time. Unlike Johnson's forces, Hobson's were untrained in law enforcement. Hobson himself trained his volunteers in a series of six training sessions in the week before the March. Many of the March organizers were secretly glad that Hobson was preoccupied "playing Napoleon marching his troops up and down," and not otherwise interfering with their planning.

Three of the training sessions in August were held on site at the Monument and Lincoln Memorial. The training was said to be mostly in "non-violent tactics." The plan for the day of the March was for the marshals to surround any violent demonstrator to isolate him or her from the remainder of the throng. If the marshals were then unable to get the individual to "refrain from misbehavior," they were to summon D.C. police who would make the arrest. None of the marshals were armed, nor did any have police powers. They were identified on March day by sashes across their torso.

To aid the marshals, a communication system was set up by 10 radio experts. A central radio station was set up inside the Lincoln Memorial, with 36 satellite stations in the demonstration area. In addition to guiding the marchers along the line of march, the marshals carried instructions as to the location of the nearest rest rooms, eating places, medical facilities, and water foutains. The marshals also assisted in meeting incoming trains and buses and directing those disembarking to the staging area at the Monument. As things worked out on the day of the March, Johnson´s forces and Hobson´s forces worked well together and were praised by police officials and the March leaders.

Early in the morning of Friday, August 9, President Kennedy´s three-day-old son Patrick, died of a breathing impairment in a Boston hospital. The President spent considerable time in Hyannisport that month as his wife recovered from her difficult pregnancy. He was, of course, kept advised of developments and demonstrations. That weekend, for example, his brother-in-law, Peace Corps Director Sargent Shriver, sent by a special messenger a letter he had received from the National Conference for Interracial Justice. Shriver was on the National Executive Committee of the Conference, and had received the letter which had gone out to all local councils.

Shriver referred the President especially to page two of the letter, where the anticipated figure of 250,000 marchers appeared. It also stated that there would be none of the feared "lobbying" in Congressional hallways. The President could breathe a sign of relief. His decision to have his administration get involved in the March was apparently paying off, both in number of participants and in peaceful tactics.

But as if purposely ill-timed, August 9 was the day that federal felony indictments were handed down against nine civil rights leaders from Albany, Georgia, for leading peaceful picketing of a grocery store. It was an action that angered many black leaders, in particular SNCC leader John Lewis. The Washington Star editorialized that the indictments showed that Attorney General Kennedy had not betrayed his trust in "seeking votes" by siding "with the Negro against the white man.'

The Albany indictment story began with the 1961 shooting of a handcuffed Negro minister, Charlie Ware, who later sued his assailant, Sheriff Warren L. Johnson of Baker County. In April of 1963, the civil suit came to trial, and an all white jury refused to find the Sheriff liable. One of the jurors, Carl Smith, was a grocer in an all-black section of Albany. His store was among those that had been boycotted and picketed by Negroes for a period of a year. When Smith closed his business soon after the trial, the FBI began looking into connecting the picketing to Smith's service as a juror in the Ware trial. Although the picketing demonstrators carried signs protesting Smith's refusal to hire blacks, and few if any knew he had any connection with the Ware trial, the FBI and Justice Department diligently pursued the matter. Thirty-eight agents were at various times assigned to the case, and Attorney General Kennedy himself announced the indictments of the leaders of the Albany Movement for obstruction of justice and perjury.

Justice Department lawyers assisted the local U.S. Attorney at the criminal trial. The gorvernment exercised peremptory challenges for any blacks on the jury panel - that is striking without cause any potential black jurors. Eight of the nine were found guilty and most given lengthy jail terms for what was essentially peaceful picketing of a merchant who would not hire Negroes. The convictions were later overturned on appeal.

In a further affront to Georgia blacks a few days after the Albany indictments were handed down, the Justice Department announced that the FBI had found no evidence of police brutality in Americus, Georgia, despite press reports of police beatings with baseball bats, and the use of electric cattle prods on demonstrators. An FBI agent stated that the allegations were "analyzed thoroughly and were found to be gross distortions and complete untruth." He also denied the fairly well-documented allegation that FBI offices in the south were staffed with pro-segregation agents.

While the Kennedys mulled over these matters in Hyannisport, the weekend of August 9-11 was another active but not so peaceful weekend for civil rights demonstrators throughout the nation. Scores of arrests were made that Friday night in the cities of Williamson and Goldsboro, North Carolina. Negroes were charged with trespassing for entering segregated facilities, or parading without permits.

Further north, a melee developed in Elizabeth, New Jersey, where Negroes were picketing a segregated construction site. On Saturday pickets staged an all-night sit-in at the Levitt housing site in Bowie, Maryland. On the west coast more arrests were made Saturday and Sunday at a segregated housing project in Torrance, California. Minority hiring was the issue at a demonstration outside the Hotel Syracuse in upstate New York. Six arrests were made in Baltimore when Negro youths attempted to integrate a private swimming quarry. There were also demonstrations in scores of other localities, the largest in Farmville, Virginia, and Jefferson City, Missouri.

All of these actions across the country and numerous unreported incidents were relatively spontaneous outbursts of activism by individuals and small groups, most of whose past involvement in demonstrations were minimal. Unlike the limited media attention of earlier events, demonstrations were a hot news item that summer, and as the news spread, so did the demonstrations. There was often no single sponsor like CORE, SNCC, the NAACP or SCLC. Nor were the leaders of the local demonstrations well known, since most of the national leaders were busy working on the March. Dr. King made few public appearances in August, as he was vacationing and writing in upstate New York.

Some cities and towns saw protests by newly formed local groups without any outside affiliation. Further, the local contingents of the major civil rights organizations were independent, and in most cases did not seek any approval or support for their local actions.

These newly formed ad hoc groups were also significant in building support and numbers for the Washington March. They heard about the March through news reports, and flooded the March committee headquarters with requests for details. Some letters were simply addressed "A. Philip Randolph, March on Washington Committee, New York, New York." The post office delivered the mail to the Harlem headquarters. Other inquiries were sent into the national offices of the NAACP and CORE, which forwarded the letters to Rustin. All received encouragement, and the

Committee's organization manual. This made for some dificulty in discipline, as a number of the local groups still had in their head a sit-in in the halls of Congress. Indeed, they were ready to transform their local tactics into mass action at the seat of national government.

Meeting in Chicago over that weekend of August 9-11, the American Bar Association Convention passed a hotly debated compromise resolution calling for respect for the law by both sides in the civil rights controversy. The ABA refused to take a stand on the proposed Civil Rights Bill. Earlier that year, at the suggestion of Robert Kennedy and others, a group of liberal but establishment lawyers, mainly on the east coast, had formed the Lawyers' Committee for Civil Rights. The influential group, unlike the ABA, became a strong vocal supporter of the Administration's rights policies. But liberal attorneys were unable to have passed a pro-civil rights resolution by the conservative ABA.

The outgoing ABA President, James Satterfield of Mississippi, told the convention delegates that President Kennedy's bill would mean the "destruction of the United States of America as we have known it. The President-elect (and later Supreme Court Justice) Lewis F. Powell, Jr., of Richmond was considered more of a moderate on civil rights issues.

The same day that the AFL-CIO Executive Council was making its final decision not to get involved in the March, Tuesday, August 13, the March committe received a cable of support from an unwanted source, the Chinese Communist government in Peking. The support was unwanted because it seemed to fuel the fires of conservatives who were speaking out loudly about the March being Communist-led, and part of a world-wide Communist plot to unsettle democracies.

Undoubtedly, as President Kennedy had warned King in June, there were communists involved in soliciting support for the March. J. Edgar Hoover had scores of FBI agents out gathering data on Communist support all summer. Negroes would complain that the G-men should have been deployed protecting peaceful protestors in the South and investigating attacks by white racists on Southern Negroes.

The conservative press seized on the communist participation and attempted to portray it as communist domination, which it clearly was not. On the same day Peking was sending its telegram of support, William F. Buckley´s conservative National Review was printing a quote from Political Affairs, a leftist publication:

"...The fight for Negro freedom has become the focal point, which at this juncture holds the key to all other struggles, including the fight for peace. What is demanded, therefore, is that all progressive and left forces, and especially all Communists, throw themselves into the battles which lie ahead on this front. More specifically, it is necessary, first to mobilize all possible support for the administration´s civil rights legislation...what is called for is bigger demonstrations and espcially a mass outpouring on August 28, such as has never before been witnessed."

The President and his brother, the Attorney General, both militantly anti-Communist, would be very surprised at the suggestion that they were somehow "duped" into introducing civil rights legislation by communists. But opponents of the bill would not hesitate to employ communist support for the bill as an argument against it.

The Communist Party, U.S.A. had long lent its support to certain liberal causes, particularly civil rights legislation, probably because its members supported the specific issue as right, just, moral, and probably also because, as the National Review said, civil rights demonstrations were "a natural attack on the social fabric, attuned to Communist ends." By 1963, most Americans were planning themselves on a particular side of an issue on the issue's own merits, and not on the basis of where the Communist party stood. This was evident by the widespread support for civil rights legislation and the later protests by varying groups opposed to involvement in Vietnam. Nonetheles, the National Review found "respectable demonstrators are indeed morally implicated by the coincident Communist purposes."

In any event, the March leaders felt bound to reply to the Peking cable, rejecting the endorsement. Roy Wilkins was chosen for the task, and he sent a return cable a few days later. He first thanked the Chinese for their good wishes but proceeded to refute every accusation the Chinese had raised in their cable concerning the President and Congress. Wilkins specifically praised President Kennedy's support for the March and civil rights legislation. He also condemned the lack of freedom in China: "We await the opportunity to send our felicitations to Chinese citizens gathered in a huge demonstration in your Nation's Capital to protest living conditions under your government and welcomed there by your heads of state." Wilkins' cable was released to the press and publicized, and there was no further comment from the Chinese Communists.

Closer to home the charge of communism was being leveled directly at Bayard Rustin. Senator Strom Thurmond of South Carolina opened a virulent attack on the same day as the Peking cable, August 13. Thurmond harped on Rustin's past communist affiliations, and threw in the fact of Rustin's 1953 arrest on a morals charge. Thurmond demanded further investigation of communist influence in the March: "I am not satisfied and many people across this country are not satisfied with the Attorney General's efforts to whitewash the question of communist influence or involvement in these Negro demonstrations." Robert Kennedy had consistently publicly downplayed the supposed communist influence. In private he winced, and was pleased that Hoover kept the flow of reports coming.

Randolph jumped to Rustin's defense on the morals charges, voicing his complete confidence in his character, integrity, and extraordinary ability. "Twenty-two arrests in the fight for civil rights attest, in my mind, to Mr. Rustin's dedication to human ideals. That Mr. Rustin was on one occasion arrested in another connection has long been a matter of public record, and not an object of concealment. There are those who contend that this incident, which took place many years ago, voids or overwhelms Mr. Rustin's ongoing contribution to the struggle for human rights. I hold otherwise."

Rustin issued a lengthy reply which mostly concerned Thurmond's allegations that Rustin was a Communist and a draft dodger. Rustin pointed out that he had registered for the draft in World War II as a conscientious objector, in line with his Quaker background: "I did not dodge the draft. I openly and vigorously opposed it. Twenty-eight months' imprisonment was the price I willingly paid for my convictions."

Rustin had joined the Young Communist League in 1938 while a student at City College of New York because he shared their pacifist and racial justice ideals. He promptly left the League in 1941 when the league advised him that there would be no more protests about integration in the U.S. military. America was now a Soviet ally, Hitler having attacked Russia. In his reply to Thurmond, Rustin noted that he had always been opposed to "totalitarianism and undemocratic elements everywhere — in Russia as well as South Carolina."

Rustin had long broken all ties with communism by 1963, as had many other Americans who had joined the Communist Party in the dark days of the thirties. Thurmond's charges were, for the most part, patently false and, as Rustin said, "a measure of the desperation of the segregationist cause."

There has never been produced even a shred of evidence that the March on Washington or, for that matter, the numerous smaller demonstrations of that summer of 1963 were "Communist led" or "Communist inspired." A review of the unpurged files of the March Committee and the personal files of Rustin and Randolph relating to the March confirm this. No contributions, no letters, no phone calls, and no volunteers in any way reveal that the March on Washington had anything to do with the Communist Party or any similar organizations.

In the final two weeks before August 28, further efforts were made to insure participation by the largest possible number of District of Columbia residents. These marchers would be able to get on a bus, or even walk to the Monument grounds, swell the size of the crowd, participate in the rally, and go home without unduly taxing health, food, transportation, or lodging resources. The organizers put out the word that they wanted 50,000 D.C residents to participate.

On the night of the 14th, the District Mobilization Committee met again to discuss these efforts. It was determined to individually contact every church and organization in the area and invite them to participate. Other than this attempt at group involvement, the Mobilization Committee's efforts to attract D.C. residents were not singularly aggressive. They decided against the use of sound trucks in the ghetto "because such a public appeal would be contrary to the dignity and solemnity of the occasion." The publicity would come through the church pulpit, radio stations, and word of mouth. If no one told the residents of Talley's Corner, the March would still go on. Indeed, the organization efforts in the District appeared to be lending a middle class air to the event.

The committee did organize a telephone and letter campaign to local, private employers, urging them to go along with the federal government's announced liberal leave policy for

the 28th.   It proved to be only moderately
successful.

Another scheme to attract local interest
was to make Home Rule for the District of
Columbia a demand of the marchers.   For years
citizens   of   the   District   had   been
disenfranchised, and had to rely on the good
will of Congress for legislation and funds.
Often this meant the good will of Committe and
Sub-Commiittee Chairmen on the Hill, who
invariably were conservative southerners from
safe Congressional districts who had built up
years of seniority.   With Washington now a
predominantly Negro city, the image of the
southern committee Chairman running a plantation
easily flashed through the locals´ minds.   When
the head of the District branch of the American
Civil   Liberties   Union   announced   his
organization´s support for the March, he also
called for Home Rule as a demand.   It was one
thing the local leaders, Fauntroy, Hobson,
Tucker, and Hailes, had no trouble agreeing
on.   New York went along in principle, and
allowed signs bearing home rule slogans to be
printed by the committee and carried in the
March.

There was deep concern in Washington about
getting the demonstrators to the staging area of
the Monument without having them march through
the downtown area.   This, of course, was part of
the paranoia city officials - and some March
organizers - had developed about the possibility
of violence or even looting by uncontrollable
demonstrators.   There was a more reasonable
basis for concern, however.   Union Station was a
good 20 blocks from the Monement and a walk from
that area by demonstrators getting off trains
would skirt a commercial area, and further
impede   traffic   on   several   major

thoroughfares: North Capitol Street, Massachusetts Avenue, Pennsylvania Avenue, and Constitution Avenue. With nearly 30 trainloads carrying an expected 1,000 marchers each into Union Station, city officials feared a large parade to the Monument grounds which would upset their plan to have the remainder of the city functioning normally and the bulk of its roadways open.

Downton Washington merchants were very apprehensive about the upcoming March, and many feared rioting and looting. Some even stored much of their stock in secure warehouses away from downtown during the week of the March. In the weeks before the March, the Metropolitan Washington Board of Trade, in an effort to ease tension, urged member businesses to remain open on the 28th, since it anticipated the March to be peaceful. It did urge that store employees living in Virginia be released early on the 28th. by 3:00 p.m., in order to avoid traffic jams.

It would not be a profitable day for merchants, seemingly a perverse result for a city with a couple of hundred thousand extra visitors. But the logistics were purposely designed to keep the demonstrators out of the stores. There were those who argued that the merchants should be compensated for their anticipated losses by the federal government, since the Kennedy Administration was such an important force behind the March. Northern Virginia Congressman Joel Broyhill and conservative columnist David Lawrence were very vociferous about this.

While Police Chief Murray continued to downplay the possibility of violence, Chief Judge John Lewis Smith, Jr., of the Court of

General Sessions of the District of Columbia,
was not taking any chances. On August 14, Judge
Smith publicly expressed his concern about mass
arrests on the day of the March, and took
measures to assure his Court would be able to
handle any unusual load. He advised his 15
fellow judges of the possibility of 24-hour duty
on the 28th:

"In view of the large number of
visitors expected here for the civil
rights March on August 28,
arrangements are being made to keep
the courts in session as long as
necessary. It is requested that all
judges not on leave be available for
emergency duty and night hearings if
necessary."

The preparation of area hospitals for the
March was being coordinated by D.C. Health
Director Murray Grant. With at least 100,000 or
so extra individuals expected in the city that
day, the hospitals were asked to be prepared
whether or not violence resulted during the
March. While the city hospital, D.C. General,
was to absorb most of those needing treatment,
the private hospitals were also placed on
alert. Administrators of those hospitals
claimed staffing would be a problem on the 28th
because so many of their employees were
requesting leave to attend the March. Thus non-
emergency surgery was postponed, and routine
outpatient treatment was rescheduled.

At the Memorial and Monument, plans were
made by Dr. Grant for 50 doctors and 100 nurses
to staff 15 on-site first aid locations, an
extraordinary number of on-the-scene medical
personnel for any such event. In addition, a

group of doctors from New York City, known as the Medical Committee for Civil Rights, planned facilities at the Willard Hotel near the White House for constant staffing by medical personnel on the day of the March.

On another front, the Washington Senators announced that, with American League approval, night games set for August 27 and 28 in D.C. Stadium with the Minnesota Twins would be postponed, to be replayed as a doubleheader on August 29. The reason cited by Police Chief Murray in requesting this was the inability of the police to provide service at the Stadium because all officers would be at the March that day. There were few voices raised in objection to postponing the games. The Senators were languishing 34 games back in 10th and last place, true to the popular slogan of the time: "Washington: first in war, first in peace, and last in the American League."

Elsewhere on August 14, the Bishops of the Protestant Episcopal Church decided to back the March at their meeting in Toronto, even though there were strong dissents. The Episcopal Bishop of Alexandria, Virginia, a Washington suburb, told the Star that he voted in favor of the resolution but that he did not favor personal involvement by clergymen in the March.

Everywhere church groups continued to announce their support, and on the 15th former President Eisenhower went so far as to say he saw nothing wrong with the March:

"Any demonstration that is merely aimed at calling attention to injustices and is made in peaceful assemblage has my approval."

By then, "calling attention" had become the major, if not the sole aim, of the March, and before the first marcher arrived in town, that aim had succeeded.

But there were other ways of calling attention, and not all eyes that were watching this historical civil rights struggle in mid-August, 1963, were focused on the August 28 March. In the Washington area, and elsewhere, demonstrations continued. Construction site pickets were out in force in Elizabeth, New Jersey, New York City and Chicago that week. In the latter city comedian Dick Gregory and others were arrested, and a number of persons injured amid cries of police brutality. The Chicago Police Superintendent stated he had a duty to arrest demonstrators who block vehicles and that his department would "meet force with force."

On the night of the 14th racial violence, including rockthrowing, broke out again in Goldsboro, North Carolina. Two thousand whites watched 600 black and white integrationists stage a parade and then attacked them. No arrests were made.

On Thursday morning, August 15, before dawn, 11 members of CORE's Brooklyn chapter led by activist Isaiah Brounson, set out with sleeping bags and pup tents for a 230-mile walk to Washington to arrive in time for the 28th.

That was also the day that most of Washington, D.C.'s white barbers closed down their shops and attended a hearing to protest proposed non-discrimination regulations affecting barber shops. The barbers claimed they were not trained to cut Negroes' hair. One of the proposed regulations required that barbers familiarize themselves with techniques for cutting all types of hair, regardless of the race of the customer. Needless to say, Local 239, Journeyman Barbers and Proprietors International Union (Teamsters) was not among the local unions supporting the March on Washington.

In Maryland, five youths were arrested on the 15th for swimming in an all-white pool in Baltimore County. A Prince George's County, Maryland Judge enjoined all picketing at the now familiar Levitt housing site in Bowie. In downtown Washington pickets marched in front of the main branch of American Security and Trust Company, across from the Treasury Department, alleging discrimination in hiring.

A similar cry was heard at the same time in East St. Louis, Illinois, where 200 demonstrators were being arrested for lying down in front of a bank. An accord satisfying the demonstrators' demands was reached the next day between rights' leaders and bank officials. An accord was also reached in Pittsburgh after pickets marched in front of the electric company's headquarters. Also on the 15th, school protests continued in Chicago and six pickets were arrested outside a segregated cafe in Danville, Virginia. On the same day in an eerie precursor of an event which would occur a few blocks away exactly a month later, a white man threw a tear gas bomb among a crowd of blacks lunching at a newly integrated Birmingham, Alabama, department store.

6

If you want to organize anything, assume that everybody is absolutely stupid. And assume yourself that you're stupid. What would I do under the circumstance? Or if this happened? There is something about people moving in numbers that reduces their ability to function efficiently."

– Bayard Rustin

On Friday, August 16, the March leaders met in New York City to discuss a myriad of planning problems. There were apparently no more buses left to charter and, against the organizers' earlier wishes, car pools were being organized. Adequate fringe parking for these cars was being sought by federal officials in Washington.

There was some concern that whites might equal or even outnumber Negroes at the March. The leaders were hoping three-fourths of the marchers would be Negroes so as to demonstrate the solidarity and concern of all Negroes. Negro leaders in the local communities were asked to redouble their efforts. Some had campaigns of their own to wage, and couldn't be bothered with marching in Washington. Jackson, Mississippi, for example, did not heed the March committee's request to send a special train of marchers. The NAACP there was busy working on a gubernatorial primary on August 27, and had little funds available.

Financial problems also continuously confronted the March Committee. The $75,000 budget had now become a $110,000.00 budget.

Thirty thousand dollars in new contributions had come in from churches, individuals and labor unions, but more money was still needed. The last youth march, in 1959, had only cost $34,000. Ultimately, the Committee spent $120,000 on the March, an enormous sum for 1963.

Among other reasons, the budget was swelling because of the Kennedy Administration's demands that certain logistics be to their satisfaction. The public address system was the key "big ticket" item. The final price was over $18,000 for a one-day rental, which was split three ways between the Auto Workers, the Ladies Garment Workers (ILGWU) and the March committee.

Rachelle Horowitz, chairman of the March's Transportation Committee, gave these estimates of people coming to the March from out of town by public transportation: 2,000 buses carrying 45 persons each; 21 special trains carrying 1,000 each; and 10 airplanes carrying 50 persons each - a total of 111,000. The special trains were coming mostly from New York City and the South, but also from Newark, Philadelphia, Hartford, Pittsburgh, Detroit, Chicago and Cincinnati. The planes had been chartered in Los Angeles, San Francisco, Chicago, Cleveland, Minneapolis and Boulder, Colorado. Boston's contingent would be coming by all-night bus. Each bus was to have a bus captain who was to carry a complete list of the names of the passengers on his or her bus. Roll was to be called on the trip down, and again prior to starting back from Washington.

By that Saturday 175,000 March buttons at 25¢ each had been sold and another 150,000 were on order, as many who couldn't come wished to show that they would be there in spirit. March headquarters, located in Harlem, was not immune

from the reality of street life, and at the
height of the August preparations, burglars
broke into the headquarters, stealing petty cash
obtained from button sales, postage stamps, and
five Royal typewriters.

Reflecting a turn from economic issues to a
focus on the Civil Rights Bill, the March
leaders made a late decision to delete two
speakers from the Lincoln Memorial Program who
were to focus on unemployment - one white and
one black unemployed laborer. The two-minute
speeches were deleted supposedly because of time
constraints.

Focusing on unemployment would have been at
least a mild challenge to the Kennedy Administration, and Reuther´s speech and Randolph´s
speech on the day of the March did speak forcefully about the problem. In fairness, President
Kennedy was concerned about the situation, often
spoke about it, and had introduced some legislation to improve matters. Measured relative to
later years, unemployment doesn´t seem like it
would have been much of a problem at all in
1963. That summer it hovered above 5.5% nationwide.

In Spartanburg, South Carolina, that
Saturday night, August 17, the Ku Klux Klan held
a cross burning rally where Imperial Wizard
Robert Shelton said the Klan was fighting the 4
K´s: Khruschev, Martin Luther King, and Jack
and Bobby Kennedy.

August 18 was a historic day for
Mississippi. James Meredith was awarded a
degree in political science from the University
of Mississippi at Oxford, Mississippi, some
eleven months after his registration there had
touched off a pitched battle between
segregationist forces led by Governor Ross

Barnett and federal marshals sent by the Attorney General. Governor Barnett made a last ditch effort to prevent Meredith from becoming a fellow alumnus, urging University officials to deny him his degree because of Barnett's claim that Meredith had violated a school directive against "inflammatory statements," apparently referring to statements in Meredith's speeches or news conferences. On a close 6-5 vote, University officials granted him his degree, and the graduation was a quiet affair. Meredith had said that Mississippi would be a "showplace" in twenty years, that since it had the largest percentage of Negroes of any state, it would solve its problems. Meredith went on to Columbia University in New York City to get a law degree. He remained active in the civil rights movement and was shot and wounded several years later by a white sniper while on a one-man "freedom march" through Mississippi. Meredith, however, was considered a conservative as far as protest tactics were concerned. He did not attend the March and, in fact, had denounced it at a speech at the NAACP convention in July.

On Sunday, August 18, a 27-year old black professional skater from Chicago, Ledger Smith, left the Windy City on roller skates bound for Washington and the March - a distance of 698 miles. He wore a sash saying "Freedom" and carried a sign reading "I'm Skating to Washington, D.C. for Civil Rights. N.A.A.C.P." He made it in time for the March, and Time magazine carried his picture in its cover story the week of the March.

As the last full week before the March began on Monday, August 19, White House Press Secretary Pierre Salinger confirmed that President Kennedy would not address the rally, but that he would meet with the March leaders sometime during the day. Meanwhile, on the same day, A. Philip Randolph sent a personal letter to all Congressmen and Senators urging them to meet with constituent marchers on August 27, the day before the March, or at the Monument grounds from 10:00 A.M. to noon on the day of the March. He specifically urged them not to see marchers on the Hill on the 28th. The March committee was fearful that this direct lobbying would get out of hand, at least in terms of numbers.

The letter was necessary because many local March organizations and civil rights groups were mailing in their final plans for participation in the March to the New York headquarters. The committee had solicited this information so it could properly plan facilities and keep an ongoing crowd estimate.

Many of the local groups listed plans to visit their senators or congressmen on the Hill on the morning of the March - in disregard of the second and final organization manual. Rustin personally wrote back to the locals with such plans, politely but firmly advising them that such tactics were not in the game plan for the 28th. Randolph, on the other end, wrote to Congress: "Only by keeping all March participants together can we avoid needless confusion and the possibility of diversions to the Capitol."

The day after Randolph's letter, the March committee sent out engraved invitations to each member of the House and Senate "cordially" inviting them to attend the program at the Lincoln Memorial on the afternoon of the 28th to hear the Marchers' "demands." A special secton of chairs near the platform had been set aside for members of Congress.

There were some complaints about the use of the word "demands." Senator Spessard Holland of Florida, for example, raised the issue on the Senate floor. He was "irritated" and said the word "demands" had "an adverse effect" on him. Holland was not considered a supporter of civil rights legislation. His complaints were countered by Senator Jacob Javits of New York and Senator Joseph Clark of Pennsylvania who stressed that the word "cordially" was also used in the invitation.

The Congressional response to the March committee's engraved invitations was less than overwhelming. Almost half sent written replies or telegrams. The typical response acknowledged receipt of the invitation, thanked the committee for it, and went on to say that due to scheduled Congressional business on the 28th they would not be able to attend. Some Congressmen or Senators added that they regretted their inability to attend, and that they supported the goals of the March, as opposed to the March itself. Many of the legislators, like Representative Gerald Ford of Michigan and Senator Thurston Morton of Kentucky, replied that they could not attend but that they would be in their offices that day to receive constituents who were in town for the March, unaware perhaps that Rustin was discouraging individual lobbying on the Hill, and apparently unaware of Randolph's letter.

Senator Goldwater wrote back that he couldn't attend because of an unspecified prior commitment on Capitol Hill. Had he attended, he would have heard at least two of the speakers align him with reactionary forces seeking to prevent passage of the Civil Rights Bill. Goldwater, to become the 1964 Republican presidential candidate, ultimately voted against passage of the final Bill.

Senator Margaret Chase Smith of Maine, the only woman in the Senate and a Republican, declined to attend due to her "long-standing policy not to leave the Hill while the Senate is in session." Senate dean and President Pro Tem Carl Hayden, Goldwater's Democratic counterpart from Arizona, declined because of Senate duties. Senator Javits of New York "accepted with pleasure," as did Senators Hart of Michigan, Williams of New Jersey, Keating of New York, Young of North Dakota, Morse of Oregon, Moss of Utah, Fong of Hawaii, Nelson of Wisconsin, Scott of Pennsyvlania, Gruening of Alaska, Randolph of West Virginia, McGovern of South Dakota, and Humphrey and McCarthy of Minnesota.

Senator Birch Bayh of Indiana praised the March in his reply to the committee but reluctantly stated he would be unable to attend as his foot was in a cast following a lawn mower accident.

Most of the segregationist Senators simply ignored the invitations, but the expression of what must have been the true feelings of most of the southern Senators was left to Senator Olin D. Johnston of South Carolina whose telegram of August 22 read as follows:

"I positively will not attend. You are committing the worst possible mistake in promoting this March. You should know that criminal, fanatical, and communistic elements, as well as crackpots, will move in to take every advantage of this mob. You certainly will have no influence on any member of Congress, including myself."

Mercifully, Senators Thurmond and Eastland did not reply to the invitation.

There were five blacks in Congress in 1963, all Democrats, and all from large cities: Adam Clayton Powell from Harlem, William Dawson from Chicago, Augustus Hawkins from Los Angeles, Charles Diggs from Detroit, and Robert N.C. Nix from Philadelphia.

Dawson, then 77, had been in the House for 20 years. He was conservative in many respects and opposed the March. He had worked his way up through Chicago's Democratic machine to be elected in 1942. Dawson worried aloud about violence at the hands of drunken demonstrators: "One incident could wipe out all the good that has been accomplished. Some of them might start drinking, for instance. When liquor comes in, good sense goes out."

Why Dawson expected a drinking crowd of his fellow Negroes was unexplained. Ultimately the decision was made by the District of Columbia Commissioners to ban the sale of alcohol on the 28th - a first for a weekday in Washington since District residents did not have the vote then, and thus there was no election ban. The greatest irony, in light of Dawson's comment on drunken demonstrators, was that on August 28, 1963, the only place in town where one could buy a drink was in Congressional dining rooms. The District Commissioners did not have authority to ban liquor on the Hill.

The other blacks in Congress were more receptive than Dawson, and Powell and Nix wholeheartedly supported the March. Diggs told the Associated Press, however, that March leaders were overrating its importance. Nix gave a lengthy speech in the House a few days before the March urging support, downplaying the possibility of violence, and stressing the March's historic importance: "Ladies and gentlemen of the House of Representatives, I appeal to you to examine your attitudes toward the August 28 March in terms of the total cause of which that event is only a symbol."

Meanwhile, a controversy was brewing over A. Philip Randolph's scheduled address to the prestigious but all male National Press Club at noon on the Monday before the March. The Press club luncheons had always been off-limits to female reporters and there were to be no exceptions made. Women reprters were free to observe only from the balcony. Elsie Carper, President of the Women's National Press Cllub, was livid: "It is ludicrous and at the same time distressing that a group fighting for civil rights has chosen a private and segregated club to discuss the march for jobs and freedom."

Randolph was apologetic, blamed his busy schedule, but wouldn't cancel his appearance: "It's a hectic time. I got the invitation and accepted. I heard the club had an all male policy afterwards. I heard from my New York office that the women sent me a telegram protesting, but I couldn't refuse to appear now. It would be uncivil." The Press Club controversy was the only public surfacing of a battle that went on within the March committee in the weeks before the March between the male leaders and women who were disappointed at the role women were being given in the March program.

The two women with the highest positions on the March committee were staffer Rachele Horowitz, who had forwarded Randolph the telegram protesting his speech, and National Council of Churches organizer Anna Arnold

Hedgeman. Hedgeman was the only woman on the admnistrative committee. In the weeks before the March, Hedgeman put in 16-hour days drumming up Protestant church participation, with speeches, phone calls and mailings. Yet she was having a difficult time convincing March leaders to place a woman on the program as a speaker at the March. The March program proposed in mid-August called for Randolph to introduce five black women to the assembled crowd: Rosa Parks, Mrs. Medgar Evers, Daisy Bates, Cambridge, Maryland leader Gloria Richardson and SNCC's Diane Nash Bevell. None were to be given the opportunity to speak.

An internal March committee document offered the rationalization that it would be difficult to find a single woman to speak "without causing serious problems vis-a-vis other women and women's groups." The "serious problems" were unspecified.

Hedgeman found the failure to provide a woman speaker during the program incredible, and sent a letter on the 16th to all the March leaders telling them so. She suggested as a compromise that at least one of the women introduce the other women on the speaker's platform. She further offered to poll the women leaders to solicit their views as to how the matter should be handled. Hedgeman's letter was apparently ignored.

At the final meeting of the March committee, Hedgeman got up and read her letter aloud. Although Wilkins expressed support, no serious changes were made in the program. Ultimately Daisy Bates was permitted to say a few words at the Lincoln Memorial program. The five women leaders were selected to head up the auxiliary line of march from the Washington

Monument down Independence Avenue to the Lincoln Memorial while the main line of march proceeded down Constitution Avenue, headed by the Big Ten. Mrs. Evers was in Boston speaking and missed the March altogether. The wives of the leaders were not permitted into the White House for the historic meeting with President Kennedy after the March. In essence, the role and importance of women in the civil rights movement was brushed aside by the March's all-male leadership.

On Monday, August 19, CORE's national director, James Farmer, was arrested in Plaquemine, Louisiana, along with 16 other demonstrators who were marching in support of a voter registration drive. The police used tear gs, and made arrests after the marchers allegedly broke an agreement not to sing. The Plaquemine jail being too small to house all the demonstrators, those arrested were bused to nearby Donaldsonville. They were charged with inciting a riot, and disturbing the peace. The arrest and confinement would keep Farmer, one of the "Big Six," away from the March on Washington.

President Kennedy held a news conference on August 20 at which he affirmed that he would not address the demonstrators on the 28th. Asked whether he would participate beyond conferring with the leaders, he said: "No ... I have been asked for an appointment and I will be glad to see the leaders of the organizations who are participating on that day."

As expected, the President was developing a core of opposition in the Senate due to his civil rights stand. Southern Democrats had almost sabotaged his domestic Peace Corps bill (VISTA) a few days before the August 20 press conference. It passed on a close 47-44 vote in the Senate. The closeness was said to serve "notice on the President that most of the Southern Democrats he has angered by pushing for action on civil rights legislation stand ready to retaliate against his programs."

As late as the week before the March, in the wake of Kennedy's firm statement that he would not address the August 28 demonstration, some erroneous news reports were saying that the Attorney General would replace his brother in addressing the crowd.

It was never a serious option for the President or his brother to address the crowd. As his chief speechwriter, Ted Sorenson, had explained, the President's political intuition told him the chances of getting an adverse reaction from that kind of crowd was great, "particularly if his remarks had to conform to a nationwide audience." For a similar reason, the President did not want to meet the March leaders prior to the demonstration. He was "afraid they would give him a list of demands he couldn't meet" and the March would turn anti-Kennedy. Thus a 5:00 p.m. meeting at the White House was arranged with the 10 March leaders.

Tuesday, August 20, was quiet as far as demonstrations went, except for continued picketing outside the Southern Governor's Conference at White Sulphur Springs, West Virginia. The leading segregationist governors, Goerge Wallace of Alabama and Ross Barnett of Mississippi, were not fairing well in their efforts to get strong resolutions passed condemning outright the Kennedy Civil Rights Bill and the March on Washington.

On the night of the 21st, Dr. King flew into Chicago to speak to a convention of Negro insurance companies, which he termed the "economic power structure" of the Negro community. They did indeed then constitute the largest industry in the Negro community. Over $10,000 was collected by the group and given to Dr. King for the SCLC. While the Negro insurance executives thought they may have been aiding the upcoming March on Washington, they were not. Despite King's promise in the spring for SCLC financial support for the March, no funds were ever contributed to Rustin's impoverished March committee by King and the SCLC. There was a measure of resentment in the movement against the publicity and financial support attracted by King at the expense of the other equally hard-working rights organizations, all of whom were more generous in their support of the March on Washington.

Violence erupted again briefly in Birmingham on the night of the 21st. No one was injured in the bombing of the home of rights leader Arthur D. Shores, but it was another ominous warning of the church bombing to come the following month. In reaction to the bombing, a riot ensued in a North Birmingham neighborhood. Schools were scheduled to integrate there in September.

In Washington, police officials held another meeting and released details of their "battle plan," including the use of 400 firemen, 250 to 500 reserve police, and 2,500 National Guardsmen. Northern Virginia's consevative Congressman Joel Broyhill continued complaining about all the assistance being given the demonstration by the "feds," and urged that federal workers, many of whom were his constitutents, be given the whole day off rather than just the option of taking unpaid administrative leave. The Star reported

Broyhill as saying: "I feel it is only right and proper to protect the interest of civil servants with as much care and consideration as that being afforded those whose presence will inevitably disrupt Government functions on that day." The Civil Service Commission stuck by its decision despite Broyhill's protestations.

The last week of August was in any event the peak time for annual leave for summer vacations, and many government workers had prior plans to be away with their families anyway. Washington area schools did not open until the day after Labor Day. Some government workers may have had their vacation plans easily decided for them, however. The nearby Delaware and Maryland beach resorts, such as Rehoboth Beach and Ocean City, announced record hotel reservations for the week of the March.

No one had so much as mentioned the possibility of rain on the 28th, and there was no "rain date" or alternative indoor site. The largest indoor arena in Washington at the time, the Washington Coliseum, formerly Uline Arena, would have accommodated less than 12,000 demonstrators. The organizers were counting on a typical hot, muggy, but rainless August afternoon for the city. A letter writer to the Star quipped: "It has yet to be determined if the weatherman is an integrationist."

As the day of the March approached, the special investigations division of the District of Columbia Metropolitan Police force increased its intelligence activities. They received daily reports from police departments all over the country and in some instances from the FBI regarding the number of demonstrators coming to Washington and possible civil disobedience. Crowd predictions steadily increased based on

the number of buses and trains being chartered
and on predictions by local organizations which
were being closely watched, if not infiltrated,
by the FBI and police departments.

The information was all forwarded promptly
to Douglas and Raywid at Justice. They were
generally dissatisfied with the quality of the
information received. The FBI reports,
reflecting Director Hoover's paranoia, were
almost exclusively concerned with the number of
and names of communist participants, regardless
of whether such individuals were prone toward
violence. Information about potential violence
or disorder was what the Justice officials
wanted but could not readily obtain from the
FBI. The D.C. police data on numbers was
adequate, but eventually proved to be an
underestimate of the number of participants.

As a result of what they considered to be
shallow reporting of such information, the
Justice officials, in the end, set up their own
intelligence network. By the day of the March,
Douglas had drafted a score of attorneys from
various divisions in the Justice Department to
act as spotters. The lawyers were fully briefed
and, some equipped with binoculars, dispatched
to the rooftops of government buildings in the
city, including several at Union Station. Other
attorneys were sent out to positions along the
Baltimore-Washington Parkway to monitor the flow
of traffic into the city and to uncover any
problems in the flow.

From these vantage points the attorney
spotters could call into Douglas and Raywid at
police headquarters or to Jack Reilly and Jerry
Bruno who would be stationed at the Lincoln
Memorial. It was another check on the situation
designed to give Justice, and ultimately the

City Commissioners and the military, all possible information in the event of a situation that could not be controlled by the police. On the day of the March, Police Chief Murray would remain, almost isolated, in a police cruiser driving in the area of the March. Douglas, who preferred to be in the background anyway, stayed at police headquarters where information from a variety of sources flowed to him.

At the Memorial, Reilly and Bruno had direct control over the loud speaker system. Unknown to the March leaders, these two men were in a position to "pull the plug" on the entire public address system if a riot ensued. The rationale behind this is unclear since communication might have been more desirable in a riot situation.

The whole issue of the sound system for the Lincoln Memorial had concerned federal officials, particularly Douglas and Raywid from the moment they become involved. Barred from financing the March, or any of the accoutrements, the feds nonetheless pressured the March leaders to provide for a top-of-the-line speaker system. They wanted to assure that everyone in the area could hear announcements and the various speakers clearly so that there would be no dissatisfaction and no crowding toward the stage area. The March leaders complied at great expense of their thin cash resources.

As it turned out, one major key to the success of the March and Lincoln Memorial program was the excellent public address system. Two huge towers were erected on each side of the Memorial with 46 massive speakers affixed. Most marchers were able to hear the speeches clearly, although those far removed from the podium had difficulty.

The sound system was augmented by a quality electric organ, valued at $6,000.00, and installed at the Lincoln Memorial prior to the March. A California organ firm donated this piece of equipment and was so taken by the success of the March that it announced several days after the 28th that it would leave the organ at the Lincoln Memorial for use on special occasions, donating it as a special tribute to the March on Washington.

The unalleviated concern about possible violence and civil disobedience, and the growing crowd estimates, led the Justice Department to prepare extraordinary documents and orders involving potential use of federal troops on the day of the March.

The orders were prepared by an Assistant Attorney General and submitted to the White House on August 23. It had been noted that President Hoover, in dispersing the Bonus Marchers in 1932, and President Wilson, in dispersing a race riot in 1919, had observed no formalities in calling out the Army, but the Justice Department was determined to go by the book. Thus, two proposed executive orders were prepred for possible use and immediate signature by President Kennedy.

The first noted that an "extraordinary assemblage of persons in the District of Columbia was constituting a threat to the lives and property of District residents," and commanded all persons so assembled to "disperse and retire peaceably forthwith." The second proposed executive order noted that the first order had been issued and not compiled with, and directed the Secretary of Defense to take all appropriate steps by use of the Armed Forces to disperse the assemblage and "maintain law and order."

The Justice Department also prepared letters to be signed by the Commissioners of the District of Columbia and Police Chief Murray requesting President Kennedy to sign the executive orders.

Joseph A. Califano, Jr., then General Counsel of the Department of the Army, suggested certain technical changes in the proposed executive orders and they were resubmitted to the White House on the morning of the 27th, the day before the March. Copies were placed in the hands of all the appropriate signatories, although there is no evidence that they were pre-signed. Actually, that would not have been necessary since telephone contacts could have been made, and all documents properly executed within minutes.

There was not time period set forth to trigger use of the second "all appropriate steps" order if the first order to disperse was not complied with. Indications are that the time period would have been negligible.

The Army was ready with its own documents. The Pentagon had forwarded three pages of detailed and classified orders to Major General Phillip C. Weble, Commanding General of the Military District of Washington. General Weble was to have 4,000 troops at his immediate disposal at Fort Myer. They were dubbed "Task Force Inside." If things got sticky, General Weble could call upon 15,000 paratroopers of the 82nd Airborne Division under the command of Major General John L. Throckmorten. This augmentation force never left its headquarters at Fort Bragg, North Carolina.

General Weble's orders were fairly standard
ones for use in civil disturbances, and not
unlike those used by National Guard units in
urban and campus riots throughout the decade.
The troops were advised to use minimum force to
the extent "such force did not jeopardize
successful completion of the mission." The
priority of force was set forth in the orders:

(1) unloaded rifles with bayonets fixed and
     sheathed
(2) unloaded rifles with bare bayonets
     fixed
(3) tear gas
(4) loaded rifles with bare bayonets fixed

Authority to use tear gas remained with
General Weble, and he was not authorized to
redelegate that authority. John Douglas of the
Justice Department was to remain with General
Weble during the day to handle public relations
and "matters having political implications."
Under no circumstances, however, was General
Weble to take orders from civilian authorities.

In the event of arrests, it was recommended
that D.C. police officers handle the booking and
detention initially, unless the resources of the
police force became exhausted. The General was
to maintain periodic telephone contact with the
Pentagon War Room from his post at police
headquarters on Indiana Avenue.

On Thursday, the 22nd, perhaps the first of
the rank and file out-of-town marchers arrived
in Wasington, thoroughly exhausted. Robert
Thomas, age 18, Robert Avery, 17, and James F.
Smith, 16, had left Gadsden, Alabama, on Sunday
for their five-day 700-mile walk and hitchike.
They also arrived penniles but were fed, housed
and put to work by Reverend Fauntroy who

obtained some rooming space on Logan Circle from
the National Beauty Culturists League. The
three, members of the Gadsden Student Movement,
were described by the Star as "veterans" of the
civil rights movement despite their youth. All
had been previously jailed for sit-in activity.

Mayor Robert Wagner of New York had
announced his participation in the March on the
20th, and offered liberal paid leave to city
employees wishing to attend. However, Negroes
in New York City were dissatisfied with his
performance on the home front.

On August 22 Mayor Wagner lost his patience
with civil rights demonstrators engaged in their
44th straight day of sitting-in outside his
office at City Hall. The previous day eight
CORE pickets had dumped a truckload of rubbish,
including a large dead rat, onto City Hall
Plaza. The pickets were complaining about the
city's vermin-infested tenements.

That Thursday, the 22nd, the pickets
chanted "Wagner, stay home," referring to his
participation in the March, suggesting that he
should stay in New York and find jobs for
unemployed Negroes and Puerto Ricans instead of
marching in Washington. The Mayor became
angered when a fracas broke out between police
and demonstrators, and ordered the latters'
eviction. He issued a statement, however,
downplaying his actions.

> "This represents no change whatever in
> the policy of my administration on
> civil rights or with regard to any
> other picketing or similar activity in
> behalf of civil rights other than
> picketing in City Hall."

The Mayor felt that after 44 days the demonstrators had made their point.

After Wagner's crackdown, the Brooklyn chapter of CORE sent an angry telegram to Cleveland Robinson at March headquarters in Harlem, asking Robinson to rescind Mayor Wagner's invitation to the March. The matter was referred to Randolph himself, who refused to rescind the invitation, announcing that he would not permit the local conflict to "detract from the unity and discipline of the March on Washington." There is some indication that Randolph or other leaders at March headquarters told CORE privately to "lay off" Wagner for the week before the March. The controversy remained muted for the next few weeks. That Thursday evening near Washington Square several thousand people held a rally supporting the upcoming March.

On Friday morning, the 23rd, the Senate Commerce Committee approved legislation which would delay a scheduled rail strike set for the night of the 28th. It was sent to the Senate floor for action on the 26th. Just in case the rail strike did strand marchers, and to account for those who, because of distance from their homes or illness, would be unable to leave the city on Wednesday night, Washington's Archbishop O'Boyle was planning to house and feed them. He set up temporary hostels at Georgetown and Catholic Universities and at eight area parishes. Staffing was to be provided by the Knights of Columbus, the Catholic Interracial Council, and area priests. The Knights of Columbus contributed $25,000.00 to set up the shelters.

There remained the problem of what the stranded marchers would sleep on. An aide to

O'Boyle approached Douglas at the Justice Department and requested a loan of army cots to be placed in the gymnasiums and parish halls for possible use. Douglas didn't like the idea because it seemed to violate the principal about direct financial support, since delivery and installation of the cots would be a direct cost to the government, not directly related to safety of the general public. It placed the government too much in a position of sponsoring the March. Douglas' suggestion was that the marchers could sleep on the floor.

O'Boyle's aide replied that it would be an insult for these people to be told that they could sleep on the floor. "For you," he told Douglas, "it might be sport to spend a night sleeping on the floor. For these people, it would be an insult." Douglas, a sensitive person, thought about it for a day and agreed that the cots should be provided. O'Boyle's aid was called and offered the cots. It was too late. He had already made other arrangements to obtain the cots from the Red Cross.

As the work week came to a close, the Washington stage was thoroughly set for the following Wednesday. President Kennedy flew out of town that Friday afternoon with his brother Ted. It would be his eighth consecutive weekend away from Washington at his family's Hyannisport retreat. First Lady Jacqueline Kennedy was still recuperating there after her difficult pregnancy and the death of her infant son.

The President left behind in Washington a hot, steamy city which was bracing itself for a very big week ahead. Appropriately, the number one popular record in town that week was Martha and the Vandella's "Heat Wave." But the number two record on the charts spoke more to the mood of those who would be descending on the city in the next few days. It was Peter, Paul and Mary's recording of Bob Dylan's civil rights anthem, "Blowin' in the Wind."

The marchers grew impatient, and began leaving the Monument grounds 15 minutes early.

The Big Ten link arms and begin the March to the Lincoln Memorial.

By noon the crowd was pressing against the barriers at the steps of the Lincoln Memorial.

"A frighteningly tight-packed assemblage."

he police and the military were out in force but had little
o do except direct traffic and exchange pleasantries.

Many in the crowd
sought respite from
the heat by wading in
the Reflecting Pool.

Dr. King: "America has given the Negro people a bad check."

The joyous crowd left the Lincoln Memorial and Washington as quickly as they had come.

7

In the final week, the ghettoes of America stirred. In thousands of homes, bags were being packed, lunches prepared, goodbyes said. In thousands of bars and barber shops, the thing was being discussed pro and con. No one knew at this point how many would be there, but the feeling was growing that everybody who could ought to be there.

                    - Lerone Bennet, Jr.

As of Saturday, the 24th, Nazi leader Rockwell was still conservatively estimating 2,000 supporters at the Monument on Wednesday for his counter-demonstration, although he said as many as 12,000 could show. D.C. Police intelligence knew otherwise and were essentiallly unconcerned. Rockwell´s show was to commence early at 4:30 a.m., on the day of the March. Another counter-demonstration was reportedly being planned from New York by a group called the National States Rights Party, which attempted to distance itself from the Nazis. There was no report that the States Rights group ever showed up on the 28th. The Reverend Carl McIntire, who represented a conservative Christian group opposed to the March, called the American Council of Christian Churches, arrived the day of the March and set up a table in the lobby of the Washington Hotel near the White House.

A fourth contingent of potential counter-demonstrators in the form of the Ku Klux Klan also failed to materialize after the Klan´s Imperial Grand Wizard, Robert Shelton, and an associate were injured when a private plane which they were taking to Washington crashed in South Carolina. The pilot was killed, and Shelton was hospitalized with multiple injuries, leaving Rockwell's Nazis alone to stand up for white supremacy.

At the other extreme, in Washington on Sunday, Black Muslims began filtering into town for an unrelated event, their annual convention, a week long affair. On a local radio show, Malcom X called the March "controlled by the government, and (it) is being used for political expediency."

A Sunday, pre-March rally at New York's Polo Grounds was somewhat of a flop, as only 2,000 persons paid $2.00 each to get in. Thirty thousand supporters had been anticipated, and the poor showing was enough to make optimistic crowd estimators for Wednesday's march very nervous. A rally at Howard University in Washington was more successful, as nearly 4,000 turned out to hear the widow of Medgar Evers encourage District residents to attend the March. Mrs. Evers was in Washington on Sunday in part to make up for her inability to attend the March on Wednesday. She had accepted a prior speaking engagement at the Negro Elks convention in Boston, where her children were receiving scholarships. Mrs. Evers would be embarrassed when watching the March on Washington on television from her Boston hotel room as her name was called as the next speaker. Someone on the Lincoln Memorial had gotten confused, but the crowd cheered for her anyway.

On Sunday evening, Dr. King and Roy Wilkins appeared jointly on NBC's "Meet the Press" in Washington for a half hour of intense, and sometimes hostile questioning. The concern about violence at the March was uppermost in the minds of the panel, as were concerns about communist influence in the March organization. Lawrence Spivak's first question to Wilkins cited the belief by "a great many people" that it would be "impossible to bring more than 100,000 militant Negroes into Washington without incidents and possible rioting", Spivak reflecting the mistaken notion that the marchers were the "militants" of the movement, and reflecting an inability or unwillingness to distinguish between the various groups and philosophies of the civil rights movement. Spivak wanted to know what gains would be made by the March that would outweigh the risks, and he emphasized: "and there are risks that you are taking." Wilkins artfully downplayed the risks in his responses, and cited the need to demonstrate to Congress the "deep concern" of millions of Americans, which city councils and state legislatures had been exposed to in the recent past. Wilkins would not give a crowd prediction, except to say that conservatively it would be more than 100,000. Panelist Frank Van der Hinden of the Nashville Banner dredged up "loyalty" allegations against Bayard Rustin, including an allegation made by the House Un-American Activities Committee that Rustin had spoken at a meeting in 1962 called to organize a fund drive to send medical supplies to Cuba. Dr. King replied that his former secretary, Rustin, had long ago denounced his communist affiliations. Dr. King similarly fielded inquiries about whether the Negroes were moving too fast, that moderation was now called for, and whether true social equality was a realistic possibility. For King, it was a generally subdued performance. Afterwards, he flew to Atlanta before returning to Washington Tuesday evening. Wilkins remained in town to help coordinate the NAACP's role in the March and to work on his speech for Wednesday.

By Sunday evening, the New York March
headquarters had shifted to Washington's Statler
Hilton Hotel on 16th Street. A block of 15 rooms
was rented for the period August 26-29, several
of them with typewriters and work tables
provided by the hotel management. Some
operations were being handled out of WUST radio
station on V Street. The next day, Monday the
26th, March public relations director Seymour
Posner met an eager Washington press corps to
discuss Wednesday's activities. Posner was
urging everyone to come by private auto if
necessary, despite the D.C. police's objection
to that. Posner also announced that 2,000 poor
southern Negroes would be unable to attend the
March as previously planned due to financial
difficulties. The March committee was out of
funds for such free transportation. At the last
minute, the SCLC sent $2,000.00 to its Atlanta
headquarters to pay for 200 Negroes to come up
from Albany, Georgia, and 100 more from
Savannah. But most of the impoverished would be
staying home, leaving unaccomplished the goal of
making the March on Washington a broad based
demonstration. Some SNCC workers in Atlanta
complained that the NAACP was actually selling
bus and train seats reserved for the poor and
"keeping the profits for themselves". The SNCC
workers complained to March headquarters, which
sent down directives about the allocated seats.
Nonetheless, SNCC felt that a grossly inadequate
number of poor southern Negroes, the most
oppressed of America's Negroes, were being
accomodated by the March leaders.

Posner's relationship with the Washington
press corps had not always been amicable that
summer, as he felt that the Negro press was
being systematically excluded from coverage of
March activities. The Washington press intended

to handle the March as it did other news
stories. The best spots, hook-ups, and other
perks would be reserved for veteran reporters
from national, influential publications.
Reporters from Negro publications had no
priority. For example, flatbed trucks had been
rented to hold reporters and television and
movie cameras, and to proceed directly in front
of the first line of march. Posner and the Negro
reporters had to fight to get a few spots for
the Negro reporters on the trucks. Of the
allotted 200 radio hook-ups for the Lincoln
Memorial programs, very few were initially
designated for Negro radio stations, many of
which wanted to cover the entire program, in
contrast to the more powerful white-owned
stations that wanted the hook-ups for a few
brief excerpts from speeches for news summaries.
Eventually, a larger number of hook-ups for the
Negro stations were allocated.

Although many would have preferred it
otherwise, local civil rights protests continued
even into March week. On Sunday in Plaquemine,
while CORE leader James Farmer languished in
jail, Negroes staged kneel-ins at two white
Protestant churches. In High Point, North
Carolina, two separate marches were staged
through the downtown area . Unrest continued in
Danville, Virginia. In Brunswick, Georgia the
week of the March, radio station WMOG ran a
series of ads sponsored by a segregationist
group called the Glynn Society for Democratic
Action. The blatantly racist appeal for funds
began with: "The niggers are now marching in
Washington", and included a plea to "keep the
schools for white people". The ads were extreme
enough to alarm most moderate whites who heard
them. The station was flooded with protests, and
finally agreed to delete "nigger" from the
spots.

On Tuesday the 26th, there were some minor incidents along Maryland's highways leading into Washington. On U.S. Route 1 near Waterloo, a Brooklyn CORE worker, part of a contingent hiking to Washington, was attacked by a white man, who stepped from his car, hurled obscenities at the marchers, struck the youth, and fled. He was not seriously injured.

On Tuesday afternoon, 20 or so SNCC members began a vigil outside the Justice Department at 10th and Pennsylvania Avenue. Bob Moses, Curtis Hayes, and Hollis Watkins, all SNCC workers from Mississippi, began the lonely picketing demonstration. They were joined by a couple of white SNCC volunteers, Casey Hayden and Sheila Kessler, and by several teenagers from Albany, Georgia. Moses, the venerated SNCC theoretician and organizer, carried a crude sign which read: "When there is no justice, what is the state, but a robber band enlarged?" One of the Albany youths carried a sign which read: "Even the federal government is a white man". Albany had been the scene earlier that summer of many documented incidents of police brutality, but for which the Justice Department could find no evidence. The demonstration outside the Justice Department lasted all night Tuesday and did not break up until 8:00 a.m. on the morning of the March. Tuesday evening several of the picketers walked the few blocks to the White House and briefly picketed there.

An influx of a couple of hundred thousand demonstrators for a late-August, mid-week affair in hot, muggy Washington would seem to be a godsend for local hotels and motels. Curiously however, hotel business greatly suffered on the 27th and 28th as the normal contingent of businessmen and tourists stayed away from Washington due to the March, and because most participants complied with the plans for a daytime only visit to the city by the marchers.

On the afternoon before the March, Dr. King and his wife flew in from Atlanta and checked into the Willard Hotel, King's choice of accomodations whenever he came to Washington. Knowing this, the FBI would commence their infamous wiretapping program of King the following January during a stay at the Willard. But there were apparently no taps on King's room during the week of the March. Had there been, the special agents listening in would have been privileged to hear King and his advisors labor over his speech to be delivered the next day, which he began putting together that evening.

A holiday eve atmosphere prevailed in Washington on the eve of the March — so many of those residents who hadn't already gone off on vacation would have a mid-week holiday on the 28th. The Senators had cancelled their home basesball game that evening in deference to the March, but there were other available leisure activities for residents or early-arriving marchers. Cleopatra with Elizabeth Taylor and Richard Burton, and How the West Was Won were the most popular movies in town. John Coltrane was appearing at the Bohemian Caverns, while the Kalin Twins were packing them in at the Rocket Room on New York Avenue. At Shady Grove Music Fair in the Maryland suburbs, Dorothy Lamour was appearing in Pal Joey. Indeed, night-time entertainment was at its summer zenith in Washington that week, and some of the celebrity participants in the March had been booked on local stages for concerts that week: Peter, Paul, and Mary, and Odetta, at the Carton Baron Amphitheatre, for example. In Georgetown, at the Shadows, Woody Allen was fronting for comedian Danny Meehan.

Meanwhile, the final pre-March meeting of the Big Ten took place that Tuesday evening in a meeting room at the Statler Hilton. It was closed to the press, although there were hundreds of reporters around, many in town just for the March, and looking for a story. They would get one in the controversy that arose later that evening over John Lewis´ prepared speech, news of which quickly spread around town. But while the Big Ten met, most reporters were left to discoursing in the lobby for several hours with Malcom X and several of his Black Muslim followers, who were staying at the same hotel in connection with their own annual convention. Malcom X expounded on his theories of racial separation: " I am not condemning or criticizing the March, but it won´t solve the problems of black people. "

Inside the meeting, Rustin, Kahn, Horowitz, and the other staffers were presenting their final reports about facilities, emergency lodging, the weather, and communications. The most important concern was the size of the crowd. Anything less than 100,000 would mark the March as a colossal failure and give solace to the Civil Rights Bill´s opponents. Rachelle Horowitz stood up to give her final report about chartered buses, trains, and airplanes. When the figures were totalled, they exceeded 120,000. Roy Wilkins questioned her sharply: "Are you certain you have that many people booked?" Yes, Horowitz was certain. Wilkins grinned, and told his fellow leaders: "Gentlemen, we are going to have at least 250,000 marchers tomorrow. All over the east coast, Mrs. so and so is going to get up early, and say to Mr. so and so: ´It´s a nice day pop, we´re going to drive down to Washington for the March.´ The people will be here." Wilkins retired to his hotel room before midnight to chat with his wife and relatives and friends who dropped by, and to put the finishing touches on his speech.

While Wilkins was tailoring his speech at the Statler Hilton, Martin Luther King, Jr., closeted with aides Andrew Young, Walter Fauntroy, Wyatt T. Walker, and Ralph David Abernathy at the Willard. He was to speak last, but each of the Big Ten had been allotted only seven minutes by Randolph and Rustin. It was not to be an afternoon of long speeches, forcing the rally into the evening hours, and disrupting plans to have the demonstrators out of town by nightfall.

King's original idea was to give a rousing talk about his dream for race relations in America, expanding on a theme he had discussed at the mass rally in Detroit in June, but it was thought that the seven minutes allotted would not permit such a discourse. The speech he and his aides worked on that night thus centered on the "bad check" Negroes had been given by America, which check the Negroes were now bringing to Washington to make good.

Coretta and King's advisors have always insisted that the "I Have A Dream" language was not included, or at least was not the focus of the speech he stayed awake all night to prepare. But after Coretta dozed off at 3:00 a.m., and his aides had left King alone to contemplate the majesty of Washington's monuments through his hotel room window, thoughts of his dream for America must have returned, as the most dramatic of waking dreams occur to people late at night. The next day at the Lincoln Memorial, no seven minute time limitation would dissuade King from sharing his dream with America.

8

"It was a bad, radical speech.
Lewis and Forman wrote it.
They're a very radical bunch."

   - Burke Marshall, 1964

The uproar surrounding a prepared speech by
SNCC leader John Lewis, and what amounted to
coerced changes in the text of that speech by
the "Big Ten" has proven over the years to be
the most controversial feature of the March on
Washington. Some saw the forced changes in
Lewis' speech as a symbol of the sell-out of the
civil rights leaders to the Kennedy Administration. Others have viewed the whole controversy as overblown.

Throughout 1962 and 1963, SNCC was having a
rugged go of it in the South, and even more
difficult problems with the Kennedy Administration. There was a continuing ambivalence of
each toward the other - SNCC still wanted the
Federal Government's support and protection, but
was appalled at the government's seeming
hypocrisy. The Administration wanted to display
its sympathy for civil rights advocates, but did
not want to place itself in a position of
excusing lawbreakers or fostering civil
disobedience. The problem was most acute for
Attorney General Kennedy, whose Justice
Department had the constitutional duty to
maintain law and order. He was in no position
to support civil disobedience, whatever his
philosophical leanings.

In early 1962, three SNCC field workers
were arrested in Baton Rouge, Louisiana for
"criminal anarchy," a charge which had been used
in the past to discourage unionization as well
as to go after supposed communists. It was

generally defined in law as espousing that a government be overthrown by force, assassination of government leaders, or by any unlawful means. The state would allege that a civil rights worker, by advocating civil disobedience, sitting in at a segregated lunch counter for example, or advocating removal of segregated facilities which had become a way of life in the south, was seeking to overthrow the government of the particular state. It was a preposterous charge, but it also carried severe penalties, and was not taken lightly either by prosecutors or civil rights workers.

Responding to these indictments, SNCC members at Howard University decided to picket the home of segregationist Senator Allen Ellender (D-La.). The Howard group was actually entitled the National Action Group (NAG), but it was generally affiliated with the National SNCC organization. In a decade of acronyms, NAG has generally been forgotten, but it exerted an important influence, and its original membership reads like an honor roll of the black student movement: Stokely Carmichael, H. Rap Brown, Courtland Cox, Cleveland Sellers, Edward Brown, among others.

A few weeks later NAG conducted a sit-in at the Justice Department, in the Attorney General's outer office, protesting the lack of intervention in the Louisiana situation and elsewhere. Burke Marshall had a dialogue with Carmichael and the other students, and Justice officials were reluctant to forceably remove the demonstrators.

Thereafter, SNCC staffers deluged the Justice Department and the Attorney General with letters and telegrams throughout 1962 pleading for protection and federal intervention.

Arrests and assaults on SNCC workers were increasing throughout the South as their voter registration campaign picked up steam. The Justice Department essentially ignored the students' pleas. It was unwilling at that stage to get involved in a showdown with Southern authorities. Critics said it was because the Kennedy Administration still needed Southern support for its programs and for reelection in 1964. John Kennedy had carried the South in his 1960 victory over Richard Nixon.

In July 1962, Marion King, the wife of jailed rights' leader Slater King, was beaten when she attempted to deliver packages to civil rights workers in an Albany, Georgia jail. Arrests for disorderly conduct or vagrancy of SNCC workers seeking to register rural black voters were common, as were attacks by Klan-like groups on individual organizers, particularly in Georgia and Mississippi.

Throughout, the federal government took a limited view of its powers and intervention in these local disputes. It was only when things got out of hand, such as in Oxford in 1962, that the Kennedy Administration was willing to send in marshalls to maintain order.

A critical event in SNCC/Administration relations occurred in January 1963 when seven workers filed a civil suit in the United States District Court for the District of Columbia against Robert Kennedy and J. Edgar Hoover. The suit was in the nature of a mandamus action seeking the Court to compel Kennedy and Hoover to prosecute southern officials and individuals who were harassing and unlawfully arresting and detaining civil rights workers. At the time such an action had little precedent, and it was promptly dismissed for technical reasons by the

Court. There was undoutedly some embarassment and resentment as far as Robert Kennedy was concerned.

The following month when the first version of the Administration's civil rights bill was introduced in Congress, it contained no provisions for expanded federal protection of civil rights workers. To SNCC this made the bill little more than meaningless. The voting rights provisions were weak in themselves, providing for temporary federal referees to determine qualifications only in those counties where less than 15% of the blacks were registered. If the federal government was taking the position that its powers of intervention were so limited, yet was also saying that it supported the goals of the civil rights movement, why did it not seek greater powers from Congress?

In the early spring of 1963, two months before King's protests in Birmingham gained national attention, the hotspot was Greenwood, Mississippi, where SNCC workers were conducting a voter registration campaign against a backdrop of white violence. In February, a Negro named Jimmy Travis was gunned down, and on March 6, four SNCC workers were fired upon while sitting in a car outside their Greenwood office. On March 26, shots were fired into the Greenwood home of two SNCC workers.

Two days later, SNCC workers staged a protest march to the Greenwood courthouse. Their leaders, including Robert Moses and James Forman, were arrested and jailed. Finally, John Doar of the Justice Department was dispatched to Greenwood to lean on local officials. An injunction was sought in federal court against harrassment of the SNCC workers. A partial compromise was reached, and the leaders were released.

As the summer of 1963 approached, and as civil rights demonstrations multiplied, the relations between SNCC and the Kennedy Administration went from bad to worse. It was if the Administration needed a whipping boy to demonstrate it had not gone overboard in its support for civil rights. The youthful SNCC organization became that whipping boy.

SNCC had no direct role in Birmingham, but while King was leading the demonstrations there, John Lewis was leading equally "tumultous" demonstrations in Nashville. Across the state in Knoxville, Tennessee, SNCC leader Marion Barry was leading demonstrations against segregated theatres. SNCC was also involved in major demonstrations that spring and summer in Pine Bluff, Arkansas, Gadsden, Alabama, Danville, Virginia, and Atlanta, Greensboro, Raleigh, Jackson, Savannah, and Cambridge, Maryland, and Americus, Georgia. The demonstrations in the latter two cities proved, along with those in Danville, to be the most violent.

In Cambridge, the Maryland National Guard was called out to restore order in June. Given its proximity to Washington, D.C. and the resultant media attention, the Administration kept a close eye on the Cambridge situation and the Attorney General himself decided to become personally involved. A short-lived truce was worked out in late July by Justice Department officials.

The trouble in Americus began on August 8, 1963, when armed police waded into a peaceful crowd of singing teenage demonstrators. There were numerous beatings and arrests. SNCC field secretary Don Harris and two others were held under high bail for the capital offense of attempting to incite insurrection. They remained jailed, facing the death penalty until November, when a federal court ruled the Georgia statute unconstitutional.

The next day, August 9, brought another demonstration, this to protest the police brutality of the previous evening. An eye-witness gave this account of the response by Americus officials: "They left the church and walked four blocks in orderly columns of twos, not blocking the sidewalk. The police officers were armed with guns, two-foot clubs, electric cattle prodders and blackjacks..... The City Marshall and Police Chief asked them if they had a permit to parade and asked them to disperse. But before any response could be given, the officers started bludgeoning groups of boys and girls with clubs and cattle prodders, which give a severe shock and leave burn marks on the flesh."

The brutality of the Americus police was widely reported in the press. Yet when FBI agents investigated, they could find no evidence. An agent told the press at a news conference that the allegations of brutality were "analyzed thoroughly and were found to be gross distortions and complete untruths." J. Edgar Hoover staunchly defended his bureau's southern agents against claims of racial prejudice. SNCC workers were unable to separate in their minds Robert Kennedy's Justice Department and its investigative arm, the FBI. Indeed, the same week the FBI was unable to find brutality in Americus, Justice was obtaining the federal indictments for "jury tampering" in Albany, Georgia against civil rights leaders there.

It was against this background that the SNCC workers viewed the 1963 Civil Rights

March. It would have been ludicrous to expect John Lewis to give a modest speech in praise of a piece of proposed legislation by the Kennedy Administration.

In the weeks before the March, the leaders made several decisions about the speeches to be given at the March. One of these was the seven minute time limit designed to assure completion of the Lincoln Memorial program in time to get the throngs on their way home before dark. Rustin recalled, as did Norman Hill, at least three other understandings reached by the leaders concerning speeches: there would be no attacks on individual senators or congressmen, or political parties, no violent language, and no prior release of speeches to the press.

This latter recollection of Rustin conflicts with numerous accounts which have put forth the notion that Lewis´ speech was edited after a compulsory exchange of speeches by March leaders on the evening before the March. Rustin´s recollection is much more credible since, in fact, none of the other leaders´ speeches were exchanged. Indeed, Wilkins is said to have been polishing his speech late that Tuesday night, and King and his associates worked nearly until dawn on his. SNCC staffers, it appears, violated this understanding by distributing copies of Lewis´ speech.

Lewis, a young, but already veteran activist and organizer, was respected by his associates as a leader. He had been arrested scores of times by the summer of 1963, beaten, and jailed. He had recently replaced Charles McDew as head of SNCC. He was not considered, and did not consider himself a gifted speech-writer. Thus he delegated much of the writing of his speech to be given at the March to his associates. For the most part the speech was composed in SNCC´s Atlanta office at 8-1/2 Raymond Street. Lewis made an initial draft, to which Julian Bond and SNCC staffer Sheila Kessler Michaels made extensive revisions. James Forman also added a number of phrases including the "one man, one vote African cry" language. Tom Kahn and Courtland Cox made further minor revisions shortly before the 28th.

According to Rustin, there would have been no pre-March editing of the speech, and Lewis could have given it as originally written if SNCC staffers "had played it straight."

A meeting of the March leaders had been set for 8:00 p.m. at the Statler Hilton on the 27th, although the meeting was rather late in getting started. By early evening a number of copies had been made of Lewis´ prepared text, probably by Julian Bond, then SNCC´s publicity director. Rustin recalls that James Forman, justifiably excited about the speech, began distributing them at the Statler Hilton, even giving one to Malcom X, who was in town for the Black Muslim Convention, and to observe the March he had been condemning for weeks. Forman recounts his meeting with Malcom X that evening in his book, and Malcom X must certainly have been impressed with the prepared text.

Others were not so impressed, and the trouble arose when Bond or Forman apparently left several undistributed copies on a table outside the leaders´ meeting room. An aide to Archbishop Patrick O´Boyle, of Washington, who was scheduled to give the invocation at the Lincoln Memorial the following day, picked up a copy and took it down the street to the Mayflower Hotel where Archbishop O´Boyle was hosting a private reception for a group of bishops from Virginia and West Virginia who had come to town for the March. The aide gave it to Bishop Spence, the archdiocesan education director, who passed it on to the Archbishop. He read it, said nothing, and passed it on to his fellow bishops. There was one phrase that stuck out in the Archbishop's mind, and in the minds of the other bishops who conveyed their feelings to him at that reception. That phrase about, as O'Boyle recalled years later, "Sherman marching to the sea." The actual prepared text went as follows:

> "We will march through the South, through the heart of Dixie, the way Sherman did. We shall pursue our own scorched earth policy and burn Jim Crow to the ground nonviolently."

The meaning of the last word, "nonviolently", was somehow lost. O'Boyle consulted with his fellow bishops, all of whom agreed that he should not give the invocation unless the speech was changed. There was some discussion about another element of the prepared text, which at the very outset suggested that SNCC could not support the civil rights bill because "it was too little and too late." But the suggestion of condoning violence is what actually bothered O'Boyle and his fellow bishops and, as he would say later, "a night of hectic telephoning began."

O'Boyle, a conservative when it came to church dogma, was a liberal on civil rights. He had been ordained a bishop in January 1948, and appointed to head the new Washington, D.C. diocese, which had been carved out of the Baltimore diocese.

O´Boyle was shocked to find a southern city when he came to Washington, with segregated public and and parochial schools and Negroes accustomed to sitting in the back of churches. The situation in the southern Maryland counties, which were part of his diocese, was particularly disturbing. Negroes there had to enter church through side door entrances.

In his first summer, he announced that diocesan Catholic high schools were to be desegregated by fall. Pleased with the cooperation he received, the following year he quietly began desegregating parochial grade schools - still five years before Brown v. Board of Education, and the desegregation of Washington´s public schools. There was some grumbling among wealthier Catholics, but there were no disorders. To foster desegregation in the high schools, O´Boyle took his allotted scholarships and sent inner city blacks to affluent private Catholic schools.

O´Boyle´s largely unheralded efforts were not confined to education alone. He lobbied the District Commissioners for action to put an end to discrimination in housing; he developed a program for exchange visits between Negro and White Catholic families; he founded and chaired the Washington Interreligious Committee on Race relations. In the 1950´s, long before such efforts were popular, or even heard of, O´Boyle, drawing on his labor union contacts, helped establish an apprentice training program for Negroes in the construction trades. He also pressured local churches to place unprecedented anti-discrimination clauses in church building contracts. In southern Maryland he built new churches with only one entry door, so that Negroes and whites, who now had to enter through the same door, began sitting next to each other.

But it was O'Boyle's pastoral letters on race relations which were read in the Catholic Churches on Sunday that were most memorable, along with his initiation of compulsory recitation at Sunday masses, in the early 1960's, of a special prayer for racial justice. Frances Kearns remarked in Commonweal on O'Boyle's efforts in her story on the March:

> At the parish church I attend - where sermons had in the past been concerned largely with the importance of the second collection, the dangers of communism, or the deficiencies of Protestant theology...the shock of relevance was overwhelming."

In the weeks before the March, O'Boyle had been of great assistance on logistics and in setting aside facilities for overnight sleeping if necessary. He urged Catholics to support and attend the March.

Thus it must have been surprising to Walter Reuther to be called out of the March leaders' meeting around 10:00 p.m. by Jack Conway on that Tuesday night. "We've got a problem," Conway told Reuther, who passed the message along to Rustin. Burke Marshall was being alerted by his friend, Auxilliary Bishop Phillip Hannan. Marshall was alarmed by the speech's non-support of the civil rights bill. An aggressive radio reporter had picked up the story in the Statler Hilton lobby, and by morning the wire services had spread the news of the controversy.

The question of revising the Lewis speech was first discussed around midnight at a meeting called by Rustin. Randolph, King, Blake, Lewis, Wilkins, Reuther, Cox, Abernathy and others attended. The first change was made that night and it was an easy one. The word "whole-heartedly" was inserted into the sentence "We cannot support the administration's civil rights bill." In fact, that change had been discussed among SNCC staffers several days previously, but the change had not made its way into the prepared text.

Actual opposition to the Civil Rights Bill, as the text seemed to call for, was a bit extreme. SNCC members had spent much time in jail and in hospitals recovering from clubbings by police and white segregationists during sit-ins. The public accommodations section of the Civil Rights Bill, for the most part, answered their protests. The Bill did not go as far as they would have liked it to, but SNCC members were in no position and of no mind to actually oppose the Bill.

John Lewis, who in his own mind thought the controversy overblown, would say that his speech was intended to present the views and feelings of the people he worked with, essentially Negroes in small towns and rural communities in the South. As to the Civil Rights Bill itself, SNCC hadn't joined the March coalition to support the Bill, but had joined to support jobs and freedoms. "I didn't see the March on Washington during the early stages, when we were trying to organize it, as to support any particular piece of legislation."

Lewis recalled the midnight meeting as more than merely an attempt to placate O'Boyle. Most of the other leaders had reservations about his speech. Dr. King told Lewis: "I think I know you well. I don't think this sounds like you." Rustin, even though the understandings about the speeches had been violated, was sympathetic to Lewis' feelings and backed him, although not as

forcefully as some of the students would have
liked. Randolph refused to condemn the speech
either, and noted that he used the words
"revolution" and "masses" in his speeches,
including the speech he would give the next
day. Tired, and with a big day ahead of them,
the midnight meeting was adjourned with a fresh
look at the speech to be taken in the morning by
an appointed committee.

The single revision regarding the Civil
Rights Bill appeased Burke Marshall, and
apparently the Attorney General, whose own copy
of the Lewis speech had underlined only one
phrase, that about not supporting the Civil
Rights Bill. In a 1964 interview, Kennedy
recalled that the speech "attacked the
President."

At 7:00 a.m. the next morning Robert
Kennedy personally called Archbishop O´Boyle to
plead with him to go forward with the invocation. Robert Kennedy and Marshall, however,
had missed the point of O´Boyle´s objections.
The support or non-support of the particular
piece of legislation was not of great conse-
quence to him. O´Boyle wanted a toning down of
the rhetoric which he perhaps misperceived as
advocating violence.

Marshall and aides began working on
suggested changes of their own, and Marshall
himself rushed to the Lincoln Memorial with a
redraft immediately before the program began.
This was unnecessary, however, since the second
revisions were made by the March leaders with
Lewis´ somewhat reluctant consent. The
Committee was unable to even discuss changes
until around 12:30 or 1:00 p.m. The leaders had
had a busy morning and were unable to get

together until immediately before the program was to begin at the Lincoln Memorial.

Dr. Eugene Carson Blake was now the most vociferous in his criticisms, insisting that the talk of "revolution" and "scorched earth" be removed. Blake also wasn't satisfied with "wholeheartedly" and preferred the phrase "with reservations." Again Randolph defended Lewis, but in the end it was Randolph who got Lewis to back down. "John, for the sake of unity, we've come this far. For the sake of unity, change it." The SNCC staffers agreed. Cleveland Sellers wrote later:

> Our first impulse was to say 'the hell with them, John. Go ahead and give the speech the way you wrote it.' After thinking about the situation, however, we realized that we were not in a position to do that.
>
> SNCC was the smallest and least influential of the major civil rights organizations. And there was no way we could force the other organizations to let John give his original speech. More important, we did not want to make a big fuss and show the nation that there were serious divisions in our ranks."

While the Lincoln Memorial program was starting, James Forman was rewriting Lewis' speech for the final time, to everyone's satisfaction, in the small storage room behind Lincoln's statue. Despite press accounts of major modifications, the "with reservations" clause and the "Sherman scorched earth" phrase were the only material alterations.

In retrospect, the episode seems a bit trivial, as if some controversy was needed in an otherwise peaceful, near perfectly executed demonstration of strength and unity. John Lewis' speech reads today as militant and uncompromising as the day it was given, to America's largest live audience, and thanks to television, to one of the largest worldwide audiences that had ever heard any speech. SNCC staffers need not have been concerned about getting their message across and demonstrating where they stood.

Lewis' actual words as he gave them, as transcribed from films and recordings of the March itself, were as follows:

> We march today for jobs and freedom, but we have nothing to be proud of. For hundreds and thousands of our brothers are not here. For they are receiving starvation wages or no wages at all. While we stand here, there are sharecroppers in the Delta of Mississippi who are out in the fields working for less than three dollars a day. While we stand here, there are students in jail on trumped up charges. Our brother, James Farmer, along with many others, is also in jail. We come here today with a great sense of misgiving.

> It is true that we support the administration's Civil Rights Bill in the Congress. We support it with great reservations, however. Unless Title Three is put in this Bill, there is nothing to protect young children and old women who must face

police dogs and fire hoses in the
south while they engage in peaceful
demonstrations. In its present form
this Bill will not protect the
citizens of Danville, Virginia who
must live in constant fear of a
police state. It will not protect
the hundreds and thousands of people
who have been arrested upon trumped
charges. What about the three young
men - SNCC field secretaries - in
Americus, Georgia who face the death
penalty for engaging in peaceful
protest?

As it stands now, the voting section
of this Bill will not help thousands
of black people who want to vote. It
will not help the citizens of
Mississippi, of Alabama and Georgia
who are qualified to vote but lack a
sixth grade education. 'One man, one
vote' is the African cry. It is ours
too. It must be ours.

We must have legislation that will
protect the Mississippi sharecropper
who is put off his farm because he
dares to register to vote. We need a
bill that will provide for the
homeless and starving people of this
nation. We need a bill that will
ensure the equality of a maid who
earns five dollars a week in the home
of a family whose income is $100,000
a year. We must have a good FEPC
bill.

"My friends, let us not forget that
we are involved in a serious social
revolution. By and large, American
politics is dominated by politicians
who build their careers on immoral
compromises and ally themselves with
open forms of political, economic,
and social exploitation. There are
exceptions, of course. We salute
those. But what political leader can
stand up and say, ´My party is the
party of principles?´ For the party
of Kennedy is also the party of
Eastland. The party of Javits is
also the party of Goldwater. Where
is our party? Where is the political
party that will make it unnecessary
to march on Washington? Where is the
political party that will make it
unnecessary to march in the streets
of Birmingham?

"Where is the political party that
will protect the citizens of Albany,
Georgia? Do you know that in Albany,
Georgia, nine of our leaders have
been indicted not by the Dixiecrats
but by the Federal Government for
peaceful protest? But what did the
Federal Government do when Albany´s
Deputy Sheriff beat Attorney C.B.
King and left him half dead? What
did the Federal Government do when
local police officials kicked and
assaulted the pregnant wife of Slater
King and she lost her baby?

"To those who have said be patient
and wait, we must say that we cannot
be patient, we do not want our

freedom gradually. For we want to be free now. We do not want to go to jail but we will go if this is the price we must pay for love, brother-hood, and true peace.

"I appeal to all of you to get in this great revolution sweeping our nation. Get in and stay in the streets of every city, every village and every hamlet of this nation, until true freedom comes, until the revolution of 1776 is complete. We must get in this revolution and complete this revolution. For in the Delta of Mississippi, in southwest Georgia, in the black dust of Alabama, in Harlem, Chicago, Detroit, Philadelphia, and all over this nation, the black masses are on the march for jobs and freedom.

"They talk about slowing down and stop. We will not stop now. All of the forces of Eastland, Barnett, Wallace, and Thurmond will not stop this revolution. If we do not get meaningful legislation out of this Congress, the time will come when we will not confine our marching to Washington. We will march through the South, through the streets of Jackson, through the streets of Danville, through the streets of Cambridge, through the streets of Birmingham. But we will march with the spirit of love and with the spirit of dignity that we have shown here today."

Lewis and the SNCC staffers were on top of the feelings and mood of rank and file Negroes, and the speech reflected the heated and sometimes pitched battles that had been waged all that summer of 1963 in places like Americus, Albany, Birmingham, Cambridge, and Danville. It was accurate in pointing to the Administration's ambivalence or outright hypocrisy in the Albany indictments, in its reluctance to protect civil rights workers from local officials, and in the Administration's reluctance to totally alienate southern Senators like James Eastland of Mississippi.

It was a speech that foretold future battles born in the frustration of young blacks -and Lewis was the only speaker to consistently use "black" rather than "Negro" in his speech at the March.

A reporter from the Nation had seen Lewis at March headquarters a few weeks before the March, and had written:

> "I listened one day at the March office to John Lewis, the shy young chairman of SNCC, telling me that he expects a new generation of leaders even younger than himself to emerge from the rural south in the days ahead, and to emerge from those whose prospects will have been broadened by the experience of the March itself. 'Everything we have done so far', he said to me, 'has been preliminary, almost a rehearsal. On August 28, the curtain goes up on the first act of the revolution.'"

That revolution, led by SNCC workers like Stokely Carmichael who stayed in Mississippi with the poor that summer of 1963, would soon pass even John Lewis by. But for the moment, while Dr. King's speech was the most memorable and moving, Lewis' speech was the most vital.

Lewis was interrupted 14 times by rousing applause, more times than any other speaker except King. One of Dr. King's biographers recalled that when Lewis finished his speech, he turned and walked past the rows of leaders and dignitaries on the platform. Every Negro speaker on the platform "shook his hand and patted him on the back, and every white speaker stared vacantly at the horizon".

"There had never been such a
crowd. There were society women
in new hats and old women in
Sunday go-to-church black; there
were bright young men from the top
level of the agencies, looking
important and hurried, and lost;
there were pretty girls and plain
ones, priests, preachers, and
rabbis, union members,
seminarians, housewives and
teachers."

 - Lerone Bennet

Buses from Boston left at 11:00 p.m. on
Tuesday night for a long, 8-hour ride to
Washington, but there were others who took
longer bus rides from places like Milwaukee,
Little Rock, and St. Louis. New York City was
active throughout the night in a scene
reminiscent of a holiday eve. Port Authority
Bus Station and Penn Station were crowded with
travelers, rare for the middle of the night on a
Wednesday in August. At Penn Station, where
special trains had left at 2:00 a.m., and again
shortly after dawn, authorities reported the
largest early morning crowd since the end of
World War II. At 1:30 a.m. buses began leaving
Yankee Stadium for the 5-1/2 hour drive to
Washington. Buses left Queens at 1:00 a.m.,
Yonkers at 4:00 a.m., and Brooklyn at 5:30
a.m. All of these charters were sponsored by
the NAACP. The buses from Westchester County
left at 2:00 a.m., the riders exhausted by the
time they reached Washington at 9:00 a.m., since
few had slept due to all the excitement. In
addition, other chartered buses were leaving
from all over the city, most from the 143rd

Street Armory, where an incredible 450 buses had assembled. The Lincoln Tunnel had a middle of the night traffic jam when the buses started rolling at 1:30 a.m.

From the CORE staging area on 125th Street, buses left at dawn. Not all supporters could come to Washington - some had to work, some had children to take care of, some could not afford the $7.00 cost of transportation. In an impulsive, inspirational display, however, thousands who couldn't go to Washington showed up at dawn in a show of solidarity for those who were going. As the lucky ones boarded the buses, the sidewalks and streets were jammed with bystanders, cheering and yelling: "You tell them - you tell them for me."

Buses left from all over the Philadelphia area at 7:00 a.m. They then rendezvoused outside the city on U.S. Route 40. Chartered trains had left Philadelphia's 30th Street Station by 6:15 a.m. A number of busloads of marchers left Rodney Square in downtown Wilmington at 7:00 a.m. on the morning of the March. There was one incidence of the feared attacks on the special buses streaming into Washington. In fact, it occurred right outside of Washington, in Bladensburg, Prince Georges Country, Maryland, rather than in the South as expected. Three juveniles were arrested by police for throwing stones at a bus on the Baltimore-Washington Parkway. A window was broken, but there were no injuries. The incident was not even attributed to a racial motive, as police reported that trucks and buses were pelted with rocks by out of school youngsters all summer. In Jessup, Maryland, however, Howard County Police arrested a motorist who attempted to sideswipe marchers walking toward Washington. By dawn, State

Police in Pikesville, Maryland reported traffic very heavy on U.S. 40, the Pulaski Highway, between the Delaware state line and Baltimore, and even heavier on the Baltimore-Washington Parkway: "Almost a continuous line of buses on the expressway," police said. By 8:00 a.m., 100 buses an hour were streaming through the Baltimore Harbor Tunnel.

Baltimore's participation was pegged by the press at a somewhat disappointing 10,000 as it was only a 45-minute drive down the Parkway to Washington. Actually, that estimate of 10,000 is suspect, since there was no way of counting the private individuals who hopped in their cars at the last minute on the morning of the March to come to Washington. Four thousand people gathered in downtown Baltimore at Lafayette Square to board buses, which began pulling away at 8:00 a.m. Marchers came to the square by transit bus, walking, or by car pool. The mood was festive and marchers were greeted personally by Mayor Theodore McKeldin, who spoke briefly to the Lafayette Square crowd shortly before 8:00 a.m., citing his support for the March and the Civil Rights Bill. McKeldin joined, in the lead car, a massive car caravan through the city to the expressway. However, he left the car caravan outside the city limits and did not attend the March.

The well-organized Maryland March committee, led by activist Troy Brailey had long since exhausted the charter bus supply, necessitating the car caravan. The 50 or so buses making the trip carried standing room only crowds. In the days before the March, participants were told to come to the square with cars if they had them. Impromptu car pools were arranged by a harried Brailey and his staff on the morning of the March. The car and bus caravan moved slowly at first through the city, picking up additional cars and buses at schools, churches, and union halls.

Annapolis, Maryland´s capital, sent seven busloads. Organized groups also chartered buses in Frederick, Hagerstown, Westminster, Havre de Grace, Salisbury, Easton, Chestertown and Cambridge. All morning the chartered buses rumbled off the Baltimore-Washington Parkway onto New York Avenue, and into downtown, headed toward the Washington Monument. In so doing they passed through the black areas of Northeast and Northwest Washington, where from windows, porches, and steps, Washington´s Negroes waved at and cheered on the incoming marchers.

Throughout the night, countless people worked on last-minute arrangements. Television crews set up their equipment at both the Lincoln Memorial and the Monument. Park Police directed traffic in the Monument area throughout the night as Park Service workers and volunteers put the finishing touches on temporary facilities, including the 120 portable chemical toilets and the 16 first aid stations set up under Army tents. At March headquarters there was still much to do. Somehow, six hundred signs had been erroneously prepared reading: "We demand an FECP law now." It should have read: "We demand an FEPC," referring to the demand for a Fair Employment Practices Commission. Volunteers cut and pasted to correct the signs before dawn.

The first out-of-town demonstrators to arrive at the Washington Monument were said to be four people from New York City who arrived at about 2:45 a.m. after leaving New York at 10 o´clock the previous evening. They spread out their lawn chairs and had a picnic breakfast even before the sun rose. Some early arriving marchers simply camped out on the Washington Monument grounds or in the city's other parks. No one asked them to move on.

At the Bible Way Church at 1130 New Jersey Avenue, N.W., Bishop Smallwood Williams was directing an all-night vigil and religious service. It started at 8:00 p.m. and broke up around dawn. The service actually picked up participants as the night wore on, with demonstrators arriving in the middle of the night from out of town and directed there by various sources, including police. Indeed, for many there was too much excitement to sleep the night of August 27.

By dawn the scene on Washington's streets was a mixture of military occupation and cherry blossom parade. Military jeeps were everywhere, with burly soldiers with MP bands on their arms directing traffic. If the city was under siege it was a gentle one. There were few unkind words, tension, or irate motorists. As if to give some relief to city officials there was, in fact, no rush hour in Washington that Wednesday as a vast number of federal workers took administrative leave for the day. Fewer than one-half of the 162,000 federal and District of Columbia workers reported for work downtown. Since marchers coming to Washington spread their arrival time over a seven-hour period from 4:00 a.m. to 11:00 a.m., the feared traffic jam never materialized. Downtown Washington outside the March area would resemble a ghost town throughout the day. The only traffic tie-up in town throughout the morning was on Constitution Avenue itself, most of which had been cordoned off for the parade. Police and National Guardsmen swarmed throughout the area all morning but they had very little to do except test their communication equipment, exchange pleasantries with the demonstrators, answer a few questions and take in the amazing scene. Army helicopters hovered overhead all morning, looking for trouble spots. They found none, but probably took a lot of good photographs of Washington's monuments and the petitioners. The weather, for an August morning in Washington, was ideal. The humidity was unseasonably low, and there were refreshing breezes. However, the heat and humidity would build as the day wore on.

All over town on the morning of the March special church services and breakfasts were held by various denominations for both out of town and local marchers. The services were a significant element, both in legitimizing the March for those individuals who had never taken part in a demonstration before and in increasing the number of participants. From St. Stephens and the Incarnation Episcopal Church at 16th and Newton Streets, N.W., a group marched three abreast down 16th Street to Lafayette Square, where they joined the congregation from St. John's Episcopal Church, and then marched to the Monument. After a mass at St. Patrick's Catholic Church at Tenth and G Street, N.W., Catholic University students, faculty members and alumni marched under a Catholic University banner to the Elipse. Out-of-town church members hooked up with sister churches in the District to coordinate activities. At the Chevy Chase Presbyterian Church on Chevy Chase Circle, members of that congregation greeted 40 visitors from several Burlington, Virginia churches and they all went to the March together, after a ham and egg breakfast. National Protestant religious leaders held a breakfast meeting at a downtown hotel, where March committeewoman Anna Arnold Hedgeman spoke briefly.

At 7:00 a.m. Washington's Union Station was practically deserted, but ready for the crush of people. It could handle the crowds – the 760 foot long, 45 foot high concourse was then probably the one of the largest rooms in the world, big enough "to accommodate the Washington Monument sideways." In the '40's, it had handled crowds of up to 175,000 at one time. In the '50's it employed 5,000 people to operate what must have been one of the original indoor shopping malls, containing a "bowling alley, mortuary, bakery, butchery, YMCA hotel, ice house, resident doctor, liquor store, turkish baths, first class restaurants, basketball court, swimming pool, nursery, police station and silver-monogramming shop." By 1963, however, declining rail traffic had made Union Station a less active marketplace. But it still was equipped to efficiently handle the crowds, and direct incoming passengers on their way. August 28 would be no different than any Thanksgiving or Christmas eve. Twenty-one extra chartered trains in one 3-hour period that morning posed no real problem.

At 8:00 a.m., the chartered trains began to arrive, the first from Pittsburgh. The incoming crowd sang freedom songs as they milled around the concourse. As succeeding trains pulled in regularly every few minutes thereafter, the crowds swelled and greetings and songs were exchanged. Thirteen of the 21 trains were from New York, with one each from Pittsburgh, Philadelphia, Chicago, Gary, Detroit, Miami, Jacksonville, and Cincinnati. Seventeen hundred people came on the Chicago train, but hundreds more were left behind because the train simply couldn't accommodate them. Three hundred marchers from Chicago had come on chartered planes. Thousands more demonstrators arrived

from various points along the east coast on
heavily booked, regularly scheduled trains. The
special freedom train from Detroit had 319
persons aboard, and included Protestant,
Catholic, and Jewish clergymen, and a large
group of high school and college students. The
Detroit train also carried probably the youngest
articulate marcher, four-year old Charles Dolby,
who told a Star reporter he was going to
Washington to "get some more freedoms." At 9:30
a.m., the chartered train from the farthest
point arrived, when the Miami freedom train
pulled into Union Station, with 775 people
board. It had left Miami at 9:30 the previous
morning, Tuesday, with 35 passengers, and
gradually added traveling marchers along the
way. It was a festive ride. At each of the 12
stops along the way cheering crowds lined the
platform as the cars pulled in. They were
supporters without the finances or time to go to
Washington, but who wanted in some small way to
show their solidarity. Nowhere was this more
evident than in Savannah Tuesday night, where
thousands of Negroes and whites created a crush
on the platform, and sent up a huge roar as the
train pulled in. Those aboard and those in the
station then loudly began chanting "Freedom!
Freedom! Freedom!" Before the train pulled out
of Savannah, having been augmented by another
contingent of marchers, their supporters on the
platform broke into "We Shall Not Be Moved."
And so it went throughout the day and night at
places like Jacksonville, and the troubled town
of Albany, Georgia.

A Star reporter who rode the train wrote
that few passengers had gotten any sleep because
of the enthusiasm and excitement: "During the
night, passengers formed human chains, marching
up and down the aisles of the cars and singing

freedom songs to the cadence of their rhythmic handclapping." But when the Miami train arrived in Washington, the marchers had enough energy left to sing "We Shall Overcome" as they hit the platform. On the trains, the buses, the planes, the private automobiles, it was not time for sleeping, reading, or private thoughts. The marchers talked, perhaps argued, joked, but above all, they sang the freedom songs which knit them all together.

By 6:00 a.m., Nazi leader Rockwell and a small group of followers had arrived at the base of the Washington Monument. Almost immediately D.C. police ordered them to move to a grassy area behind the Monument which would be completely out of sight of demonstrators arriving at the staging areas and the entertainment stage set up for those who would be performing prior to the March. While Rockwell and his group milled around the small area to which they had been assigned, 200 policemen and National Guardsmen completely surrounded them. The Nazis did not wear their uniforms nor display Nazi emblems. Their failure to obtain a parade permit precluded this. The previous day, several of Rockwell's followers had, without incident, picketed Negro radio station WUST, which housed a temporary March headquarters.

Rockwell continued to wait for his ranks to swell, but they never did. Police estimated that a maximum of 72 Nazis appeared during the course of the morning. At about 11:00 a.m., Deputy Nazi Commander Karl Allen attempted to make a speech to the small gathering, ignoring police warnings that such a speech was prohibited. He was promptly arrested and taken away. There were some boos from the Nazis but no attempt to intervene. Allen got as far as saying: "We are here to protest by as peaceful means as possible the occupation of Washington by forces deadly to the welfare of our country." Police Captain Herlihy told him to stop, but Allen continued, and the arrest was immediate. Rockwell then lead his followers in a march across the 14th Street Bridge, in the opposite direction of the Civil Rights March, and into Virginia. Few of the civil rights marchers even knew that the Nazis had been in the area. Rockwell's attempt to attract thousands of counter demonstrators had failed miserably. He told reporters: "The right-wing, I'm sorry to say, is the most cowardly thing in the world. The Negroes are brave enough to go out and be arrested by the thousands." It was probably the only nice thing Rockwell ever said about his hated adversaries.

Karl Allen was found guilty three days after the March in a District of Columbia court and fined $50.00 for giving a speech without a permit.

On Capitol Hill, things almost had the appearance of business as usual, at least as the day began. Capitol Hill police were vigilant lest anyone dare scoff the congressional ban on demonstrations in the Capitol area. A group of 75 marchers from Wisconsin were cautioned while walking to the Monument grounds after getting off their bus in the Capitol Hill area. It seems that some of the marchers had the temerity to hold their placards above their heads while walking past the Capitol. Alert Capitol Hill police quickly advised them of the rules, and the marchers were said to have quitely complied.

If there would be no march to Capitol Hill, there would at least be a March contingent from

Capitol Hill. About 100 Capitol Hill employees
assembled west of the Capitol to march to the
Washington Monument even as the civil rights
leaders were meeting with congressional
leaders. About half were said to be staff
members of various congressional offices while
the other worked in the barbershops and
cafeterias on the Hill.

NAACP lobbyist Clarence Mitchell had
previously arranged for early morning meetings
between the Big Ten and Congressional leaders.
Mitchell accompanied the civil rights leaders to
the Hill in two rented limousines, which were
paid for by the March committee. The first
meeting was at 9:00 a.m. with Senator Majority
Leader Mike Mansfield. The group meeting with
Mansfield included Randolph, Reuther, Wilkins,
King, Ahmann, Blake, John Lewis, Rabbi Prinz,
Whitney Young, Floyd McKissick of CORE, attorney
and rights activist Joseph Rauh, and Arnold
Aronson, Secretary of the Leadership Conference
on Civil Rights. McKissick was replacing the
imprisoned James Farmer. The March committee
was apparently somewhat embarrased about James
Farmer remaining in jail. They had allegedly
pressured Lulu Farmer, his wife, to get him out
of jail on the day before the March, telling her
his remaining there was "granstanding." But
another leader told Newsweek: "I think he was
the victim of an element in CORE that was
unhappy about the March from the moment we ruled
out any civil disobedience. I think he wanted
to be here." At 9:30, the group met with
Minority Leaders Everett Dirkson and Charles
Halleck, and at 10:00 a.m. with House Majority
Leader Carl Albert and Speaker John McCormack.
Wilkins was the chief spokesman for the group at
the private meetings, as Randolph was described
as "visibly tired" having had a hectic final
week before the March.

Mitchell had arranged the congressional meetings, in lieu of the original plan for lobbying by rank and file marchers on Capitol Hill. Mitchell was experienced on Capitol Hill and feared a backlash against the Civil Rights Bill if unorganized lobbying took place. Earlier in the summer, reaction to the announcement of a proposed congressional sit-in had been muted. The Southern senators merely doubted that any great numbers would come. Capitol Hill police had said they would handle any crowds routinely. The Senate galleries held 275 spectators, the House 600, with a 15 minute rotation of all visitors if crowds were waiting. Those breaking the rule against silence would be removed. No incidents occurred at the Capitol on the day of the March.

At least two senators made the March from the Washington Monument to the Lincoln Memorial that morning. Senator Hubert Humphrey of Minnesota had breakfasted that morning with United Church of Christ ministers and laymen from Minnesota. At noon he and his fellow Minnesota Senator Eugene McCarthy marched with the religious delegation to the Memorial. Also, an inter-religious group from St. Louis met with Missouri's senators that morning on Capitol Hill, and later with the State's representatives on the House side. The meetings on Capitol Hill that morning carried on so long that word finally came that the marchers down at the Washington Monument were getting impatient and getting ready to march without the civil rights leaders in front of them. On hearing this, the leaders broke off their meetings and made a mad dash for taxicabs and other transportation, the limousines having been apparently forgotten. Clarence Mitchell stayed at the Capitol to tie up some loose ends, including his arrangements to get interested senators and congressmen to the Lincoln Memorial for the afternoon program. Mitchell had arranged with the Capital Transit Company for one bus. However, many congressmen apparently became fascinated with the idea of going to the March at the last minute, the bus quickly filled, and Mitchell himself and a few others were unable to get aboard. Fortunately, the Capitol Police provided him with an escort to the Lincoln Memorial.

One coincidence resulted when the legislators finally arrived at the Lincoln Memorial, which perhaps resulted in the original idea of the March on Washington being fulfilled. So many legislators showed up that there was some difficulty in finding a special section where they all could sit together. One was finally found at the foot of the Lincoln Memorial. However, it was necessary to bring the legislators through a special entrance and to have them walk single file down the steps of the Memorial in front of the crowd to the special section. When the crowd massing at the Lincoln Memorial observed these congressmen and senators marching down the steps, somebody struck up the chant, "Pass the Bill, Pass the Bill". The chant was taken up by the massive crowd and was described to be very impressive as far as the attending legislators were concerned.

But as one reporter noted, the distance between the Lincoln Memorial and the U.S. Capital is 11,470 feet. Most of the nation's lawnmakers did not hear that chant, and apparently did not care. For on Capitol Hill that day, for the most part, it was business as usual. With the more liberal or perhaps more courageous members of both Houses packed off to the Lincoln Memorial, the House and Senate settled down to their awesome work, in this instance that consisted of making August 28, 1963, seem like any other day on Capitol Hill. The men of the cloth chosen that day to give the invocation in each chamber knew their audience. In the Senate a Reverend Frederick Brown Harris reassured his listeners: "In these most dangerous days the Republic has ever known, subdue, we pray, all selfish clamor, that amid our national confusion the voice of Thy guidance may be heard. Thou who art the author of liberty has taught us that the essence of our freedom is not in having rights but in fulfilling them. In Thy lights may there be revealed to this bewildered generation, with all its moral failures, that to insist on grasping for that which may be justly claimed and then to use such blessings for self-gratification and indulgence is but to prove that those thus oblivious to responsibility are unworthy of such inheritance." On the House side a Reverend Bernard Braskamp divinely warned against too much law making: "Grant that we may be so devoted and loyal to our form of government ... that it will become increasingly less necessary to multiply legislation and enact laws to govern our character and conduct."

Although the House of Representatives had at least one reason for meeting that day, the final vote on the Railroad Arbitration Bill to avoid the impending railroad strike, the Senate, it was said, had absolutely nothing to do that day. "If it had not been for the March, the Senate would almost certainly have voted itself a day off, August 20." In all events, both Houses went out of their way it seemed to avoid any discussion of civil rights.

The House deliberated on the Railroad Bill from 12 o'clock until after 3:00 p.m. At about

1:30 p.m., the time at which the Lincoln
Memorial program was beginning, a Representative
Snyder of Kentucky suggested the absence of a
quorum. The roll was called and all but 92
members responded. Many, if not most, of those
were at the Lincoln Memorial. So it would be
known who stood where, a Representative Bass of
Tennessee requested that the names of the 92
absentees "be spread upon the Journal". The
House was not ready to adjourn as yet. There
was a resolution to be debated and passed
requesting the President of the United States to
issue a proclamation declaring the first week in
March every year to be Save Your Vision Week.
"Of all the impairments among civilized man"
Representative Rogers of Colorado argued,
"vision tops the list." The Negro situation in
America was not to go without comment, however,
that day in the House. A Representative Gary of
Virginia was permitted to introduce into the
record a letter and editorial he had apparently
clipped from the conservative Richmond Times-
Dispatch. The letter was from a Negro named
Zeak Crumpton of Hampton, Virginia: "I am glad
that my ancestors were Negro slaves. My race
has made tremendous progress since they came to
live in this country. I own my own home which
is neatly furnished and is fitted out with all
modern appliances. I have steady employment and
hard work as a section hand, I shall retire next
year on a good pension from the railroad. I
enjoy good health and have no grievances. For
Sunday dinner, we can afford such foods as
black-eyed peas, grits, cabbage, corn muffins,
and fried chicken. Had my ancestors not been
slaves, life for me would be different. I would
walk around in my bare feet with a metal ring in
my nose. On holidays we would feast on
elephants´ toes, roasted grasshoppers, and the
milk of a coconut. I get on my knees each night

and thank God for permitting my ancestors to come to America as slaves." The Times Dispatch editorial concluded: "Here is a man who is a credit to his race ... we salute him as the sort of man who has made this country great."

While the House was adding to its official record this auspicious document, the Senate was dealing with a revamped statute for licensing practical nurses in the District of Columbia, expressing the appreciation of the Congress to the American Association of State Highway Officials for its numerous contributions to American transportation over the prior 50 years, and approving a number of promotions in rank for members of the military. Only Senator Sam Ervin of North Carolina was willing to add to the civil rights debate in the Senate that day. For some time he ranted about a Defense Department directive granting certain military commanders the authority to put certain segregated public places close to bases off limits to base personnel. Ervin claimed such a directive had the effects of "converting the military and naval commanders of the nation into political arms of the Executive Department of the Federal Government." Meanwhile, while all this non-debate was continuing, a judiciary subcommittee of the House tabled pending civil rights legislation for two more weeks. In fact, no serious attempt to deal with the civil rights legislation would be made until after President Kennedy's death three months later. On August 28, the legislators had plenty of time and plenty of willing audiences to give their reactions about the March on Washington. The obvious success of the March was said to have intensified Senator Thurmond's displeasure with the Civil Rights Bill. That evening Thurmond told television audiences that Negroes had more

automobiles, refrigerators and other goods and
were better off here than in any other
country. Senator Russell Long of Louisiana
referred to the demonstrators as a mob.
Congressman Broyhill of Virginia complained
again that District of Columbia merchants had
lost millions of dollars due to the "nuisance"
of the March. Senator John Stennis of
Mississippi saw a perverse reason for joy:
"This is going to help defeat the Bill."
Senator Thurmond was distinguished for holding
the record for the longest Senate speech, 24
hours and 18 minutes, set in 1957 in a
filibuster against civil rights legislation.
The filibuster was a major weapon of the
Southern Democracts opposed to the Civil Rights
Bill. Senator Richard Russell of Georgia had
developed a disciplined platoon system to assure
continued, perhaps unending debate on the Bill
in a planned attempt to wear out supporters.
Cloture, the parliamentary mechanism for cutting
off debate, would not be invoked until the
following June. Russell was one of the most
powerful members of the Senate, and
"traditional" in his view of Negro rights. When
asked on Meet the Press a few weeks before the
March why he thought there was no need for a
public accomodation section in the Civil Rights
Bill, Russell responded: "There are Negro
restaurants in every town in the south of which
I have any knowledge where they have any
considerable number of Negroes, and it is not at
all unsual to send down to get some of their
barbecue and some of their other specialities.
They are very fine cooks."

Some of the southern legislators were said
to be "visibly shaken as they watched the March
proceedings in a House cloakroom from a tiny
Japanese television set. But none of the

Southern conservatives changed their minds as a result of the March.

March headquarters at WUST radio station remained a beehive of activity throughout the morning and into the early afternoon. Staffers there missed the March and much of the program, and some missed all of it. Police directed newcomers there for information, and crude maps were drawn for those who didn't know how to get to the Monument. The mood there, however, was exhilarating. It seemed that the whole world had come to Washington. A drum and bugle corps made up of the CORE workers who had walked to Washington from Brooklyn, plus some local recruits, spent the morning going though Washington neighborhoods literally drumming up last-minute participation.

The media needed no last-minute encouragement. One thousand six hundred and fifty-five special press passes were given out at the special press tent at the Washington Monument. These were in addition to the over 1,200 regular press passes possessed by full time Washington correspondents. The total coverage exceeded any prior Washington event, including John Kennedy's inaugural two years earlier. On a day of very little crime in Washington, a few press badges were reported stolen. With thousands of reporters swarming the area, it would be expected that they would at least turn up one ugly incident of racial hatred or vandalism. Amazingly, not a single such incident was reported, an extraordinary fact for any event with over 250,000 participants. One reporter said later: "The March was disciplined; throughout a long and weary day I saw not a single act of discourtesy, nor did I hear even one expression of irritation."

Many of the special passes went to foreign correspondents who took an extraordinary interest in the March. Around the world, sympathetic demonstrations were held on August 28 in such places as Berlin, Munich, London, Amsterdam and Kingston, Jamaica. There were also demonstrations of support in cities across the United States. For example, in Akron, Ohio, hundreds of families flew American flags to show their support for the marchers. There were also demonstrations of support in Los Angeles and in Austin, Texas. The Honolulu, Hawaii branch of the NAACP, while they were unable to send any representatives, shipped 15 authentic Hawaiian leis to the Washington branch of the NAACP. They were flown into National Airport and delivered to the Lincoln Memorial just before the speeches began.

Izvestia, Moscow's afternoon daily, devoted its entire front page to the March. The BBC covered the March live. Film crews from Canada, Japan, France, and West Germany covered the entire event as well. Many foreign newspapers flew in top correspondents to cover the March, including London's major dailies, as well as papers from Australia, India, Korea, West Germany, France, Switzerland, Holland, Spain, Japan, Canada, and Cuba. The Voice of America also covered the March as its lead story, portraying it as a reaffirmation of the United States Constitution, and as an accepted means for making an appeal in a democracy.

The pre-March program at the Washington Monument was to begin at exactly 9:30. Bayard Rustin, however, advised Ossie Davis, the master of ceremonies, to delay the program because only two dignitaries had been able to fight their way through the crowd to get to the stage. Ninety thousand persons now spread out over the

Washington Monument lawn looking for their groups, making new acquaintances and holding early morning picnics. The longest line in the area was not for the comfort stations but for an enterprising ice cream vendor who had somehow managed to drive his truck to the area directly in front of the Washington Monument. While the demonstrators were waiting for the on-stage entertainment to begin, many restless youngsters began holding impromptu concerts of their own. In front of a large green tent that served as March headquarters, a group of young black teenagers with CORE t-shirts were standing in a circle clapping and singing: "I´m Going to Walk the Streets of Jackson," one girl sang. "One of These Days´ her friends answered. "I´m Going to be the Chief of Police," another girl sang. "One of These Days," the surrounding crowd now answered.

Finally, folk singer Joan Baez´ voice came over the loud speaker, "Oh Freedom" she sang, and the March program had begun. The crowd steadily increased. Perhaps the largest noise of the day arose when Carol Taylor, the nation´s first black airline stewardess, was introduced to the crowd at the Washington Monument. She spoke briefly and then told the demonstrators that she wanted to hear the crowd yell "Freedom" loud enough to be heard all over the world. She held her hands above her head, waited patiently, and dropped her arms to signal the crowd. "Freedom" they screamed in one voice that could be heard miles away.

As Odetta launched into "I´m on the Way to Canaan Land", Josh White arrived on stage. Perhaps fearing he would miss a chance to perform altogether, he walked up to the microphone to sing with Odetta. Then Baez joined them, along with the Freedom Singers and Peter, Paul, and Mary.

Besides the entertainers who performed songs at the Monument, Davis introduced a variety of celebrities, including performers Lena Horne and Bobby Darin, and Rosa Parks, the Negro woman who had started the Montgomery bus boycott in 1955 by refusing to move to the back of a city bus. Davis also introduced Daisy Bates, another brave Negro woman who had escorted the nine teenagers who integrated Central High School in Little Rock, Arkansas amid extensive civil unrest in 1957. Miguel Abreau Castillo, the head of the San Juan Bar Association, gave a short speech in Spanish. When Davis told the crowd at 11:45 that the March to the Lincoln Memorial was about to begin, he was in error. It had begun at least 20 minutes earlier.

Impatient marchers had already begun moving down Constitution Avenue to the Lincoln Memorial before the Big Ten had returned from their trip to Capitol Hill. By 11:30, it had become a steady stream, and there would be difficulty in getting the leaders into the line. Television coverage was about to go live, so Ed Brown of the March's Washington office, and Publicity Director Posner, with the aid of a group of parade marshals waded into the throng, and blocked off the line of marchers so the leaders could jump in. The flatbed trucks full of camera equipment then recorded the famous picture of the line of leaders, King, Randolph, Young, Reuther, Rauh, Wilkins, and the others, their arms linked, starting out on the March to the Lincoln Memorial. They linked arms as much to hold back the surging crowds, as to display their brotherhood.

The Hollywood contingent fell in at some point behind the March leaders and attracted almost as much attention. The flatbed trucks also followed their progress. Harry Belafonte, Charlton Heston, Burt Lancaster, Marlon Brando and Sidney Poitier led the group, also locking arms as much for security as for solidarity. The crush of demonstrators wanting to get a glimpse of the stars as they walked became overwhelming. A cordon of D.C. police had to be formed to hold back the crowds, most of whom had never seen a movie star in the flesh. The stars remained good natured, and shook every hand that was flung at them and exchanged greetings.

The march itself was described as a dignified walk, the silence of the demonstrators not broken by idle chatter or militant slogans, but only occasionally by the familiar strains of "We Shall Overcome." One group carried a coffin in the parade labelled Jim Crow, signifying death of southern segregation ordinances. Ledger Smith, the NAACP member from Chicago who had rollerskated to Washington, gave one more performance as he rollerskated down Constitution Avenue to the Lincoln Memorial. Jay Hardo, an 82-year old Dayton, Ohio, man deserved an award for endurance for bicycling all the way from his hometown. One 20-year old, Bruce Marzhan bicycled even further - from Tulare, South Dakota. However, he fell off his bike on the morning of the March, and was treated for a lacerated scalp at one of the first aid stations. A group of denim clad youngsters from Plaquemine, Louisiana, where CORE director Farmer remained in jail, danced down Constitution Avenue. There were fathers and mothers with infant children, and many elderly couples. In a day before the world "hippie" had entered the language, both Time and U.S. News and World Report reported the presence of "beatnik types - bearded young men and young women with hair trailing over their shoulders, wearing tennis shoes and dungarees."

Who in fact made up the crowd that day? Most estimates were that about one-fourth of the participants were white and one in six were students, mostly college students. Albert Gollin of the Bureau of Social Science Research in Washington conducted an on-site survey of March participants in order to determine the demographics of participation. Gollin found that Negro participants in the March were predominantly northern and urban, and distinguished by high education and income, by membership in active civil rights organizations, and by high rates of prior activism in local community politices. Most of the marchers said they were chiefly concerned about equal job opportunities and school desegregation. Two-thirds of the black participants held white collar occupations, although the fact that the March took place in Washington and many participants were federal government workers holding office jobs makes this finding unsurprising. Gollin concluded that the burden of direct action protest was being carried by students and the rising Negro middle classes. Twenty-eight percent were college graduates, and an additional 25 percpent had some college, compared with 10 percent of all blacks nationally in 1963. The median family income of the 1963 marchers was almost $6,000, which was said to be 1.7 times higher than the median of non-white families throughout the United States that year. In a relative sense, black participants were clearly more affluent than the average Negro in America in 1963.

Practically no one watched this parade from the sidelines, except for District and Park policemen. At Bacon Drive, the Constitution Avenue line of march took a rolling left turn toward the Lincoln Memorial. A displaced, regular White House picket sat silently on that corner holding a sign predicting the end of the world. As the line of march reached the Lincoln Memorial, the newly installed organ donated by a private firm incongruously played "Stars and Stripes Forever", the organist having misplaced his copy of the music for "We Shall Overcome." Recurrent choruses of the latter were being sung by each group of marchers as they made the turn in front of the Lincoln Memorial toward the Reflecting Pool. Marshals directed the rank and file in that direction, after separating the leaders and V.I.P.´s, and sending them directly up the front steps of the Memorial.

Inside the open air Memorial, the leaders exchanged pleasantries with celebrities and reporters. There was much photographing, and some on-the-spot interviews, before the leaders retired to a back room for the final meeting about John Lewis´ speech. By noon, the growing crowd was "pressing against the barriers at the steps of the Lincoln Memorial, stretching far down on both sides of the Reflecting Pool".

"A cast of entertainers no entrepreneur could possibly have assembled for profit."

— Washington Star
September 1, 1963

The rather considerable influence of Hollywood stars and other entertainers on American politics has been a curious phenomenon for at least several decades. In 1963, there appeared to be a genuine consensus of support among these celebrities for the Civil Rights Bill and an abolition of discriminatory practices. Nowhere was that consensus more apparent than in Washington on August 28. Numreous celebrities poured into the city for the big March: whites, Negroes, Republicans, Democrats, singers, actors and writers. It appeared as if they felt that their failure to appear would be interpreted as softness on the issue. Thus did Burt Lancaster, Josephine Baker and James Baldwin, after themselves leading a march in Paris on the 21st in support of the Washington march, fly into Washington shortly before the March to join their fellow celebrities.

Many, like Baldwin, Joan Baez, Peter, Paul and Mary, Harry Belafonte, and Sammy Davis, Jr., had long records of support for liberal political causes, and civil rights demonstrations in particular. A rumor that Hollywood stars were being urged not to attend the March by agents and producers fearful of a white backlash at the box office was given little credence. There was not a shred of evidence that such a backlash later occurred.

The formal organization of Hollywood's participation in the March began on July 30 with a meeting at Charlton Heston's home. Director Billy Wilder and actors Marlon Brando, Tony Curtis, James Garner, Mel Ferrer, Tony Franciosa, Peter Brown and Burt Lancaster all attended, and each agreed to try to drum up further support within the film industry. Heston was elected Chairman of the group, and spoke to the press after the meeting: "We will march because we recognize the events of the summer of 1963 as among the most significant we have lived through, and we wish to be part of these events, and of this time when promises made a century ago will finally be kept."

Ironically, on the following day the NAACP announced in Hollywood plans to seek from the National Labor Relations Board decertification of several movie industry unions that were alleged to be practicing discrimination. In fact, in 1963 there were no black members of the various technical trade unions in Hollywood connected with film production. Heston had met earlier in July with Dr. King and other civil rights leaders, and with leaders of the trade unions in attempts to get the unions to break down their discriminatory barriers. In reality, a white person unrelated to a current member of one of the technical trade unions had nearly as insurmountable a task as a Negro breaking into the closed shops in 1963, such was the structure of those unions at the time. Heston, who had involved himself in civil rights picketing over the prior year, suggested to King and the others that an artists' group be formed to coordinate involvement by those interested in participating in the upcoming March on Washington.

Whatever Hollywood's internal racial problems were, support for the March on

Washington was not difficult to garner, although many actors and show people did shy away with the explanation that demonstrations were not their style. Another meeting was held a week later, on Sunday, August 7, with Heston chairing, and sixty celebrities in attendance.

Heston called several more meetings throughout the month of August to assess the group's progress. A smaller steering committee met regularly at Heston's or Brando's home or dressing room. On one occasion a meeting was "staged" for the benefit of network news cameras which had missed a meeting on the previous night at Heston's home. The arts contingent realized from the outset that their chief role in the general scheme of the March on Washington was to draw attention to the March and its goals, and in that sense the use of their names and faces for publicity purposes was welcomed. When Heston was obliged to go to New York for rehearsals in the latter part of August, James Garner filled in as chairman of the group.

This ad hoc celebrity group was not always in accord on tactics, and there were frequent disputes. Brando and others tended to favor a more "theatrical display" rather than just solemn participation in the March. Generally however, as befitted the spirit of that summer, harmony prevailed as individuals acceded to the consensus of the group. This is exemplified by the statement that Heston read on behalf of the arts contingent on the day of the March at the Lincoln Memorial. Roles were assigned to the various participants, and it was decided that a writer, James Baldwin, would prepare a statement, and an actor, Heston, would read it. The fiery Baldwin of course held much more radical views than those of most of his fellow artists, and these had been widely publicized in his various books. On the plane from New York to Washington for the March, Heston and Baldwin argued over the tone of the statement. Yet when Heston was handed Baldwin's creation the night before the March, which he received with some trepidation, he found its content and tone to be most acceptable.

Ossie Davis signed on early with the March committee to coordinate participation of the various entertainers and, along with Heston, was largely responsible for their active support. Davis was both an actor and a writer, having produced a book on Frederick Douglass among other efforts, and was actively involved in the civil rights movement, along with his wife, actress and writer Ruby Dee.

Some of the actors were not content to wait until the 28th to get directly involved in the events of that historic summer. Brando, Franciosa, Paul Newman, and William Frye were in Gadsden, Alabama on the 23rd for the stated purpose of mediating the ongoing dispute between Negroes and city officials and businessmen. Over 1,000 civil rights demonstrators were arrested in Gadsden that summer. The actors hoped to establish a dialogue between the groups, but were rebuffed by the town's Mayor, who refused to speak with the "rabble rousers".

On the Friday night before the March, a number of entertainers took part in a fund raiser for the March committee at the Apollo Theatre in New York City. At ticket prices from $3.00 to $100.00 per person, it was the only large scale fund raising effort undertaken by the financially strapped March committee. Tony Bennett, Cozy Cole, Herbie Mann, Quincy Jones, Thelonius Monk, Carmen McRae, and Billy Eckstine all donated their time.

Initially, it had been planned that the Hollywood stars would be chauffered to the Lincoln Memorial stage from the various hotels on the day of the March. However, Heston and the others insisted on taking part in the March itself from the Washington Monument to the Lincoln Memorial. On the morning of the March, J. Edgar Hoover had several of his FBI agents calling Hollywood stars at their hotels urging them not to participate for fear that violence would ensue, but the celebrities had come too far to take Hoover's advice.

A stage had been set up for the pre-march entertainment of the crowd which assembled at the Monument in the early morning hours. Davis was the master of ceremonies for the show, spending much of the time simply introducing the various celebrities who wandered up to the stage as well as making the usual anouncements about lost children, misplaced groups, and rearranged meeting places.

Those who arrived an hour before the March's scheduled 11:30 commencement were treated to an outstanding free concert by some of the greatest names in American folk music, among them Josh White, Odetta, Bob Dylan, Joan Baez, the Freedom Singers, and the most popular act of the summer, Peter, Paul, and Mary. The latter trio had only been together for two years at the time of the 1963 March, but had become immensely popular on the strength of their hits, including "If I Had a Hammer", "Go Tell it on the Mountain", and their version of Bob Dylan's "Blowin' In The Wind".

Mary Travers was born in Kentucky in 1936, but grew up in New York City. She attended "progressive" schools, and started folk singing as a youth. She also started demonstrating at a very early age. She had worn out a pair of shoes marching in Washington before, as a teenager protesting the Rosenberg executions in 1953, and had gone home committed to activist causes. Noel Stookey was born in Baltimore in 1937, and used the name "Paul" to give the right "ring" to the trio's name. Peter Yarrow was a New York City native, born there in 1938. Peter, Paul, and Mary started performing together in the spring of 1961, first in New York, but later in coffee houses and on colleges campuses across the country. They put out their first album in 1962, as well as their first single, Pete Seeger's "If I Had A Hammer", which became a classic. Peter, Paul, and Mary were political and proud of it. Hitting the top of the pop charts did not change that. In 1963, they had performed at several rallies in the South, and at least one where Dr. King had spoken.

The Freedom Singers were four former SNCC field secretaries: Chuck Neblett, Cordell Hull Reagan, Bernice Johnson, and Ruth Harris. They started performing together at rallies and concerts in 1962 to raise funds for SNCC. Throughout 1962 and 1963 they traveled the country singing and performing on hundreds of stages, and raising thousands of dollars for SNCC. They sang gospel and protest songs a capella, and were very popular particularly among students and folk music fans. In the summer of 1963, they performed at the Newport Folk Festival with Bob Dylan, Joan Baez, and Peter, Paul, and Mary.

Odetta Filious was born in Birmingham in 1930. After going to school and breaking into a music career in California, she relocated to New York in the 1950's. There she met Harry Belafonte and Pete Seeger, who influenced her career, and gave it a boost. She was an accomplished guitarist and actress as well as a folk singer. She entertained and recorded simply as "Odetta". The morning of the March "the mighty Odetta, in a fantastically resounding voice that reached almost to the Capitol nearly two miles away, sang ´If They Ask You Who You Are, Tell Them You´re A Child of God´".

Joshua Daniel White was born in Greenville, North Carolina in 1908. When he was a child of eight, he left home to travel with and assist a series of blind singers including the legendary blues figures Blind Lemon Jefferson and Leadbelly. It was from masters such as these that he learned his trade. He became a blues and folk star in the 1940´s, and even performed at the White House for President and Mrs. Roosevelt. His career waned in the 1950´s as a result of McCarthy era blacklisting. But he became a popular figure at civil rights rallies throughout the country in the early sixties.

In the summer of 1963, and for sometime thereafter, no one symbolized the era more for young white Americans than Bob Dylan. Said to be less than knowledgeable about politics, he nonetheless quickly adopted the civil rights cause, the injustices to Negroes having been brought home to him by friends and associates. While young idealists would seethe about a particular injustice, Dylan would go home and seemingly effortlessly fashion a memorable song about it. No one could measure how intensely he captured the spirit of that generation, but his influence was certainly widespread.

Dylan, who came east from his native Minnesota in 1961, is said to have first become interested in the civil rights movement through the influence of a girlfriend, Suze Rotolo, who worked in the New York office of CORE. Dylan wrote his first civil rights song in 1962, "The Ballad of Emmett Till", a traditional folk ballad about a 14 year old Chicago youth who was murdered in 1955 while visiting relatives in Mississippi, by whites who claimed young Till had made a pass at a white girl. Dylan also recorded "Oxford Town" in 1962 about James Meredith's ordeal at the University of Mississippi. In April, 1962, Dylan had written "Blowin' In The Wind", an instant classic and civil rights (and later anti-war) anthem. It was subsequently recorded by scores of artists from Odetta to Stevie Wonder. Peter, Paul, and Mary's version was the most successul recording of Dylan's simple melody of desperation about war and injustice.

Dylan had met folk singer Joan Baez in Greenwich Village in 1961 and they became close friends. She sang many of his songs at her concerts, and Dylan accompanied her on her concert tour in the summer of 1963. By then, Baez's voice was already legendary, but she was also becoming known for her political activism, frequently appearing at fund raisers and rallies for civil rights. With Baez and Dylan on tour that summer, there was plenty of diversions for politics, and the pair attended several rallies in the South. In July, Dylan sang with Pete Seeger, Josh White, and Theodore Bikel at a Greenwood, Mississippi rally to support the voter registration drive. Dylan met and became friends with many of the young Negro workers in Jackson during his trip, including SNCC's James Foreman.

The morning of the March at the Monument, Baez sang "We Shall Overcome", and that afternoon, Dylan sang a new song he had written after Medgar Evers' death in June, "Only A Pawn

In Their Game". He had sung it publicly only once before, at Greenwood in July. A month after the March, Dylan recorded "The Lonesome Death of Hattie Carroll", about a slain Baltimore bar maid and her white murderer, William Zantzinger, who received a wrist slap six-month sentence for the crime on the very day of the March on Washington, fifty miles away in Hagerstown, Maryland.

After the march from the Washington Monument to the Lincoln Memorial, the entertainers gathered in a special section near the speaker's podium. Few of the celebrities who came to the March were given the opportunity to speak to the crowd during the afternoon program, the schedule being already quite crowded, but most were at least introduced. Some of those intimately involved in the civil rights movement, such as Sammy Davis, Jr., and James Baldwin, were said to have been disappointed at the inability to fit them into the program. One who was not on the program but who was asked to speak briefly was reluctant to do so. Comedian Dick Gregory had been involved in demonstrations all summer. "There was some bad feeling among whites toward me for demonstrating and I didn't want to bug anyone in their living room that day. I didn't want the least little thing to mar this beautiful day". After the March leaders "insisted", Gregory said "a few humorous words".

A skit had been prepared by Ossie Davis about the struggle for freedom. It was to be performed on the Lincoln Memorial stage in the afternoon with Marlon Brando and Harry Belafonte playing the lead roles. Time limitations due to the steadily expanding program caused the skit to be scratched.

Marian Anderson was scheduled to sing the National Anthem to kick off the afternoon program at the Lincoln Memorial. She was unable to get to the platform in time however, due to the crowds. The decision was made to have Carmilla Williams, a gospel singer from Danville, Virginia, do what Marian Anderson had done at her Lincoln Memorial concert on Easter Sunday, 1939, and again at the Prayer Pilgrimage in 1957. When Mrs. Anderson did arrive, in tears, she sang a stunning version of "He's Got the Whole World in His Hands". In a print dress and Chinese coolie hat in deference to the hot sun, her voice carried easily to the end of the Reflecting Pool. She sang as always, with eyes closed, concentrating fully on the words of the song.

A somewhat surprising, but crowd pleasing appearance was made at the Lincoln Memorial by Josephine Baker, then 60 years old, who had flown in from Paris the night before the March. Miss Baker had grown up in St. Louis and became a famed jazz singer. She had always been more popular in France, where she had lived since the 1920's. In World War II, she served in the French Army and in the Free French forces. She was decorated with the Legion of Honor, and wore her Free French uniform and medals on the day of the March. She addressed the crowd at the Lincoln Memorial and called it the greatest day of her life. Miss Baker, who had roundly condemned American race relations over the years, was caught up in the spirit of what she viewed as a changing America: "You are a united people at last...I'm glad that in my home this day has come to pass. Today you are on the eve of complete victory. Tomorrow time will do the rest. The world is behind you."

Marlon Brando spoke briefly to the crowd, brandishing a cattle prod, which was then a favorite weapon of southern police officials. He displayed the device to call attention to police abuses in the south.

Harry Belafonte had been at the Lincoln Memorial before, and was a moving force behind the integration and youth marches in Washington in the late 1950´s. Belafonte was born in New York City in 1927, and lived in the West Indies as a child before returning to New York. He did a stint in the Navy as a janitor, and later was a Greenwich Village restauranteur while dabbling in dramatics and folksinging. By the late 1950´s he had become a folk star. He was an active and generous contributor to the civil rights movement.

The highlight of the day, as far as entertainment was concerned, occurred late in the afternoon when a lady with a huge flower in her coat and a funny looking hat came to the speaker´s podium. Mahalia Jackson was probably the greatest name in gospel music in the 20th century. She was born in New Orleans in 1911, but lived most of her adult life in Chicago (where she died in 1972). She first recorded in 1934 and although she might have had a more commercial career, she never sang or recorded anything but religious songs. By the late 1950´s she had become active in the civil rights movement, and a friend and associate of Martin Luther King, Jr. She sang at the Lincoln Memorial Prayer March in May, 1957. President Kennedy was a fan of hers, and she had sung at his inaugural celebration in 1961. Her greatest moment however, was August 28, 1963, when she faced a joyous but restless crowd of 250,000 near the end of the day´s ceremonies.

In a lingering afternoon of sometimes tedious and repetitive remarks, Mahalia Jackson´s rendition of the Negro spiritual "I´ve Been ´Buked and I´ve Been Scorned" brought the crowd to life, and set the stage for Dr. King´s "I Have a Dream" speech which followed:

"I´m gonna tell my Lord
When I get home
Just how long you´ve
Been treating me wrong ...
I´ve been ´buked and I´ve been scorned
Trying to make this journey all alone."

Lerone Bennett described the effect on the Negroes who heard Mahalia Jackson sing that day:

"There is a nerve that lies beneath the smoothest of black exteriors, a nerve four hundred years old and throbbing with hurt and indignation. Mahalia Jackson penetratd the facades and exposed the nerve to public view ...

"A spasm ran through the crowd.

"The button-down men in front and the old women in the back came to their feet screaming and shouting. They had not known that this thing was in them and that they wanted it touched. From different places, in different ways, with different dreams, they had come and now, hearing this sung, they were one."

The importance of music and song to the civil rights movement at that time cannot be overstated. Witness the wrath it incurred among southern police officials who would brutally come down upon peaceful, even prayerful civil rights paraders the moment they started to sing. Agreements worked out between city officials and protesters that summer often contained clauses that promised that demonstrators would not sing.

On the morning of the March, as George Lincoln Rockwell´s Nazi gathering on the far side of the Washington Monument grounds fizzled, it was the music, not the police, that finally drove him from the scene. Time reported that Rockwell "raged helplessly: I can´t stand niggers. I can´t stand to hear ´We Shall Overcome´".

That civil rights anthem, which Joan Baez led the morning crowd in singing, was the most loved – and most feared – rhythm of all, and it was sung over and over again that summer and on August 28. That and the other freedom songs of the period were described as "common denominators of the Negro people". The songs´ effects on crowds were explained in terms of welding "individuals with individual doubts and terrors and weaknesses into a dynamic and inexorable striking force". As one of Dr. King´s biographers put it: "This was not the kind of singing one can listen to immobile and in silence. These were strutting and handclapping songs. They spoke to the vital core of the blacks, and they communicated the joy of pristine brotherhood to the whites".

The presence of so many talented and recognized entertainers at the March on Washington did not, of itself, give legitimacy to the March – it already had Presidential approval. But it demonstrated both the popularity and urgency of the movement. Never would there be such a unity of purpose and commitment in the entertainment world as there was for the March on Washington.

11

"You got religion today. Don't backslide tomorrow."

- Roy Wilkins

At 1:15 p.m. the Lincoln Memorial rally commenced with the singing of the Star Spangled Banner. Archbishop O'Boyle, the matter of the Lewis speech resolved, then gave his invocation. At this point, and continually interspersed throughout the afternoon, protest leaders and celebrities were introduced to the appreciative crowd. Some gave short unscheduled speeches, like Birmingham's Fred Shuttlesworth, who spoke first, King's associate, the Reverend Ralph David Abernathy, comedian Dick Gregory, and Josephine Baker. Charlton Heston read the statement prepared by James Baldwin regarding the support of the artistic and entertainment community. Burt Lancaster unfurled a scroll he and Baldwin had brought from Paris signed by 1500 overseas Americans in support of the March.

The largest public demonstration ever held in the nation's capitol fittingly received the most extensive world-wide television coverage ever accorded to that time. Part of the reason was that this was one of the first major events broadcast by live transmission to Europe via Telestar satellite. This coverage was, of course, unprecedented for any political demonstration in this country. If the March did not quite receive the non-stop coverage devoted by all of the networks to a political convention or a space shot, it did receive more than casual treatment of everyday news. Thirty-five cameras were employed on the scene and the three networks were said to have spent more than $300,000.00 in covering the event for that one day - twice the March committee's budget.

By all accounts the day's events were well watched by daytime televesion standards. Overnight Nielson ratings of the New York market, for example, showed a 46% increase in viewing for the same daytime period the week before. Only CBS provided "gavel to gavel" coverage of the Lincoln Memorial program from 1:30 to 4:30 p.m. CBS covered all the speeches with relatively few commercial interruptions. Roger Mudd anchored ably, although one critic commented that he needlessly summarized each speech at its conclusion. "Mudd was talking while the cameras were finding some of their best crowd shots - a little girl's rapt face, or singers with linked hands." CBS sacrificed one day of "As the World Turns," "Password," Art Linkletter's "House Party," "To Tell The Truth," "The Edge of Night," and the "Secret Storm" to bring America this historic event.

The other networks, ABC and NBC, gave periodic reports between game shows and soap operas, and provided excerpts of the speeches after the Lincoln Memorial program concluded at 4:30. Curiously, Frank McGee anchored the NBC coverage from New York rather than Washington. Richard Bate and Howard K. Smith anchored ABC coverage from Washington. After viewing the marchers with the placards for some time, including one sign which read "Dogs have TV shows, Negroes don't," the networks returned to their regular programming, CBS coming back to the March as the Lincoln Memorial program began. One CBS camera was perched atop the 550 foot high Washington Monument, affording impressive views of the entire crowd. CBS cameramen also captured the unforgettable sight of the numerous marchers seeking relief by dangling their feet in the Reflecting Pool as the hot afternoon wore on.

The first scheduled speaker was, fittingly, the Chairman of the March and its originator, A. Philip Randolph, who needed and received no introduction. Randolph's speech reflected his economic oriented view of the civil rights debate, and in that sense was the closest to the original intent of the March on Washington. He called the marchers "the advance guard of a massive moral revolution for jobs and freedom," but noted that he saw it not as a Negro revolution or civil rights revolution, but a revolution of all liberal-minded people against unemployment as well as freedom for all Americans: "We know we have no future in a society in which six million black and white people are unemployed and millions more live in poverty."

Open accomodations would be meaningless if Negroes could not afford them, and Randolph asked what good an FEPC bill would do "if profit-geared automation destroys the jobs of millions of workers, black and white." Randoph cited the need to create full employment, and his desire to "put automation at the service of human needs, not at the service of profits."

Randolph defended the tactic of street protest, citing its historic acceptance and validity, its use by the labor movement and how "Jesus Christ led the multitude through the streets of Judea." Randolph noted that before Birmingham, the federal government had been indifferent to their demands, but he carefully avoided direct criticism of President Kennedy. He blasted those who, under the guise of contempt for protest tactics, really were seeking to sabotage the civil rights movement:

"Those who deplore our militance, who
exalt patience in the name of a false
peace are in fact supporting
segregation and exploitation. They
would have social peace at the expense
of social and racial justice."

Randolph finally laid a pointed attack at
Dixiecrats and conservative Republicans who
opposed Medicare, and other social welfare
programs, telling the Marchers that these were
the Negros´ true enemies. He urged support of
President Kennedy´s civil rights program, and
promised that the March on Washington was only a
beginning, that they would return in "ever
increasing numbers, until total freedom is
ours."

After Randolph´s seven minute speech, the
program proceeded pretty much as scheduled. The
"Tribute To Women" followed, Randolph intro-
ducing Daisy Bates, the absent Mrs. Medgar
Evers, SNCC founder Diane Nash Bevel, Cambridge
rights leader Gloria Richardson, Montgomery bus
boycott originator Rosa Parks and Mrs. Herbert
Lee, widow of a civil rights worker murdered in
Liberty, Mississippi by a white Mississippi
politician. Bob Dylan sang his "Only A Pawn In
Their Game" after the thunderous applause for
Mrs. Evers. Then Odetta, Joan Baez and Peter,
Paul and Mary sang again. A series of speeches
followed this interlude of introductions and
entertainment, beginning with that of Dr. Eugene
Carson Blake.

It was a day of confession as well as a day
of protest and a day of celebration. Dr. Blake
recognized in his speech that he and his fellow
churchmen shared the blame for the plight of
American Negroes in that the churches had failed
to put their own houses in order. Talk alone

was no longer sufficient, and in fact talk had
masked the churches´ past failures:

"For many years now the National
Council of Churches and most of its
constituent communion have said all
the right things about civil rights.
Our official pronouncements for years
have called for a non-segregated
church in a non-segregated society.
But as of August 28, 1963, we have
achieved neither a non-segregated
church nor a non-segregated society.

"We do not therefore come to this
Lincoln Memorial in any arrogant
spirit of moral or spiritual
superiority to set the Congress or the
Nation straight or to judge or to
denounce the American people in whole
or in part. Rather, we come late,
late we come, in the reconciling and
repentant spirit in which Abraham
Lincoln of Illinois once replied to a
delegation of morally arrogant
churchmen who came to see him. He
said: ´Never say God is on our side,
rather pray that we will be found on
God´s side.´ Yes we come to march
behind and with these amazingly able
leaders of the Negro Americans who to
the shame of almost every white
American have alone and without us
mirrored the suffering of the Cross of
Jesus Christ. You have offered your
bodies to jail, to fire hoses, to dogs
and, some of you, to death."

John Lewis ironically followed Blake, who
had demanded changes in Lewis´ speech, to the

podium to give his caustic indictment of the
American system. He was sandwiched between
Blake and another white member of the Big Ten,
United Auto Workers President Walter Reuther.
Reuther was short of stature, but a great
speaker in the tradition of American Labor
leaders. Perhaps picking up on the emotion
generated by Lewis, he thumped the podium
repeatedly, and spoke loudly into the
microphone, his voice and his pounding easily
carrying the length of the Reflecting Pool, and
drowning out even the jets from National Airport
that roared continuously overhead. His speech
was repeatedly interrupted by applause. He
began with a call for immediate progress, lest
any labor leaders or any white liberals be
confused about the meaning of "now":

> "Brother Randolph, fellow Americans
> and friends; I am here today with you
> because with you I share the view that
> the struggle for civil rights and the
> struggle for equal opportunity is not
> the struggle of Negro Americans, but
> the struggle for every American to
> join in. For one hundred years the
> Negro people have searched for first
> class citizenship, and I belive that
> they cannot and should not wait until
> some distant tomorrow. They should
> demand Freedom now! Here and now! It
> is the responsibility of every
> American to share the impatience of
> the Negro Americans."

Reuther generally supported the Kennedy
Administration but he was no apologist for its
actions or lack of action. His speech was
politely but pervasively critical of Kennedy's
inability to improve an increasingly worsening

economic situation that was harmful to black and
white workers, and what he viewed as lack of
full committment on civil rights. Reuther
called Kennedy's bill comprehensive but
moderate, and in need of strengthening. In
particular, Reuther complained in his speech
about the lack of an FEPC bill. In a timeless
observation, as far as the job situation was
concerned, Reuther wanted to know why only war
could bring full employment: "If we can have
full employment and full production for the
negative ends of war, then why can't we have a
job for every American in the pursuit of
peace." But the most searing yet disguised
criticism of the President was in Reuther's
comparison of the federal government's
reluctance to intervene to protect demonstrators
in the South and the President's famous pledge
to the people of Berlin that summer to stand
behind them in their struggle to maintain their
freedom: "We cannot defend freedom in Berlin so
long as we deny freedom in Birmingham." His
voice cracking, and his throat congested as he
drew to a close, Reuther pounded out a warning
of the result if their crusade should fail, a
prophecy that would ring true in the summers to
come:

> "If we fail, the vacuum of our failure
> will be filled by the Apostles of
> Hatred who will search for answers in
> the dark of night, and reason will
> yield to riots, and brotherhood will
> yield to bitterness and bloodshed and
> we will tear asunder the fabric of
> American democracy."

After Reuther's speech, Randolph, now
acting as a master of ceremonies, announced the
police department's crowd estimate: "I am glad

to report to you that the official count is that we have over 200,000 Negro and white workers." It was greeted with a roar of approval.

The figure which Randolph read over the public address system at 2:00 p.m. was a police estimate obtained at noon. Randolph refused to cite any other figure unless he received an official written report. Unfortunately, the police made no later crowd estimate. At noon marchers were still streaming up Constitution Avenue, while others were still grouping together on the Monument lawn. Chartered buses were still coming into town from distant points. Individuals continued to drive themselves or come by scheduled carriers, unable to be booked on earlier sold-out flights or trains. Most significantly local residents had not as yet appeared in force at the time of the police estimate. Police officials later agreed that local residents continued to swell the crowd as the afternoon wore on, as they were released from work or made late decisions to attend.

Estimates over the years of attendance at the March on Washington have ranged from 200,000 to half a million. Of course, the exact amount could never be known. As one social scientist put it, in describing the difficulty in counting participation at demonstrations: "There is a constant ebb and flow in such massive demonstrations; people move between active and passive roles, or leave the scene as their committments, personal and social, interact with the events´ changing character." So it was August 28, but all indications were that the crowd actually grew as the afternoon wore on. It is doubtful that many people left that moving scene early, but it is definite that even after 2:00 p.m., many more arrived. The number of

District of Columbia residents participating was pegged at about 45,000. Many were said to be latecomers, who watched the beginning of the March on television, and wandered over the Memorial to take part, while others joined when they were let out of their jobs early.

Police estimates are based on the number of square feet which a crowd occupies divided by a number of square feet estimated to be occupied by each individual. Thus a very closely packed crowd will produce an underestimate since police estimates assume several square feet of space for each individual in counting a crowd. In mid-afternoon, actors Woody Allen and Marlon Brando, for example, observed a man near them go "beserk" after becoming claustrophobic from the crowd. All observers were unanimous about the density of the crowd, and one periodical called it a "frighteningly tight packed assemblage."

The consensus of most on the scene observers with some degree of experience was that the actual crowd by mid-afternoon was much closer to 400,000 than 200,000. Considering the normal ebb and flow of participation, it is not an exaggeration to state that 400,000 persons took some part in the March on Washington and the program at the Lincoln Memorial.

The next scheduled speech after Reuther's was that of the imprisoned James Farmer. CORE Chairman Floyd McKissick, as fiery and emotional a speaker as Farmer, was the perfect choice to read a message said to be composed by Farmer himself in his Louisiana jail cell. It was not quite King's letter from the Birmingham jail, but it was a timely message which McKissick read well:

"From a South Louisiana parish jail, I
salute the March on Washington for
Jobs and Freedom. 232 freedom
fighters here with me also send their
greetings. I wanted to be with you
with all my heart for this great
day. I cannot come out of jail while
they are still in, for their crime was
the same as mine, demanding freedom
now..."

Farmer first decried violence:

"In an age of thermonuclear bombs,
violence is outmoded as a solution to
the problems of men. It is a truth
that needs to be shouted loudly, and
no one else anywhere in the world is
saying it as well as are American
Negroes through their non-violent
direct action demonstrations."

Farmer wanted to make it clear that the
violence of 1963 was the violence of white
racists, not that of civil rights demonstrators. The press had a penchant for blaming
the victims of the violence, even as if they
deserved what they received by reason of their
decision to make their views known. Farmer
insisted that if the press didn't know these
facts, the world did:

"the tear gas and the electric cattle
prods...the fire hoses and dogs...are
giving to the world a tired and ugly
message of terror and brutality and
hate...of pitiful hopelessness from
little and unimaginative men to a
world that fears for its life. It is

not they whom the world is listening
to today. It is to American's
Negroes..."

Farmer, by his absence that day, a living
embodiment of committment, told those who
listened that the road ahead would not be an
easy one, that there were other problems that
had to be faced besides the overt discrimination
in the deep South. The flight for economic
equality would be more difficult than even
perhaps Farmer envisioned:

> "We will not slow down, we will not
> stop our militant, peaceful
> demonstrations. We will not come off
> the streets until we can work at any
> job befitting our skills any place in
> the land...until our kids have enough
> to eat and their minds can study and
> range wide without being cramped in
> Jim Crow schools.

> "Until we can live wherever we choose
> and can eat and play with no closed
> doors blocking our way. We will not
> stop till the dogs stop biting us in
> the South and the rats stop biting us
> in the North."

Randolph then introduced the "brilliant
executive director" of the Urban League, Whitney
Young, Jr. a new face in what might have been
called the protest arm of the civil rights
movement, as the March probably was the Urban
League's first involvement in the politics of
direct action. Young began his speech by
thanking the other organizations for their
"increased respect for the Urban League's
role." Young then blasted the opponents of

civil rights legislation, and those willing to compromise on any section of the administration's bill, including those with constitutional objections, citing the "shame" of "those who would make deals, water down civil rights legislation, or take cowardly refuge in technical details around elementary human rights...Civil rights which are God-given and constitutionally guaranteed are not negotiable in 1963."

Young was unwilling to accept automatically as sincere the presence of whites at the March, including those white leaders with whom he shared the platform, Young alone that day presenting a specific challenge to those liberals and religious leaders:

"One should not seek here to atone for his past failures as a responsible citizen of the majority group. The evils of the past and the guilt about it cannot be erased by a one-day pilgrimage, however magnificant. Nor can this pilgrimage substitute for an obligation to tomorrow by these same citizens. And so this March must go beyond this historic moment..."

The focus of Young's organization was, of course, on the cities, and he recognized that the March on Washington and even the Civil Rights Bill would do little to change conditions in the nation's ghettoes. He called for future marches, but not of the type A. Philip Randolph envisioned. Young recognized that the politics of street demonstrations had its limits:

They must march from the rat-infested,
overcrowded ghettoes to decent,
wholesome, unrestricted residential
areas dispersed throughout our
cities. They must march from the
relief rolls to the established
retraining centers...They must march
from the cemeteries where our young,
our newborn die three times sooner and
our parents die seven years
earlier...They must march from the
congested, ill-equipped schools which
breed dropouts and which smother
motivation...and finally they must
march from a present feeling of
despair and hopelessness, despair and
frustration, to a renewed faith and
confidence..."

In so speaking, Young catalogued what would
be the failure of the 1960s, and foresaw, as had
Reuther, the consequences:

"The hour is late, the gap is
widening, the rumble of the drums of
discontent resounding throughout this
land are heard in all parts of the
world."

Young delivered his speech rapidly, perhaps
overly conscious of the seven-minute time limit,
and he was not interrupted by applause.
However, his speech when read or listened to
later is quite impressive. But it had little
visible impact on the dense crowd by then
sweltering in the August heat, many waiting
almost for the speeches to end. Many sought the
shade of the huge trees lining the Reflecting
Pool, but the trees could not cover all of the
crowd. Some took dips in the shallow, murky

Reflecting Pool. Everyone fanned himself or herself. Approximately 1700 people were treated during the afternoon at the 24 first aid stations set up around the area. Most of the ailments were minor – cuts, stomach aches, headaches, and many faintings due to the heat and long hours in the sun. Only three of the 1700 marchers who sought first aid had to be hospitalized. All three were from the New York area, two of them were elderly, and all had medical problems. There was one death at the March. Fifty-six year old Charles Schreiber from Manhattan was listening to the speeches at the Lincoln Memorial when he suffered a heart attack. He was taken immediately to George Washington University Hospital several blocks away, but died shortly after his admission.

The sight of so many clergymen at the March led some opponents to challenge the authenticity of the wearers of clerical garb. The rumor broadcast by some radio stations went that New York costume and clergy supply houses sold out of clerical garb in the weeks before the March, and that tailors were sewing black cloth as quickly as they could. Thus it was pressed that many of the marchers faked their religious affiliation to heighten acceptance of the participants.

The rumor was fired by the statements of Ohio Republican Congressman William H. Ayres, an opponent of the March. Ayres claimed a friend of his in New York who owned a costume shop had called him with the information about the run on clerical garb. Ayres contacted the FBI demanding an investigation. What crime would be under investigation was unclear, and nothing came of Ayres' request. Ayres claimed that one such false minister came into his office to lobby and that he had seen others parading on the Capitol grounds. How did Ayres know they were not ministers? The Congressman, son of a Methodist minister, replied: "I can tell a preacher when I see one." No one has ever produced facts to support Ayres' claim.

The next speaker after Whitney Young, Jr., was the least well-known of the Big Ten, Matthew Ahmann, a white layman and Executive Director of the National Catholic Conference for Interracial Justice:

> "Where is a man - white or Negro - whose heart has not been touched by the revelation in past months of racial sores among the people of our country? Where is a man so callous that in some deep way his conscience has not yet been moved to see the evil effects of racial discrimination and segregation upon both the Negro and the white man? Who can call himself a man, say he is created by God and at the same time take part in a system of segregation which destroys the livelihood, citizenship, family life and very heart of the Negro citizens...

Ahmann's heart, like those of the other white speakers, was undoubtedly in the right place, but his words were essentially empty. They lacked a militant call for action, the sense of urgency, the sense of "Now" so vital to blacks in the summer of 1963. William k. Miller, one of Dr. King's biographers, described the problem: "Many blacks undoubtedly appreciated the good intentions of the white speakers, and they responded with polite applause. But the smell of the white liberal

hung over them...of the four religious leaders
(including O´Boyle) only Blake had been arrested
- once - and thus gained a wisp of insight into
the experience of a John Lewis, arrested twenty-
two times, beaten a dozen times, born on the
wrong side of the color line. Men without
prejudice, they lacked the experiential insights
of even the most moderate of their black
confreres."

It was now the NAACP´s Roy Wilkins´ turn
and Randolph introduced him as "the acknowledged
champion of civil rights in America." He was
warmly welcomed, and began by thanking the crowd
for fulfilling his previous night´s prediction
of the size of the crowd at the meeting of the
Big Ten:

> "First of all, I want to thank all of
> you for coming here today because you
> saved me from being a liar. I told
> them you would be here. They didn´t
> believe me because you always make up
> your mind at the last minute. And you
> had me scared. But isn´t it a great
> day?"

Wilkins´ speech focused on the pending civil
rights bill and the struggle ahead to get it
passed. Wilkins was not timid about challenging
the extent of the Kennedy Administration´s
commitment, but his challenge was limp next to
John Lewis´:

> "The President´s proposals represent
> so moderate an approach that if it is
> weakened, the remainder will be little
> more than sugarwater. Indeed as it
> stands today, the package needs
> strengthening. And the President

should join us in fighting to be sure
that we get something more than pap."

Wilkins questioned the apparent inability
of the federal government to protect from police
abuse, civil rights workers, voting registration
workers, and demonstrators in the South:

"It is simply incomprehensible ...
that the United States Government,
which can regulate the contents of a
pill, apparently is powerless to
prevent the physical abuse of citizens
within its own borders."

Finally, Wilkins reminded the crowd that
the previous day, W. E. B. Du Bois, the
legendary Negro leader and theorist, and founder
of the Niagara Movement which spawned the NAACP,
had passed away in Africa. Wilkins paid tribute
to the author of "The Souls of Black Folks":

"Regardless of the fact that in his
later years Dr. Du Bois chose another
path, it is incontrovertible that at
the dawn of the 20th century, his was
the voice calling you to gather here
today in this cause."

In closing Wilkins urged that the
demonstrators return home to keep up the work,
that their task was far from finished:

"Well my friends, you got religion
here today, don't blackslide
tomorrow. Remember Luke's account of
the warning that was given to us
all: No man having put his hand to
the plow, and looking back, is fit for
the kingdom of God."

It was immediately after Wilkins' speech that Mahalia Jackson brought the then listless crowd to life with her dramatic rendition of "I've Been 'Buked and I've Been Scorned": "As the sun beat down and the afternoon wore on, hundreds of marchers began to drift back to their buses, but they lingered a moment when gospel singer Mahalia Jackson came to the microphone to sing..." It was enough to save most of the crowd for Dr. King's dramatic conclusion of the rally. There was one speaker remaining before him, however, Rabbi Joachim Prinz. The short, slight, graying President of the American Jewish Congress was then 61 years old. He had been born in Germany, but expelled by order of Gestapo official Adolph Eichmann in 1937, for his public speeches in support of Zionism, and criticism of the early Nazi leadership. Prinz came to America and settled in Newark, New Jersey and was an active lecturer, and Jewish historian.

Prinz alluded to Germany of the 1930s in warning of the danger of silence in the face of injustice:

> "The most urgent, disgraceful and shameful problem is silence ... America must not become a nation of silent onlookers. It must speak up and act from the President on down, not for the sake of the image, the dream, the idea, the aspiration, but for the sake of America itself."

Like Ahmann and Blake, Prinz's remarks lacked any sense of urgency, and listeners could "conclude that Prinz was referring to nothing more than expressing one's opinions to friends or writing to one's congressman". America in fact had become a silent nation long before Prinz warned of this danger. Throughout the entire 20th century up until 1963, white Americans had essentially ignored the "Negro problem". Much more was required now than a lack of silence, and Prinz´s historical lesson, well meaning though it was, had little relevance in 1963.

Martin Luther King had started writing his speech several days before the march, in Atlanta, with the assistance of SCLC publicity man Ed Clayton. The final revisions were of course made the night before at the Willard. It was said to have been "more carefully prepared than any he had made before". At the Lincoln Memorial, it was Publicity Director Posner´s job to "remind" the speakers of the seven-minute time limit. He stood with Ossie Davis near the microphones, both of them timing the program as it proceeded. It was 20 minutes to four when King rose to speak, and the program was ahead of schedule. Posner knew King would speak longer than seven minutes, and so did several of the March leaders, and Posner had no intention of "pulling King´s coat" if he rambled on.

After Rabbi Prinz had finished, the crowd knew from the program that had been distributed that Dr. King would speak next. They began to chant "Martin Luther King, Martin Luther King."

Randolph then stepped to the podium to introduce him. "I have the honor to present to you the moral leader of our nation." The crowd cheered as Randolph went on: "a great dedicated man". More cheering and clapping: "the philosopher of the nonviolent system of behavior in seeking to bring about social change...I have the pleasure to present to you Dr. Martin Luther King jay-ar. As Dr. King arose, a great roar

went up from the crowd. He waved for thirty
seconds, or so as the crowd cheered, and then as
he began his prepared speech, a hush fell over
the crowd:

> "I am happy to join with you today in
> what will go down in history as the
> greatest demonstration for freedom in
> the hisotry of our nation. Five score
> years ago a great American in whose
> symbolic shadow we stand today, signed
> the Emancipation Proclamation. This
> momentous decree came as a great
> beacon light of hope to millions of
> Negro slaves who had been seared in
> the flames of withering injustice. It
> came as a joyous daybreak to end the
> long night of their captivity."

Mrs. King has said that her husband was
tremendously moved by the reception he
received: "I could tell by the line of his back
and the sound of his voice - a little husky at
first, then going out in a strong beautifully
resonant tone that came when he was inspired to
his best." To read the speech later is a moving
experience. To hear a recording of it is
something beyond moving. To those who were
there, the experience is difficult to put into
words:

> "It is impossible to describe the
> basic fervor with which the text was
> laid out in Martin King's resonant
> voice - the level from which the
> emphases rose with cumulative power up
> to the sermonic crests at the end.
> But he carried every ear and every
> heart along that rise of intensity and
> into the emotional heights as well.

The crowd more than listened, it
participated, and before he had
reached his last phrase, a torrent of
applause was already welling up."

There would be no mention by King of the
Civil Rights Bill - it had been thoroughly
discussed by the other speakers. There would be
no mention of specific reforms, nor condemnation
of specific individuals by name in King's
speech, nor any mention of any concrete action
the marchers should take. King's speech would
be the true benediction of the March on
Washington. He began with the extended metaphor
of the bounced check America had issued to its
Negroes:

"In a sense we have come to our
nation's capitol to cash a check.
When the architects of our republic
wrote the magnificent words of the
Constitution and the Declaration of
Independence, they were signing a
promissory note to which every
American was to fall heir. This note
was a promise that all men, yes black
men as well as white men, would be
guaranteed the unalienable rights of
life, liberty, and the pursuit of
happiness. It is obvious today that
America has defaulted on this promissory note insofar as her citizens of
color are concerned. Instead of
honoring this sacred obligation,
America has given the Negro people a
bad check: a check which has come
back marked 'insufficient funds'. But
we refuse to believe that the bank of
justice is bankrupt. We refuse to
believe that there are insufficient

funds in the great vaults of opportunity of this nation. So we have come to cash this check - a check that will give us upon demand the riches of freedom and the security of justice."

Dr. King had the crowd in his hands now, and the speech continued to build to its climax. Mrs. King recalled that at this point in the speech, "when he got to the rhythmic part of demanding freedom now, and wanting jobs now, the crowd caught the timing and shouted now in cadence. The response lifted Martin in a surge of emotion to new heights of inspiration."

"We have also come to this hallowed spot to remind America of the fierce urgency of now. This is not the time to engage in the luxury of cooling off or to take the tranquilizing drug of gradualism. Now is the time. To make real the promises of democracy. Now is the time. To rise from the dark and desolate valley of segregation to the sunlit path of racial justice, now is the time. To lift our nation from the quicksands of racial injustice to the solid rock of brotherhood, now is the time. To make justice a reality for all of God's children."

For those who thought the summer of 1963 would pass on to quieter times, that the thousands of protests, and the hundreds of arrests were an aberration, Dr. King had a warning:

"It would be fatal for the nation to overlook the urgency of the moment and to underestimate the determination of the Negro. This sweltering summer of

the Negro's legitimate discontent will
not pass until there is an invigorat-
ing autumn of freedom and equality.
1963 is not an end, but a beginning.
Those who hope that the Negro needed
to blow off steam, and will now be
content will have a rude awakening if
the Nation returns to business as
usual. There will neither be rest nor
tranquility in America until the Negro
is granted his citizenship rights.
The whirlwinds of revolt will continue
to shake the foundations of our Nation
until the bright day of justice
emerges."

Next, King had a response to those at the
other extreme, those who he perceived as
apostles of hatred, and perhaps those black
separatists, who saw evil in permitting whites
in the movement:

"But there is something that I must
say to my people who stand on the warm
threshold which leads into the palace
of justice. In the process of gaining
our rightful place we must not be
guilty of wrongful deeds. Let us not
seek to satisfy our thirst for freedom
by drinking from the cup of bitterness
and hatred.

We must forever conduct our struggle
on the high plane of dignity and
discipline. We must not allow our
creative protest to degenerate into
physical violence. Again and again we
must rise to the majestic heights of
meeting physical force with soul
force. The marvelous new militancy
which has engulfed the Negro community

must not lead us to a distrust of all
white people, for many of our white
brothers, as evidenced by their
presence here today, have come to
realize that their destiny is tied up
with our destiny and their freedom is
inextricably bound to our freedom. We
cannot walk alone."

Then in a response that reached the heart
and soul of every Negro in the nation, no matter
his status, or where he lived, King answered the
congressmen and columnists who wanted to know
that summer when the Negro would be satisfied:

"And as we walk, we must make the
pledge that we shall always march
ahead. We cannot turn back. There
are those who are asking the devotees
of civil rights, ´when will you be
satisfied?´ We can never be satisfied
as long as the Negro is the victim of
the unspeakable horrors of police
brutality. We can never be satisfied
as long as our bodies, heavy with the
fatigue of travel, cannot gain lodging
in the motels of the highways and the
hotels of the cities. We cannot be
satisfied as long as the Negro´s basic
mobility is from a smaller ghetto to a
larger one. We can never be satisfied
as long as our children are stripped
of their self-hood and robbed of their
dignity by signs reading ´For Whites
Only´. We can never be satisfied as
long as a Negro in Mississippi cannot
vote and a Negro in New York believes
he has nothing for which to vote. No.
no we are not satisfied, and we will

> not be satisfied until justice rolls
> down like waters and righteousness
> like a mighty stream."

His alloted seven minutes were now up, and
King was now nearing the end of his prepared
text, and an impressive end it would have been
had it not been for what followed:

> "I am not unmindful that some of you
> have come here out of great trials and
> tribulations. Some of you have come
> fresh from narrow jail cells. Some of
> you have come from areas where your
> quest for freedom left you battered by
> the storms of persecution and stag-
> gered by the winds of police brutal-
> ity. You have been the victims of
> creative suffering. Continue to work
> with the faith that unearned suffering
> is redemptive.
>
> Go back to Mississippi, go back to
> Alabama, go back to South Carolina, go
> back to Georgia, go back to Louisiana,
> go back to the slums and ghettos of
> our northern cities, knowing that
> somehow this situation can and will be
> changed. Let us not wallow in the
> valley of despair."

The finale was extemporaneous, recurrently
interrupted by applause, and a fitting capstone
to the Negroes´ long summer of discontent. As
one of Dr. King´s biographers put it: "This was
rhetoric almost without content, but this was,
after all, a day of heroic fantasy." No one
complained that Dr. King´s speech went on for
almost 19 minutes.

"I say to you today, my friends, that
in spite of the difficulties and
frustrations of the moment, I still
have a dream. It is a dream deeply
rooted in the American dream. I have
a dream that one day this nation will
rise up and live out the true meaning
of its creed: ´We hold these truths
to be self-evident - that all men are
created equal.´

"I have a dream that one day on the
red hills of Georgia the sons of
former slaves and the sons of former
slaveowners will be able to sit down
together at the table of brotherhood.
I have a dream that one day even the
state of Mississippi, a desert state
sweltering with the heat of injustice
and oppression, will be transformed
into an oasis of freedom and justice.

"I have a dream that my four little
children will one day live in a nation
where they will not be judged by the
color of their skin but by the content
of their character.

"I have a dream today.

"I have a dream that one day the state
of Alabama, whose governor´s lips are
presently dripping with the words of
interposition and nullification, will
be transformed into a situation where
little black boys and black girls will
be able to join hands with little
white boys and white girls and walk
together as sisters and brothers.

"I have a dream today.

"I have a dream that one day every valley shall be exalted, every hill and mountain shall be made low, the rough places will be made plain, and the crooked places will be made straight, and the glory of the Lord shall be revealed, and all flesh shall see it together.

"This is our hope. This is the faith with which I return to the South. With this faith we will be able to hew out of the mountain of despair a stone of hope. With this faith we will be able to transform the jangling discords of our nation into a beautiful symphony of brotherhood. With this faith we will be able to work together, to pray together, to struggle together, to go to jail together, to stand up for freedom together, knowing that we will be free one day.

"This will be the day when all of God's children will be able to sing with new meaning 'My country 'tis of thee, sweet land of liberty, of thee I sing. Land where my father died, land of the pilgrim's pride, from every mountainside, let freedom ring.'

"And if America is to be a great nation this must become true. So let freedom ring from the prodigious hilltops of New Hampshire! Let freedom ring from the mighty mountains of New York! Let freedom ring from the heightening Alleghenies of Pennsylvania!

"Let freedom ring from the snowcapped Rockies of Colorado!

"Let freedom ring from the curvaceous peaks of California!

"But not only that; let freedom ring from Stone Mountain of Georgia!

"Let freedom ring from every hill and mole hill of Mississippi. From every mountainside, let freedom ring.

"When we let freedom ring, when we let it ring from every village and every hamlet, from every state and every city, we will be able to speed up that day when all God's children, black men and white men, Jews and Gentiles, Protestants and Catholics, will be able to join hands and sing in the words of that old Negro spiritual, 'Free at last! Free at last! Thank God almighty, we are free at last!'"

To many of the rank and file marchers, Dr. King's speech, while the best of the lot, was not then the moving experience that it became later on in hindsight. Indeed, there was almost a collective sigh of relief that respite from the heat, standing, and crowd was forthcoming. But others remember it as the most moving moment of their lives. In a larger sense King's speech forever "legitimized" the civil rights movement to those whites who had difficulty accepting it:

"In less than 15 minutes, King had transformed an amiable effort at lobbying Congress into a scintillating historic event. 'The thundering

events of the summer rquired an
appropriate climax, ´ King later wrote,
and he had provided it. His dream,
judged by its impact both on those in
Washington and on those watching on
television, had buoyed the spirit of
blacks and touched the hearts of
whites. Not all, to be sure. It
changed neither votes in Congress nor
the minds of those most opposed or
indifferent to racial equality. But,
for most, King´s eloquence and vision
offset the ugly images of black
violence that the demonstrations had
started to evoke, replacing them with
an inspiring picture of the movement
at its benevolent best. To the extent
that any single public utterance
could, this speech made the black
revolt acceptable to white America."

It was this very acceptance that critics
such as Malcolm X found demeaning to the civil
rights movement, and which gave them cause to
write off the March on Washington as a useless
display.

The March on Washington and the Lincoln
Memorial Rally did not end with Dr. King´s
speech. The marchers themselves had not yet
given their own speech, and they were given that
opportunity by Bayard Rustin. Randolph returned
to the podium:

"I want to introduce now Brother Bayard
Rustin who will read the demands of the March on
Washington movement. Everyone must listen to
these demands. This is why we are here."
Rustin told the Marchers that their leaders
would meet President Kennedy at 5:00 p.m. "to
carry the demands of this revolution. It is now
time for you to act. I will read each demand

and you will respond to it so that when Mr. Wilkins and Dr. King, and the other eight leaders go, they are carrying demands which you have given your approval to."

Rustin then reviewed the ten demands of the March. After reading each of the first few demands, Rustin asked the crowd "What do you say?" They cheered loudly, and as he proceeded with the ten demands, they needed no cue, and the cheers became louder. The demands included passage of the Civil Rights Bill without compromise or filibuster, withholding of federal funds from discriminatory programs, a ban on discrimination in housing, retraining programs to combat unemployment due to automation, an increased minimum wage, immediate school desegregation, and a Fair Employment Practices Act.

Randolph then asked all the marchers to stand while he read a pledge of personal commitment by each marcher to carry the message of the march back to their home towns.

At 4:15 p.m. the pledge was completed, and Randolph introduced Benjamin E. Mays, President of Morehouse College, who gave the benediction. Dr. Mays asked for blessings upon President Kennedy, the Supreme Court and Congress, and concluded: "Guide, keep, sustain, and bless the United States and help the weary travelers to overcome someday soon."

The organ played "We Shall Overcome" one more time, and the demonstrators solemnly sang. The March on Washington was over. The program had ended at 4:20 p.m., 10 minutes ahead of schedule, and three hours after Reverend Shuttlesworth had given the first speech.

The crowd left orderly, and almost immediately. A half hour later, D.C. police reported that only 2,000 persons were left at the Lincoln Memorial, although the steps of the Memorial and the area surrounding the Reflecting Pool was strewn with litter long after the crowds had gone. Government workers had been released at 3:15 p.m., an hour before the demonstration ended. Thus there was no crush of traffic at any time throughout the afternoon. Commuters had cleared town before the marchers began their exodus. Indeed traffic was so light in Washington that day that a Star reporter called it "a harried motorist's dream of heaven". By 7:00 p.m. nearly all of the buses and trains, and most of the private vehicles had left town. By dusk the city seemed strangely deserted. The visitors had mostly left, and the inhabitants were either out of town, or still afraid to come out of doors. At 9:00 p.m. the police considered things back to normal and extra police and national guardsmen were released from duty.

At the rally's conclusion, limousines were waiting for the Big Ten on the side of the Lincoln Memorial for the scheduled trip to the White House to meet President Kennedy. Marshals led the leaders to the cars through a small but surging crowd who had fought their way to the area near the podium as the crowd began to drift away.

The President, for his part, was described as relieved and happy when the leaders arrived. He had watched the Lincoln Memorial program on CBS thoughout the afternoon, and the Attorney-General, the Vice President, Assistant Attorney-General Marshall, and Secretary of Labor Willard Wirtz were with him in the oval office. It was a joyous occasion. Roy Wilkins later called it "rewarding", saying that the President was "bubbling over with the success of the event".

The President had been genuinely moved by Dr. King's speech as he watched it on television. Their oratorical styles were not that different, and as the President shook King's hand as he entered the oval office, he said to King, "I have a dream". When King modestly asked the President if he had heard Walter Reuther's outstanding speech, the President joked that he had heard Reuther plenty of times before.

The President knew of the leaders' activities that day, their meeting with Congressional leaders that morning, and their rush back to Constitution Avenue to lead the line of March. He also knew there had been no time for lunch. The Big Ten had not complied with their own directive that each marcher bring a bag lunch and a bag dinner. The President, however, had ordered sandwiches and coffee from the White House mess which the leaders graciously dined on in between photographs. At first, there was small talk, discussion of the weather, the size of the crowd, the lack of incidents, and the telling of anecdotes.

President Kennedy was happy that things had gone well, but he did not merely pat the leaders on the back, and "tell them they had done a great job." Such was not this President's style or his way of achieving results. He was a man of action who knew that speeches and a massive rally would not automatically change years of hatred, tradition and racial prejudice. He stressed the hard work ahead, not only with the Civil Rights Bill on Capitol Hill, but in the local communities:

"He told the Negro leaders they faced
hard work in their districts, cities
and states, and with pencil and paper
Mr. Kennedy spelled it out for each

man how to use his influence with
labor unions, state political leaders,
and even down to the local precinct
officials. He gave each of them an
assignment, warning them this was but
a beginning. Negro leaders left the
White House subdued in their
realization that they were dealing not
only with a President who was on their
side but with a President who was
determined that their side win."

The White House meeting lasted almost an
hour and a half. Many of the leaders, including
King and Wilkins then rushed off for television
interview commitments. Later Senator Jacob
Javits hosted a party at his fashionable
Northwest Washington home. Charlton Heston,
Marlon Brando, Paul Newman, Edward R. Murrow,
James Baldwin, Harry Belafonte, and Norman
Mailer all attended along with some of the
rights´ leaders who wandered in late from their
television commitments.

Justice´s John Douglas had remained at
Police Headquarters on Indiana Avenue all day
awaiting any reports of trouble. None
developed, and Douglas and his assistant Alan
Raywid missed the March, not realizing how
dramatic an event it was nor the vast success of
the coordinating efforts until later. After the
White House meeting, and back at the Justice
Department, the Attorney General called Douglas
who was still monitoring the outlflow situation
from police headquarters. Kennedy congratulated
him on a job well done, and asked him for a list
of those others who it would be wise to personally thank. Douglas said he would compile one
and call back. He and Raywid gave it a few
minutes´ thought, and called back with nearly 30
names of police officials, local and national

organizers, and private citizens. That evening
the Attorney General called everyone on the list
to thank them for a job well done.

For A. Philip Randolph, the man whose idea
had started it all, it was "the most beautiful
and glorious" day of his active, fruitful
life. Randolph's biographer recounts what
happened when Rustin observed Randolph standing
alone on the speaker's dais at the end of the
rally:

> "As the thousands walked away from the
> Memorial singing, he had stood at the
> deserted end of the platform, looking
> out over the grounds that were slowly
> emptying. Seeing him standing alone,
> Bayard Rustin broke away from a group
> of friends, went over, and put his arm
> around the old man's shoulders. 'I
> could see he was tired,' Rustin
> recalled. I said to him: "Mr.
> Randolph, it looks like your dream has
> come true', and when I looked into his
> eyes, tears were streaming down his
> cheeks. It is the one time I can
> recall that he could not hold back his
> feelings."

12

Our March is a march for America. It is a march just begun.

— Whitney Young, Jr.

The conservative Southern press reacted predictably to the March on Washington. The Birmingham News, still recovering from the spring disorders, had nothing but contempt for those who marched: "It is a blasphemy against constitutional government that ´take it to the streets´ once again has been the procedure, and this time on the door step of the federal government."

The Nashville Banner continued to see the March as some sort of unlawful threat, and urged Congress to resist the intimidation:

"... Congress ... still sits, it is to be hoped, mindful of legislative duties in the Constitutional pattern, neither denying valid individual rights nor abdicating a responsibility under the weight of mass coercion, accusation, and threat."

The Chattanooga Free-Press hadn´t changed its mind either about civil rights demonstrators: "The marchers were not primarily seeking to gain the civil rights for themselves but to deprive others of their civil rights so that the demonstrators might have what belongs to others." David Lawrence, the conservative columnist continued his attack even after the March had successfully concluded, calling it a day of disgrace for its effect on the American image, a "step backward in the evolution of the American system of governmnet."

But elsewhere, the March was widely praised and cited as the opening of a new age in race relations in America. The previously skittish were repentant: "All the head shaking, anxieties, and misgivings over the big march on Washington seems a little foolish today," said the Miami News. "This was not an angry mob that paraded down Constitution Avenue to the Lincoln Memorial. It was not a mob at all. It was an unbelievably good-natured gathering of purposeful people, assembled to stir up the conscience of America."

But for all the exhilaration, hope, and promise of the March on Washington, rather than producing a new period of tranquility and cooperation in America, it represented the end of a period in the civil rights movement, and indeed the end of a period in American history. This period of almost youthful innocence is perhaps more accurately bordered by another date three months later, November 22, 1963, when President John F. Kennedy was assassinated in Dallas. Thereafter, the 1960s and the nation itself moved with such frightening and violent fits of quest for change - and resistance to that quest - that all prior struggles seemed mild by comparison.

Those who in hindsight have termed the March on Washington a collosal failure, point to events which soon followed, notably the September 15 bombing of a Baptist Church in Birmingham which killed four young girls, or even to President Kennedy's assassination in Dallas. Such isolated acts of terror of course have no real relation to shortcomings of the March on Washington. Did anyone genuinely expect that extreme racists or violent reactionaries would somehow see the light, and miraculously change their ways, perhaps moved by the speeches and songs of August 28? The "failure" of the March on Washington lies much deeper in the collective psyche of America. It is a failure of spirit as well as expectations, the blame for which is not easily placed.

In fact, no one had even claimed that the March would magically bring an end to racist attitudes or bigoted resistance to Negro freedom. Such a suggestion would have been foolhardy of course. Neither did anyone have to wait until the September 15 bombing in Birmingham to realize that no magical alteration of American history had occurred. On their way home from the March, three busloads of Negroes tried to use the white restrooms, waiting rooms, and restaurant at the Trailways bus depot in Meridian, Mississippi, and a fight erupted between white and black youths. Over the weekend, on August 30, 1963, white suburbanites in Folcroft, Pennsylvania, outside of Philadelphia, attacked and harrassed a Negro family moving into a previously all-white neighborhood. The following Monday, September 2, Alabama Governor Wallace ringed a public school in Tuskegee with state troopers in another attempt to delay court-ordered integration. In Plaquemines, Louisiana, the same day, state troopers, city police officers, and sheriff's deputies used night sticks, clubs, tear gas, and cattle prods to break up two civil rights marchers, and arrest 68 persons.

On Sunday, September 15, a bomb was tossed from a speeding car into the Sixteenth Street Baptist Church in Birmingham, Alabama, which was crowded with children attending Sunday school. Four young girls died in the explosion, and there were 21 injuries. Civil disturbances ensued that afternoon, and two more Negroes died, one at the hands of a white policeman.

Only the intercession of Dr. King and Reverend Shuttlesworth prevented further rioting, even though King blamed Governor Wallace for creating the climate of violence, wiring him: "the blood of four little children ... is on your hands." In a rage at King´s telegram, Wallace washed his hands of any blame for the incident. The Birmingham bombing probably did much to quash the euphoria of the March, and to direct the civil rights movement down a different road: "the traumatic shock of the Birmingham bombing changed the texture of the Negro mood ... On all sides now, men raised demands for open civil disturbance."

In a fitful, yet sobering editorial, the Washington Star had breathed a sigh of relief on the day after the March that all had gone well. It warned, however, that too much should not be made of the March´s success, that progress for the Negro would be slow:

"In the day´s speeches one line recurred again and again: ´We Want Freedom Now´. It is important that all concerned understand what these words legitimately mean - and what they cannot mean. They cannot mean that the Negro is going to achieve full status in our system now, no matter who wishes it. If he expects otherwise, he is doomed to cruel disappointment ... Long after legal segregation is gone economic and social segregation will remain. The only process that ultimately can lead large numbers of Negroes out of their trap of frustration is the hard, slow, cumulative process of education. It

will happen, but not now. Not this
year, or next year, or in this
generation.

"All intelligent Negro leaders know
this. Though no one said it at the
Lincoln Memorial yesterday, they did
sing it. The anthem of this
revolution is: ´We Shall Overcome -
Someday.´ That last word was put
there by someone who knew the
difference between truth and
demagoguery."

Such an attitude was a challenge to young blacks
in the 60s, not a roadblock. Thus the battle
lines were drawn between blacks who felt that
slow progress was no progress, and moderates and
liberals who were content to let the system take
its course. The new enemies of progress were
thus harder to define, and harder to spot than
Bull Conner, Ross Barnett, or George Lincoln
Rockwell.

In the very week of the March, Louis Harris
was conducting a poll of whites for Newsweek on
white attitudes toward Negroes. The results
indicated that the legal prohibition on open
accommodations and equal opportunities for
Negroes would indeed fall shortly, but that the
harder problems of housing, job quotas, and
social attitudes would be a long time resolving,
if they ever would be resolved. More than
three-fourths of the whites surveyed nationwide
supported legal guarantees that Negroes have
equal job opportunities; access to public
accommodations; voting rights, "good" housing;
and integrated schools. Two-thirds favored
passage of the Civil Rights Bill. On the other
hand, 97% of the whites polled opposed giving

hiring preferences to Negroes to make up for past discrimination; the vast majority of whites opposed Negro demonstrations; and 56% opposed a Federal law barring discrimination in housing: "Of all the many great issues that totally divide white America and black America, none looms larger than housing. The white Northerner and white Southerner are adamantly opposed to letting a Negro family move into their white neighborhood." Twenty years later, white neighborhoods and black neighborhoods were still a reality throughout the nation.

Many disbelieving white Americans had undoubtedly seen the March and the speakers on television, and had become believers. But these late comers also hoped there would be no necessity for future demonstrations. Barely aware of the Negroes´ plight, their support was very thin and fleeting. Murray Kempton wrote in the New Republic a few weeks after the March: "If the March was important, it was because it represented an acceptance of the Negro revolt as part of the American myth, and so an acceptance of the revolutionaries into the American establishment. That acceptance, of course, carried the hope that the Negro revolt will stop where it is. Yet that acceptance is also the most powerful incentive and assurance that the revolt will continue ..."

Some observers saw the March only as a massive pep rally – as meaningless perhaps as some sporting event: "As a morale booster, the March was a stunning success. But as an exercise in leadership, it was something less than scintillating. The March was not coordinated with anything that preceded it or anything that followed it. It led nowhere and was not intended to lead anywhere. It was not planned as an event within a coherent plan of action. As a result, the March was a stimulating but detached and isolated episode."

While this lack of a coordinated plan may have been the way things turned out, it had not been so envisioned by the organizers. Rustin of all people was insistent throughout his career that any demonstration in which he was involved have specific obtainable goals. The March on Washington Committee had indeed specifically stated its demands and had had the marchers orally, en masse, pledge their support for the specific goals. After the March, there was much talk, and well laid plans for continued lobbying in Washington for achievement of the goals. Rustin had sent a memo to all his workers a few days before the March instructing them that they were all expected back at March headquarters at noon on the 29th. They would only have off the morning after the March. On September 5, Rustin urged continuing direct action in a memo to the Big Ten, including lobbying on Capitol Hill. A filibuster against the Civil Rights Bill by Southern Senators Ervin, Thurmond, Eastland, and others was anticipated. Rustin noted in his memo that a continuing March committee could produce 1,000 demonstrators a day for lobbying at the Capitol in the event of a filibuster. But minds were directed elsewhere, and competing camapaigns sapped resources and public attention. Rustin closed the New York headquarters when no support for his plans were forthcoming, and the ongoing lobbying never materialized.

A "Council on United Civil Rights Leadership" had been founded around the time of the March on Washington in order to coordinate and channel the energies of the major civil rights organizations as had the March on Washington. Whitney Young and a wealthy young financier, Stephen Currier were co-directors. It was to be well funded and to include the SCLC, SNCC, the NAACP, and the Urban League. By definition almost, it was to be too moderate to contain the energies of the long-frustrated Negro masses. This loosely organized "Negro Summit Group" fell apart after it vetoed a series of planned civil disobedience activities and ultimately called for a moratorium on demonstrations in 1964.

But the March on Washington did produce some results, and is generally considered to have been instrumental in passage of the Civil Rights Bill, which was finally approved by the Senate, after a lengthy Southern filibuster, on June 19, 1964. The final vote was 73-27. The House of Representatives passed the final Senate version on July 2, 1964, by a vote of 289-126. That evening, President Lyndon Johnson signed the Bill into law. Dr. King attributed final approval to the March on Washington and the Birmingham campaign. Others saw passage as a tribute to the late President Kennedy. In 1965, a major voting rights bill was enacted, which would greatly increase the enfranchisement of Southern blacks.

However, 1964 and 1965 would not be peaceful years. Each summer major civil rights legislation was enacted by Congress and signed by President Johnson. Each summer the frustration of blacks over their economic position in American society led to unrest and finally large-scale urban riots. Liberal legislation, a few black high level appointments, and a strong civil rights advocate in the White House would not be enough to solve America's racial problems. When Watts, Los Angeles' black ghetto erupted in 1965, it was the bloodiest urban riot in history. Even more damaging and deathly riots would follow in later years in places like Newark, Detroit, and Washington, D.C. itself. Floyd McKissick linked the urban riots directly to the "failure" of the March on Washington: "America also failed to understand the significance of the March on Washington in August of 1963. With one last plaintive cry, hundreds of thousands of Americans - white as well as black - descended upon the nation's capital to dramatize their needs. They were ignored."

"Although few realized it at the time - for the tone of that March was one of hope and optimism - much of the idealism and romanticism of the Civil Rights Movement died that day. For that demonstration culminated years of suffering and toil - and when that cry went unheeded, Black America began a revolution."

The failure to achieve economic and social progress in the second half of the 1960s is usually explained in terms of America's involvement in Vietnam. Certainly Lyndon Johnson's "Great Society" became bogged down, fiscally and emotionally by the massive war build-up that commenced in 1965: "The heady days of the 1960s did not last of course. A nation, a city, a people can afford to be generous until it hurts - and a nation economically strained by war and recession hurts. Laws and goodwill gestures did not cure economic deprivation. Great expectations slapped against the reality of limited resources. Integration theory was replaced by separatist theory."

Bayard Rustin argued later that "separatist impulses" emerged precisely when the need for a new and sophisticated approach to coalition politics was greatest. "Oppressed groups in

society - blacks, women, hispanics, the elderly,
even the handicapped, chose to assert their
causes alone lest their particular needs be
submerged by the coalition. Thus a home for
such a broad coalition, be it the Democratic
party or elsewhere, was nowhere to be found.
The March on Washington and the 1964 election
campaign were the last gasp for the great
American liberal coalition."

In the confusion of those years of the late
1960s, the dreams that Dr. King had articulated
on August 28, 1963, the hopes of the marchers,
white and black, appear to have been somehow
lost. Even though the nation was "at war",
there were still enormous funds being spent for
social programs. The need of America's blacks
were not totally ignored. Only now,
expectations, well deserved, had far outstripped
the country's resources. However, even if the
nation's resources were unlimited, it would be
presumptious to think that money could have
solved the nation's racial troubles in those few
years, and that 300 years of oppression of black
people could have been cured by President
Johnson's well-meaning programs. The upheaval,
rioting, and seeming separatism were in a sense
part of a catharsis that was long overdue for
America's blacks. The Kerner Commission, which
in 1968 inquired into the causes of the ghetto
riots that plagued the nation saw the March on
Washington as "more than a summation of the past
years of struggle and aspiration." It
symbolized certain new directions ... and new
demands from the most militant, who implied that
only a revolutionary change in American
institutions would permit Negroes to achieve the
dignity of citizens."

Many of those involved in the March on
Washington in 1963 would be dead within a few

years at relatively young ages. An assassin's
bullet cut down Dr. Martin Luther King, Jr., at
a Memphis motel on April 4, 1968. Former
Attorney-General Robert Kennedy met the same
fate in Los Angles two months later. Whitney
Young, Jr., drowned off the coast of Lagos,
Nigeria in 1971. Walter Reuther was killed in a
private plane crash in 1970 in northern
Michigan.

Two other participants, from opposite ends
of the spectrum, neither of whom supported the
March, would die of gunfire. Malcolm X was
killed by members of a rival Muslim sect in
1965. Nazi leader George Lincoln Rockwell was
gunned down by a dissident Nazi party member in
an Arlington, Virginia parking lot on August 25,
1967, almost 4 years to the day that he angrily
led his followers away from the Monument grounds
on the morning of the March.

Randolph, Rustin and Wilkins lived and
worked in the civil rights movement for many
years after 1963, Wilkins being the most active,
and a confidant of President Lyndon Johnson.
Randolph died in 1979 of natural causes, as did
Wilkins in 1981. Rustin became Director of the
A. Philip Randolph Institute in New York City.

As far as the organizations which sponsored
the March, they had a mixed record of success in
the years following the March on Washigton. The
SCLC, until and after King's death in 1968,
pressed the campaign for equality, notably in
the famous Selma to Montgomery, Alabama freedom
march in 1965. Under King's leadership and
guidance, the SCLC alone among the major civil
rights orgnaizations, was active in opposing
U.S. involvement in Vietnam in the later
1960s. The Urban League and the NAACP continued
their moderate form of leadership, which after

passage of the civil rights legislation in 1965
contained a more economic flavor. The NAACP
seemed increasingly isolated from the feelings
of rank and file Negroes whose militancy
increased as the decade wore on.

SNCC, and for practical purposes, CORE, did
not survive as major civil rights
organizations. By 1968, with the selection of
Roy Innis as its national director, CORE had
become a black separatist organization, not
unlike Marcus Garvey's back to Africa movement
of the 1920s. Innis even joined forces with
arch-segregationist Lester Maddox, the former
governor of Georgia. Maddox had first come to
prominence when he chased Negroes away from his
restaurant by wielding an ax handle. Maddox
later distributed ax handles as souvenirs in his
race for the governorship. Innis and Maddox
wanted to reinstate a dual "separate but equal"
school system. Innis and CORE also backed a
conservative member of a whites only country
club when he was nominated to a seat on the U.S.
Supreme Court by President Richard Nixon. Innis
reasoned that the nominee would be unlikely to
vote with the "integrationist majority" on the
Court.

SNCC had internal problems as well as
growing problems of divisiveness with the other
civil rights organizations. The schism may have
initially opened with the dispute over John
Lewis' prepared speech. In the fall of 1963,
Bayard Rustin spoke at a SNCC conference:
"Heroism and ability to go to jail should not be
substituted for an overall social reform
program." Rustin appealed to SNCC to endorse a
national call for economic relief to all the
lower class, and laborers, not just Negroes.
SNCC, however, was rejecting coalition
politics. The Lewis speech dispute had arisen

because of coalition politics. SNCC´s most talented member, Stokely Carmichael, had stayed away from the March on Washington, and the forces that sided with Carmichael within SNCC were in the ascendancy.

SNCC would finally break with the other civil rights organizations in the summer of 1964 at the Democratic Convention in Atlantic City. SNCC alone refused to support any compromise over the seating of a Mississippi Freedom delegation of blacks who were willing to pledge loyalty to the National Democratic party platform that, of course, supported an expansive civil rights and voting rights program. Most Democratic party leaders favored a compromise, seating both the black and a conservative white delegation. Wilkins, King, Rustin, and even James Farmer favored some compromise. SNCC was unwilling to go along again with any deal in the spirit of "coalition politics."

By 1964, SNCC was barely a "student´ committee, most of the campus chapters having withered away. Viorst described SNCC in 1964: "The cadre which then took over SNCC´s operations was more Northern than Southern, more sophisticated, its character formed more by the hard knocks of the urban ghetto than by the love of the Christian church."

The segregationists in the drama of the summer of 1963 did not fare badly in later years. After Senator Richard Russell´s death in 1971, his colleagues named one of the huge Senate office buildings after him. Senator Thurmond became a Republican in 1964 after passage of the Civil Rights Act, and was reelected in 1966 and 1972 and 1978. Senator Sam Ervin of North Carolina was reelected in 1968 before retiring in 1975. He became highly

respected for his role as Chairman of the Senate
Watergate Subcommittee in the summer of 1973,
the beginning of President Richard Nixon's
downfall.   Joel   Broyhill   served   Northern
Virginia in the Congress until defeated by a
liberal Democrat in 1974.   Senator John Stennis
of Mississippi was reelected in 1964, 1970, 1976
and   1982,   in   the   latter   election   with
substantial black support, the Senator having
publicly dissociated himself by then from his
earlier views on civil rights.

Perhaps the most successful segregationist
of all was George Wallace, who in addition to
serving several terms as governor, ran three
increasingly successful campaigns for President
in 1964, 1968, and 1972.   In 1968, he won 5
states including Alabama, Mississippi, Arkansas,
Georgia and Louisiana, making him one of the
most viable third party candidates in American
history.   Wallace's 1972 campaign looked even
more promising until would-be assassin Arthur
Bremer   wounded   and   paralyzed   Wallace   at   a
Laurel, Maryland rally in May.   The next day
Wallace won the Michigan and Maryland primaries,
but   his   injuries   ended   his   campaign,   and   he
supported   Republican   President   Nixon's
reelection.   In the late 1970s Wallace began to
publicly moderate his racial views, so that he
sought   and   received   black   support   in   a
successful comeback campaign for the Alabama
governorship in 1982.   He received more than 90%
of the black vote, and appointed several blacks
to his cabinet.   Indeed 20 years after the March
on Washington, America had changed.

In the spring and summer of 1963, there
were said to be more than 10,000 civil rights
demonstrations, and over 5,000 persons were
arrested for participating in them.   Dr. King
argued that "to measure the gains of the summer

by doing some social bookkeeping - to add up the thousands of integrated restaurants, hotels, parks, and swimming pools; to total the new job openings; to list the towns and cities where the victory banners now float - would be to tell less than the whole story. The full dimensions of victory can be found only in comprehending the change within the minds of millions of Negroes. From the depths in which the spirit of freedom was imprisoned, an impulse for liberty burst through. The Negro became, in his own estimation, the equal of any man."

But beyond its importance in the history of black Americans, the March on Washinton was a milestone in the history of the nation itself. It legitimized mass political protest as an acceptable means of political persuasion, after years of mere lip service to the constitutional guarantee of freedom of assembly to petition the government for a redress of grievances. Later, there would be those who would challenge that right consistently, but no one would be able to undo the precedent of the mass March on Washington of August 28, 1963.

Yet the critics persist, some drawing their fire from Malcolm X´s taunt of the "Farce on Washington" in his autobiography: "Who ever heard of angry revolutionists swinging their bare feet together with their oppressor in lily-pad park pools, with gospels and guitars and "I have a Dream" speeches? And the black masses in America were - and still are - having a nightmare."

Yet, whatever its consequences, however innocent in its dream, and whatever the motives of those involved, the March on Washington deserves better historical treatment than being written off as a nostalgic remembrance of the turbulent 1960s, or as a sell out of blacks to white liberals. Times change, issues change, but although he termed it "too late", no less a radical than former Black Panther Eldridge Cleaver recognized what he termed the "truth" of the March on Washington, a haunting truth, afraid it seems to ever again burst to the surface: "(T)hat this nation – bourgeois or not, imperialist or not, murderous or not, ugly or not – its people somewhere in their butchered and hypocritical souls , still contained an epic potential of spirit which is its hope, a bottomless potential which fires the imaginations of its youth."

That spirit undeniably lives on in those who marched on August 28, 1963, and in those who celebrated with the marchers while watching on television. It is also present in those who read and study the civil rights movement and who look for respite in the words of togetherness, equality, justice, and peace uttered from the platform that day at the Lincoln Memorial.

Chapter One

Page 1:   Dr. King quote: Why We Can't Wait, p. 121.

Page 2:   "In its dignity ...": Christian Century, September 18, 1963.

Page 4:   Randolph data: Washington Post, May 18, 1979, and Anderson, Jervis.

Page 4:   Sleeping Car Porters: Washington Post, September 2, 1982 and May 18, 1979.

Page 5:   "Unique because ...": Kempton, Murray, The New Republic, September 14, 1963.

Page 6:   Urban League: Negro History Bulletin, October 1963.

Page 7:   Wilkins data: New York Times, September 9, 1981.

Page 8:   "the noise and get the publicity...": Washington Star, June 17, 1963.

Pages 8-9:   CORE data: Meier and Rudwick, p. 146-147, 224; Rustin, Strategies For Freedom, p. 20.

Page 9:   "was approachable...": Meier and Rudwick, p. 146.

Page 9:   SNCC and King: Oates, p. 155 and 197.

Page 9:   Lewis: Viorst, Fire in the Streets, p. 95.

Page 10:   King data: Washington Star, April 5, 1968.

Page 11:   Rustin data: Oral interview with author; Brooks, Walls Come Tumbling Down, p. 222-223.

Page 13:   "Rising expectations...": Brooks, p. 191-193.

Page 14:   "that while Dr. King's street demonstrations...": Anderson, p. 324.

Page 15:   Hill's role: Norman Hill, oral history, Howard University.

Page 16:   "until Pharaoh lets God's people go": Oates, p. 213.

Page 16:   Most segregated city: Kunstler, Deep In My Heart, p. 174.

Page 17:   "committing his brutality openly...": Oates, p. 212.

Page 18:   Palm Sunday events: Kunstler, p. 179.

Page 18:   Good Friday: Brooks, p. 204; Kunstler, p. 185.

Page 19:   Recruiting children: Kuntsler, p. 189.

Page 19:   "when down through the years...": Brooks, p. 206.

Page 21:   "move from protest to reconciliation": Viorst, p. 220.

Page 22:   Rustin quote: Rustin interview with author.

Chapter Two

Page 23:   Sorenson quote: Kennedy, p. 503. Navasky quote: Kennedy Justice, p. 226.

Page 23:   NAACP to direct action, Wilkins arrest; Washington Post, June 2, 1963; Brooks, p. 215.

Page 24:   Demonstrations, week of June 7: RFK papers, JFK Library.

Page 26:   Danville and Cambridge: Washington Post, June 11, 1963.

Pages 26-28: University of Alabama showdown: Wilhoit, Politics of Massive Resistance, p. 196-198.

Page 28:   Clark, G. Mennen Williams´
              memos: RFK papers, JFK Library,
              May 15, 1963 and June 15, 1963.
Page 29:   McNamara quoted in Forman, The
              Making of Black Revolutionaries,
              p. 347.
Page 29:   Johnson Gettysburg speech
              reprinted in Johnson, A Time For
              Action, Antheneum, 1964.
Page 30:   Kennedy record: Oates, The
              Trumpet Sounds, p. 176-179, 197,
              207, 222.
Page 31:   May 24 meeting: Lewis, Portrait
              Of A Decade, p. 252.
Page 32:   "Recognizing the call...":
              Bennett, What Manner of Man, p.
              156.
Page 34:   Eastland is quoted in Sitkoff, p.
              158.
Page 34:   "Seldom has a chief
              execuive...": Chalmers M. Roberts
              in The Washington Post, June 13,
              1963.
Pages 34-35: Evers data: The Washington Post,
              June 13, 1963.
Page 36:   Warnings about violence in 1963
              "had been directed at
              Negroes...": Sorenson, p. 502.
Page 36:   June 11 press conference: The
              Washington Post, June 12, 1963.
Page 37:   Wilkins and Young initial
              reaction: Hill oral interview,
              Howard University.
Page 37:   "Everyone started getting
              panicky." Marshall oral
              interview, p. 915.
Page 37:   "Well, if we can´t stop it...":
              confidential source, interview
              with author.

Page 38:   Kennedy´s remarks quoted in
              Sitkoff, p. 160.

Page 38:   Accounts of the June 22 meeting
              appear in Schlesinger, Robert
              Kennedy and His Times, p. 363-365;
              Sitkoff, The Struggle For Black
              Equality, p. 160-161; Lewis, King,
              A Biography, p. 218-219, Anderson,
              p. 326-327; Brooks, p. 216-217.

Page 39:   Lack of early organization:
              Marshall and Kennedy oral history,
              JFK Library, p. 915-919.

Page 40:   RFK on Meet The Press:
              Transcript, June 23, 1963,
              courtesy of NBC.

Page 40:   Detroit Freedom Walk: Pittsburgh
              Courier, July 1963.

Page 41:   Night rally in New York, June
              25: Brooks, p. 221.

Page 42:   Wilkins objection to Rustin:
              Anderson, p. 324-325. Wilkins
              proved to be an informant of sorts
              for the Kennedy Administration,
              continuously assuring the Attorney
              General that communists were being
              kept out of the March. Robert
              Kennedy was convinced early on
              that Communists were trying to
              play a major role in the March in
              Washington, but was later
              satisfied that Wilkins and the
              other leaders would preclude their
              involvement. RFK oral interview,
              p. 919.

Page 42:   Aiken quoted in Brooks, p. 225.

Page 42:   The Washington Star Editorial,
              June 21, 1963.

Page 43:   Meyer quoted in The Nation, July
              27, 1963, p. 42. The Nation quote
              is from the same article.

Page 43:   Public accommodations section in
             Congress: <u>Time</u>, July 5, 1963, p.
             16.
Page 44:   Kennedy losing votes: <u>U.S. News &
             World Report</u>, September 9, 1963.
Page 44:   "Militant spearhead of the Negro
             drive...": Charles Bartlett in
             the <u>Washington Star</u>, August 20,
             1963. Bartlett was commenting on
             this attitude, not stating it as
             his view.
Page 45:   King quoted in Wofford, p. 177.

                     Chapter Three

Page 47:   Kilgore´s Church: Norman Hill
             oral history. <u>Business Week</u>,
             August 24, 1963. Swados, <u>Nation</u>,
             September 7, 1963.
Page 47:   "A lithe bundle...": Brooks, p.
             224.
Page 47:   Rent: MOW Comm. files.
Page 47:   "Visitors...telephone": Anderson,
             Jervis, p. 325.
Page 48:   Salaries: MOW Comm. files.
Page 48:   SNCC workers in Washington:
             Sellers, <u>River of No Return</u>, p.
             62.
Page 48:   Rustin reprimand to Brown: MOW
             Comm. files, Rustin
             correspondence.
Page 49:   Stokely Carmichael: Viorst, p.
             355. Edward Brown oral interview,
             p. 28.
Page 49:   "It was to be a confrontation...":
             Sellers, p. 62.
Page 50:   "Basically unrelated...": Sellers,
             p. 63.

Page 50:   Hill's role: Hill, oral inteview,
                  p. 18-19.

Page 51:   "Opening on a littered
                  backyard...": Swados, Nation,
                  September 7, 1963.

Page 51:   Description of March
                  headquarters: Rustin, oral
                  interview with author; MOW Comm.
                  files; Nation, September 7, 1963.

Page 52:   "Littered with piled papers...":
                  Business Week, August 24, 1963.

Page 52:   Assignments of staff, replies to
                  letters: MOW Comm. files.

Page 53:   Vickery letter and reply: MOW
                  Comm. files, Rustin
                  correspondence.

Page 53:   Non-partisan character:
                  Organization Manual No. 1, MOW
                  Comm. files.

Page 53:   Commercial proposals: MOW Comm.
                  files, e.g., Rustin letter August
                  19, 1963 to "Freedom Shirts."

Pages 53-54:   Horowitz, Posner: MOW Comm.
                  files. Posner interview with
                  author.

Page 55:   Working for Rustin: Posner
                  interview with author.

Page 55:   "We wanted to get everybody...":
                  Quoted in Viorst, p. 224.

Page 56:   "Who the hell...": Brooks, p. 224.

Page 57:   Meany's testimony is reprinted in
                  Brooks, p. 225.

Page 58:   AFL-CIO statement: Washington
                  Star, August 13, 1963. Brooks, p.
                  225.

Page 58:   Reuther and Randolph reaction:
                  Anderson, p. 327.

Page 58:   Meany's quote: Anderson, as
                  quoted in Brooks, p. 225.

Page 59: Radio editorial: WMCA, New York
City, August 20, 1963. MOW Comm.
files.

Page 59: APR Institute: Goulden, Meany, p.
341.

Page 59: "Almost overnight...": New York
Times, July 7, 1963. Quoted in
Brooks, p. 224.

Page 60: "A stooge for the Supreme
Court": Golden, Harry, Mr.
Kennedy and the Negroes, p. 192.

Page 62: Hedgemann quote: op. cit., p.76.

Page 62: Douglas background: Douglas
interview with author.

Page 62: Douglas' task force: Raywid
interview with author.

Page 63: Meeting with police: Raywid and
Douglas interviews with author.

Page 64: Douglas v. police dogs: Raywid
and Douglas interviews with
author. Tobriner oral history.

Page 65: "One of the reasons...": Mayer,
Saturday Evening Post, p. 76.

Page 65: Conway's role: Conway oral
history, JFK Library.

Page 66: Justice Department preference for
March: Raywid interview with
author.

Page 66: Cellar reaction: New Yorker,
September 14, 1963.

Page 66: Selection of date: Rustin
interview with author.

Page 67: Memorial dedication: Greene,
Secret City, p. 199.

Page 68: Patchwork segregation: Sansing,
John, The Washingtonian, September
1982, p. 100.

Page 68: Anderson at Lincoln Memorial:
Anderson, Marion, Oh, What A
Beautiful Morning. 1956 Viking

Press. <u>Newsweek</u>, September 9,
1965. <u>Saturday Review</u>, May 1,
1965.

Page 72: Rustin quote: Viorst, p. 225.

Page 73: Hoover racism: Garrow, p. 150.
Ungar, <u>FBI</u>, p. 327-329.

Page 73: "The Director fell back...":
Schlesinger, <u>Robert F. Kennedy and
His Times</u>, p. 366-367.

Page 73-74: Sullivan quote: Schlesinger, p.
367.

Page 74: King and Levison: Garrow, p. ·48
et. seq.

Page 75: RFK to Senators: Schlesinger, p.
373.

Page 75: Hoover and King: Schlesinger, op.
cit. Garrow, op. cit., p. 106.

Chapter Four

Page 76: Population information: Green,
<u>Secret City</u>, p. 318.

Page 76: "Population Exchange": Liebow,
<u>Tally´s Corner</u>, p. 4.

Page 77: Covenants in residential deeds:
Green, op. cit., p. 204.

Page 77: Suburban segregation: Green, p.
235.

Page 77: Racial classification in newspaper
ads: Green, p. 321-322.

Page 77: Integration of employment: Green
p. 315.

Page 78: CORE boycotts: Meier & Rudwick,
p. 188.

Page 80: 1962 City championship football
game: <u>Washington Post</u>, November
23, 1962.

Page 80:   Press downplayed racial aspects:
            Author´s interview with M.A. Jost
            and J. Tumulty.
Page 80:   JFK reference to riot: New York
            Times, January 25, 1963.
Page 81:   "One small disturbance...":
            Business Week, August 24, 1963.
Page 82:   1783 demonstration: Newsweek,
            September 2, 1963.
Page 82:   Coxey´s Army: Newsweek, September
            2, 1963. U.S. News and World
            Report, September 2, 1963.
Page 83:   Suffragettes: Zinn, A People´s
            History of the United States, p.
            336-337. Newsweek, September 2,
            1963. U.S. News and World Report,
            September 2, 1963. Washington
            Star, August 18, 1963.
Page 85:   Bonus March: Washington Star,
            August 18, 1963. U.S. News and
            World Report, September 2, 1963.
Page 85:   Glassford and McLean: Washington
            Post, July 28, 1982.
Page 86:   Passage of Patman bill:
            Washington Star, August 18, 1963.
Page 86:   General MacArthur: Washington
            Star, August 18, 1963.
Page 86:   1933 Marches: Washington Star,
            August 18, 1963.
Page 87:   Second Bonus Army: Washington
            Star, August 18, 1963.
Page 87:   Segregation in government:
            Greene, Secret City, p. 252.
Page 88:   Randolph quote: Viorst, p. 204.
Page 88:   Randolph´s seeking support for
            March: A. Philip Randolph Oral
            History, Howard University.
Page 89:   Madison Square Garden: Randolph
            interview, Howard University.

Page 89:   Eleanor Roosevelt and LaGuardia meeting: Randolph interview, Howard University.

Page 90:   Randolph/FDR meeting: Time, September 2, 1963. Randolph interview, Howard University.

Page 91:   "Outwardly incredulous." Greene, Secret City, p. 255.

Page 91:   "On the run": Randolph interview, Howard University.

Page 91:   Press reaction: Washington Star, June 25, 1941.

Page 91:   Randolph to Rustin quote: Rustin interview with author.

Page 91:   1942 demands: Chronicles of Negro Protest, p. 229-230.

Page 92:   1957 March: Viorst, Fire In the Streets, p. 212. Oates, The Trumpet Sounds, p. 119. Miller, Martin Luther King, Jr., p. 62.

Page 93:   King 1957 speech: Quoted in Oates, p. 121.

Page 93:   1958 March: Viorst, p. 212.

Chapter Five

Page 95:   Headquote, Dr. King, Why We Can´t Wait, p. 121.

Page 95:   Gradualism and tokenism in civil rights: Meier, New Politics, Summer, 1963.

Page 95:   Demonstrations in last week of June: Time, July 5, 1963.

Page 96   "Week by week...": Time, July 12, 1963.

Page 97:   Gwynn Oak demonstration: Meier & Rudwick, pp. 222-223, Time, July 12, 1963.

Page 98:   Fourth of July demonstations:
                Time, July 12, 1963.
Page 99:   NAACP convention: _Time_, July 12,
                1963.
Page 99:   "infiltration": Meier, _New
                Politics_, Summer, 1963.
Page 99:   Mid-July demonstrations: _Time_,
                July 19, 1963.
Page 100:   Reaction of white liberal press:
                Washington Star, August 6, 1963.
Page 100:   Barnett Testimony: _Time_, July 19,
                1963.
Page 100-1:   Wallace Testimony: _Time_, July 26,
                1963.
Page 101:   Rusk and Kennedy Testimony: _Time_,
                July 19, 1963; Wilkins
                Testimony: _Time_, August 2, 1963.
Page 102:   JFK July 17 news conference:
                Viorst, p. 225; _Time_, July 26,
                1963.
Page 103:   JFK August 2 news conference:
                Washington Star, August 3, 1963.
Page 103:   August 2 demonstrations:
                Washington Star, August 3, 1963.
Page 104:   Soviet Delegate's reaction:
                Washington Star, August 7, 1963.
Page 105:   Big Ten meeting of August 3: MOW
                Comm. files.
Page 106:   APR to reporters: _Washington
                Star_, August 4, 1963.
Page 107:   Demonstrations of August 3 and
                4: _Washington Star_, August 4,
                1963 and August 5, 1963.
Page 108:   Wallace musing about running in
                Maryland primary: _Washington
                Star_, August 14, 1963.
Page 109:   Governor Harrison quote:
                Washington Star, August 8, 1963.
Page 109:   Manassass exception: _Washington
                Star_, August 13, 1963.

Pages 110-11: Danville: <u>Washington Star</u>, August
8, 1963; <u>Washington Post</u>, June 11,
1963; Forman, pp. 327-331; <u>From
Race Riot to Sit-in</u>, p. 224.

Page 113: Rockwell and Nazis: <u>Washington
Star</u>, August 7, 1963; MOW Comm.
files.

Pages 114-5: Guardians and Hobson: <u>New York
Times</u>, August 23, 1963; MOW Comm.
files; Author's interviews with
Rustin and Posner, and Eleanor
Whittle.

Page 116: Radio communications: <u>Washington
Star</u>, August 20, 1963; Raywid
interview with author.

Page 116: Shriver letter: RFK papers, JFK
Library.

Page 117: Star reaction to Albany
indictments: August 12, 1963.

Pages 117-8: Albany: Brooks, p. 190.

Page 118: Americus: <u>Washington Star</u>, August
14, 1963.

Pages 120: ABA Convention: <u>Washington Star</u>,
August 12, 1963.

Page 121: Quote from <u>Political Affairs</u>
appeared in <u>National Review</u>,
August 13, 1963.

Page 122: Wilkins reply to Peking Cable:
<u>New York Times</u>, August 23, 1963.

Pages 123-4: Thurmond charges and APR and
Rustin Response: MOW Comm. files,
Posner oral interview with author.

Page 126: Home Rule demand: MOW Comm.
files; Rustin letter to George
Pendleton, August 20, 1963.

Page 127: Merchants placing stock in
storage: Author's interview with
Martha Suesse.

Page 128: Judge Smith statement: <u>Washington
Star</u>, August 14, 1963.

Page 128:   Medical preparations: <u>Washington Post</u>, August 16, 1963.

Page 129:   Episcopal bishop of Alexandria: <u>Washington Star</u>, August 14, 1963.

Page 129:   Eisenhower quote: <u>Washington Post</u>, August 16, 1963.

Chapter Six

Page 132:   Rustin quote: Rustin interview with Viorst

Page 132:   Jackson NAACP plans: Letter from "June" to Tom Kahn, MOW Comm. files.

Page 133:   March expenditures: MOW Comm. files.

Page 133:   Speaker system: MOW Comm. files, APR letter to ILGWU's David Dubinsky.

Page 134:   Meeting, burglary, cancellation of unemployment speakers: MOW Comm. files.

Page 134:   KKK rally: <u>Washington Star</u>, August 19, 1963.

Pages 137-8:   Congressional replies: MOW Comm. files.

Page 139:   Black congressmen: <u>Washington Star</u>, August 19, 1963.

Page 140:   Randolph/National Press Club: <u>Washington Star</u>, August 22, 1963.

Page 140:   Internal Memo: MOW Comm. files.

Page 142:   Women at the March: King, Corretta, <u>My Life with Martin Luther King, Jr.</u>; Oates, <u>The Trumpet Sounds</u>, p. 179-180.

Page 142:   Farmer at Plaquemine: <u>Washington Post</u>, August 20, 1963; <u>New York Times</u>, August 25, 1963.

Page 143: "Notice on the President...":
Washington Star, August 15, 1963.

Page 143: Attorney General addressing the
crowd: U.S. News & World Report,
August 26, 1963.

Page 143: Sorenson: Oral History, JFK
Library, page 42.

Page 143: Governor's conference: Baltimore
News Post, August 22, 1963.

Page 144: Dr. King and Insurance
convention: New York Times,
August 22, 1963.

Page 145: Beach resorts: Salisbury Times:
August 27, 1963.

Page 145: Letter to Star: August 22, 1963.

Page 145: Intelligence reports: Author's
interview with Hurlihy.

Page 146: Justice dissatisfaction with FBI
reports: Raywid interview with
Author.

Page 146: Justice "spotters": Author's
interview with Raywid.

Page 147: Reilly, Bruno, Murray: Author's
interview with Raywid.

Page 148: Electric organ: Washington Star,
August 30, 1963.

Pages 148-50: Executive Orders, riot contingency
plans: RFK Papers, JFK Library,
declassified, 1975.

Page 150: Gadsden Marchers: Washington
Star, August 22, 1963.

Page 151: Wagner controversy: New York
Times, August 23, 1963.

Page 152: Randolph reply re: Wagner, MOW
Comm. files, APR correspondence;
Hill oral interview, p. 20.

Page 153: Temporary hostels: O'Boyle and
Raywid interviews with author;
Washington Star, August 23, 1963.

Chapter Seven

Page 155:   Head quote: Bennett, Wade In the Water.

Page 155:   McIntire: Washington Star, August 27, 1963; McIntire, in the late 1960s and early 1970s, led several pro-Vietnam war marches in support of President Nixon's policies.

Page 156:   Malcolm X on radio: Washington Star, August 27, 1963.

Page 156:   Polo Grounds rally: Cumberland Evening Times, August 26, 1963.

Page 156:   Howard University rally: Washington Post, August 26, 1963.

Page 156:   Mrs. Evers: For Us the Living, page 341.

Pages 157:   Meet the Press: Transcript, August 25, 1963, courtesy NBC.

Page 158:   Posner press conference: Cumberland Evening Times, August 27, 1963; author's interview with Posner.

Page 158:   SNCC/NAACP dispute: MOW Comm. files; letter to author from Sheila Kessler Michaels.

Page 159:   Black media and logistics: Author's interview with Posner.

Page 159:   WMOG ads: Burke Marshall papers, JFK Library.

Page 160:   Justice Department Picketing: Michaels letter to author, Washington Star, August 28, 1963.

Page 160:   Hotel business: Washington Star, August 27, 1963.

Page 162:   Meeting at Statler Hilton: Author's interview with Bayard Ru tin.

Page 162:   Malcolm X quote: Washington Star, August 29, 1963.

Page 163:   Writing King's speech: Oates, pp.
                 256-257; Coretta King, pp. 236-
                 237.

Chapter Eight

Page 164:   Marshall quote: Oral history, JFK
                 Library.
Page 166:   Marion King beating: Carson,
                 Clayborne, p. 86-87.
Page 169:   "They left the church...": John
                 L. Barnam, Jr. is quoted in
                 Forman, p. 339.
Page 170:   Decisions about speeches; Rustin
                 interview with Author.
Page 171:   Drafting of speech; Lewis oral
                 histories, Michaels interview,
                 Rustin interview.
Page 171:   "Played it straight": Rustin
                 interview with author.
Page 171:   Statler Hilton meeting: Rustin
                 interview with Author.
Page 171:   O'Boyle's meeting: O'Boyle
                 interview with Author.
Page 172:   O'Boyle objections to speech:
                 O'Boyle interview with author.
Pages 173-4:   O'Boyle and desegregation:
                 Commonweal, September 20, 1963:
                 Author's interview with O'Boyle.
Page 175:   Initial change in speech: Lewis
                 interview with Carson; Lewis oral
                 histories, JFK Library, Howard
                 University.
Page 175:   "I didn't see...": Lewis interview
                 with Carson.
Page 175:   King to Lewis, Rustin, Randolph
                 comments: Oral histories JFK
                 Library, Howard University.

Page 176:   Marshall and Kennedy: RFK Papers;
                 Marshall and Kennedy Oral
                 History. JFK Library.
Page 176:   RFK call to O´Boyle: O´Boyle
                 interview with Author.
Page 177:   Blake´s objections: Washington
                 Star, August 29, 1963.
Page 177:   Randolph´s defense: Lewis
                 interview with Carson.
Page 177:   Sellers quote: River of No
                 Return, p. 65.
Pages 178-81:   Lewis speech: "March on
                 Washington for Jobs and
                 Freedom." Motown Records, 1963.
                 When the album was reissued in
                 January 1983, the Lewis speech was
                 not included; newsreels.
Page 182:   Nation quote: Swados, H., Nation,
                 September 7, 1963.
Page 183:   "Shook his Hand...": Miller,
                 Martin Luther King, Jr., p. 163.

Chapter Nine

Page 184:   Headquote: Wade in the Water.
Page 184:   New York City A.M.: MOW Comm.
                 files; Bennett, Wade in the Water.
Page 190:   Description of Union Station:
                 Time, August 25, 1982.
Page 191:   "During the night...": Washington
                 Star, August 28, 1963.
Page 192:   Nazi incident: Washington Post,
                 August 29, 1963; Author´s
                 interview with Herlihy.
Page 194:   Lulu Farmer pressure: letter to
                 Author from Sheila Kessler
                 Michaels.
Page 194:   Newsweek quote: September 9,
                 1963.

Page 195:	Capitol Hill meetings: Clarence Mitchell oral history, JFK Library.
Pages 197-9:	The day on Capitol Hill: Rovere, New Yorker, September 14, 1963.
Page 200:	Richard Russell on Meet the Press: Transcript June 11, 1963, courtesy of NBC.
Page 204:	Beginning of March: Posner interview with Author.
Page 205:	Hollywood contingent: Heston interview with Author; Washington Star, August 28, 1963.
Page 205:	Hardo and Marzhan: New York Times, August 29, 1963.
Page 206:	Statistics: Gollin, op. cit.
Page 207:	"Pressing against...": Washington Post, August 29, 1963.

Chapter Ten

Page 208:	"Backlash": Jet, September 17, 1963.
Page 209:	Heston meeting and quote: Washington Star, August 1, 1963. Heston interview with Author.
Page 209:	NAACP suit: Washington Star, August 2, 1963. Nineteen years later discrimination was still a problem. The NAACP filed a suit against the same unions for discriminatory practices on August 3, 1982.
Page 210:	August 7 meeting: Washington Star, August 8, 1963; Heston interview.
Page 211:	Baldwin vs. Heston: Heston interview with author.

Page 211:	Gadsden: <u>Baltimore Sun</u>, August 24, 1963; <u>Cumberland Evening Times</u>, August 23, 1963.
Page 211:	Apollo fundraiser: MOW Comm. files.
Page 212:	FBI calls to celebrities: Letter from Lydia Heston to Author.
Pages 212-3:	Mary Travers: Oral interview, Mary Travers with Author.
Page 212:	Freedom Singers: Baggeloor & Milton, <u>Folk Music</u>.
Page 214:	"The mighty Odetta": Miller, <u>Martin Luther King, Jr.</u>
Page 214:	Dylan, initial interest in civil rights: Scaduto, <u>Dylan</u>, p. 132.
Page 216:	Dick Gregory: <u>Nigger</u>, p. 211-212.
Page 216:	Ossie Davis skit: MOW Comm. files.
Page 219:	Lerone Bennett on Mahalia Jackson: <u>Wade in the Water</u>. Johnson Publishing Co., Inc. Chicago, 1979.
Page 220:	Rockwell quote: <u>Time</u>, September 6, 1963.
Page 220:	"Individuals with individual doubts...": Clark, <u>Freedom Songs and The Fold Process</u> "Sing Out." February-March 1964.
Page 220:	"This was not the kind of singing...": Lewis, p. 224-225.

Chapter Eleven

Page 223:	Television coverage: <u>Washington Star</u>, August 29, 1963; <u>Cumberland Evening Times</u>, August 29, 1963; <u>New York Times</u>, August 29, 1963.

Pages 229-30: Crowd size: Posner, Hurlihy interviews; Gollin, op. cit.; B. Sharp interview; letter from Woody Allen to Author.

Page 230: "Frighteningly tight packed assemblage": The Reporter, September 12, 1963.

Page 235: Illnesses and death: New York Times, August 30, 1963.

Page 235: Clerical garb controversy: New York Times, August 31, 1963.

Page 236: White Speakers quote: Miller, pp. 163-4.

Page 239: Data on Prinz: Current Biography, 1963.

Page 239: "Conclude that Prinz...": Miller, p. 164.

Page 240: "Pulling King´s coat": Posner interview with Author.

Page 241: Mrs. King´s recollection: My Life with Martin Luther King, Jr., pp. 238-9.

Pages 241-2: "It is impossible to describe...": Miller, pp. 166-7.

Page 246: "This was rhetoric almost without content...": Lewis, pp. 228-9.

Page 249: "In less than 15 minutes...": Sitkoff, p. 164.

Page 252: "a harried motorist´s dream of heaven": Washington Star, August 29, 1963.

Page 252: Meeting with President Kennedy: Roy Wilkins oral interview, JFK Library; Sorenson, p. 505.

Page 253: "He told the Negro leaders...": Golden, p. 163.

Page 254: Douglas activity and list: Douglas and Raywid oral interviews with Author; Navasky, p. 227.

Page 255:   "As the thousands walked
                away...": Anderson, pp. 331-2.

                   Chapter Twelve

Page 256:   Young quote: Speech on August 28,
                1963.

Page 256:   Adverse reactions reported in
                Washington Star, August 30, 1963.

Page 259:   King wire to Wallace: Wilhoit,
                Massive Resistance, p. 199.

Page 259:   "The traumatic shock...":
                Bennett, What Manner of Man, p.
                163.

Page 259:   Washington Star Editorial, August
                29, 1963.

Pages 260-1:   Harris Poll: Newsweek, October
                21, 1963.

Page 261:   Kempton in New Republic, September
                14, 1963, pp. 19-20.

Page 261:   "As a morale booster...":
                Bennett, Confrontation: Black and
                White, p. 242.

Page 261:   Rustin plans and memo: MOW Comm.
                files.

Pages 262-3:   Council on United Civil Rights
                Leadership: Bennett, op. cit.,
                pp. 242-3.

Page 263:   Dr. King's attribution: Where Do
                We Go From Here, p. 58.

Page 264:   McKissick quote: 3/5 of a Man, p.
                37.

Page 264:   "The heady days...": Sansing,
                Washingtonian, September, 1982, p.
                111.

Page 265:   Rustin quote from Strategies For
                Freedom, p. 73.

Page 265:   Kerner Commission Report, p. 109.

Page 266:   Rockwell death: New York Times,
            August 26, 1967.
Page 267:   Innis and CORE: Rustin,
            Strategies For Freedom, p. 20.
Page 267:   Rustin Speech: Ed Brown oral
            history, Howard University, p. 31.
Page 268:   SNCC unwilling to go along with
            "coalition politics":   Ed Brown
            oral history, Howard University,
            pp. 41-42.
Page 268:   Viorst quote: Fire In The
            Streets, p. 244.
Page 269:   Wallace 1982 comeback: New York
            Times, January 23, 1983.
Page 269:   Statistics on 1963
            demonstrations: Wilhoit, p. 198.
Page 270:   King quote: Why We Can't Wait, p.
            121.
Page 270:   Malcolm X quote: Autobiography,
            p. 281.
Page 271:   Cleaver quote: Soul on Ice, p.
            201.

SOURCES

I. MANUSCRIPT COLLECTIONS

Kennedy, Robert F. John F. Kennedy Library.
March on Washington Committee, A. Philip
    Randolph Institute.
Marshall, Burke. John F. Kennedy Library.
Randolph, A. Philip. A. Philip Randolph
    Institute.
Rustin, Bayard. A. Philip Randolph Institute.

II. GOVERNMENT PUBLICATIONS

Congressional Record, June-September, 1963.
Report of National Advisory Commission on Civil
    Disorders, GPO, 1968.

III. ORAL HISTORY

A. John F. Kennedy Library

        Conway, Jack
        Kennedy, Robert F.
        Lawson, Belford
        Marshall, Burke
        Mitchell, Clarence
        Rauh, Joseph
        Sorenson, Theodore
        Tobriner, Walter
        Wilkins, Roy

B. Lyndon B. Johnson Library

        Farmer, James
        Wilkins, Roy

C. Moorland Springarn Research Center,
Howard University: Civil Rights
Documentation Project

    Brown, Edward
    Fauntroy, Walter
    Hill, Norman
    Lewis, John
    O´Boyle, Patrick Cardinal
    Randolph, A. Philip
    Shuttlesworth, Fred

IV. BOOKS AND ARTICLES

Anderson, Jervis. *A. Philip Randolph,* New York. Harcourt Brace Javanovich. 1972.

Baldwin, James. *No Name in the Street.* New York. Dell Publishing Company. 1973 (paperback edition).

Bennett, Lerone Jr. *Wade in the Water.* Chicago. Johnson Publishing Co., Inc. 1979.

Bennett, Lerone Jr. *What Manner of Man.* Chicago. Johnson Publishing Company, Inc. 1976.

Braver, Carl M. *John F. Kennedy and the Second Reconstruction.* New York. Columbia University Press. 1977.

Brooks, Thomas R. *Walls Come Tumbling Down (A History of the Civil Rights Movement 1940-1970).* Englewood Cliffs, New Jersey. Prentice Hall. 1974.

Carson, Clayborne. *In Struggle: SNCC and the Black Awakening of the 60´s.* Cambridge. Harvard University Press. 1981.

Chambers, Bradford. *Chronicles of Negro Protest.* New York. Parents Magazine Press. 1968.

Cleaver, Eldridge. Soul on Ice. New York.
    Dell Publishing Co. 1968.
Dorman, Michael. We Shall Overcome. New
    York. Delacorte Press. 1964.
Evers, Myrlie. For Us: The Living. Garden
    City, New York. Doubleday Company, Inc.
    1967.
Farmer, James. Freedom - When? New York.
    Random House, Inc. 1965.
Forman, James. The Making of Black
    Revolutionaries. New York. MacMillan.
    1972.
Garfinkel, Henry. When Negroes March. New
    York. Antheneum. 1964.
Garrow, David. The FBI and Martin Luther King,
    Jr. New York. Norton and Company. 1981.
Gollin, Albert E. "The Dynamics of
    Participation in the March on Washington."
    Bureau of Social Science Research. May,
    1964. Abstract in Public Opinion
    Quarterly. Winter, 1964.
Gollin, Albert E. "Poor People's Campaign and
    the March on Washington: Mobilization for
    Collective Protest." Bureau of Social
    Science Research. May, 1969.
Golden, Harry. Mr. Kennedy and the Negroes.
    Cleveland. World Publishing Company. 1964.
Good, Paul. The Trouble I've Seen. Washington,
    D.C. Howard University Press. 1975.
Goulden, Joseph C. Meany. New York.
    Antheneum. 1972.
Grant, Joanne. Black Protest: History,
    Documents and Analyses. New York. Fawcett
    Publications. 1968.
Gregory, Dick w/ Robert Lypste. "Nigger". New
    York. E.P. Dutton and Company. 1964.
Harrington, Michael. The Other America. New
    York. MacMillan. 1962.

Hedgemann, Anna Arnold. The Gift of Chaos. New
    York. Oxford. 1977.

Hedgemann, Anna Arnold. Trumpet Sounds: A
    Memoir of Negro Leadership. New York.
    Holt. 1964.

Humphrey, Hubert. The Education of a Public
    Man. Garden City, New York. Doubleday and
    Company. 1976.

Johnson, Lyndon B. A Time for Action. New
    York. Antheneum. 1964.

Kahn, Tom. "Problems of the Negro Movement."
    Dissent. Winter, 1964.

Kearns, F.E. "Marching for Justice."
    Commonweal. September 20, 1963.

Kempton, Murray. "March on Washington." New
    Republic. September 14, 1963.

King, Coretta Scott. My Life with Martin Luther
    King, Jr. New York. Holt, Reinhart,
    Winston. 1969.

King, Martin Luther, Jr. Why We Can't Wait.
    New York. Harper and Row. 1963.

Kuntsler, William O. Deep In My Heart. New
    York. Morrow. 1966.

Lewis, Anthony and the New York Times. Portrait
    of A Decade. New York. Random House,
    Inc. 1964.

Lewis, David L. King: A Biography. Urbana,
    Illinois. University of Illinois Press.
    2nd Edition. 1978.

Liebow, Elliot. Tally's Corner. Boston. Little
    Brown and Company. 1967.

Malcolm X. The Autobiography of Malcolm X. New
    York. Grove Press. 1964.

McKissick, Floyd. 3/5 of a Man. Toronto.
    MacMillan Company. 1969.

Meier, August. "New Currents In the Civil
    Rights Movement." New Politics. Summer,
    1963.

Meier, August, et al. CORE - A Study in the Civil Rights Movement 1942-1968. New York. Oxford Press. 1973.

Meyer, M. "Lone Wolf of Civil Rights, Bayard Rustin." Saturday Evening Post. July 11, 1964.

Miller, William Robert. Martin Luther King, Jr. New York. Weybaught and Tally. 1968.

Moon, Henry Lee. "A Day to Remember." Crisis. September, 1973.

Murphy, Raymond and Elinson, Howard. Problems and Prospects in the Negro Movement. Wadsworth Publishing Co., Inc. Belmont, California. 1966.

Navasky, Victor. Kennedy Justice. New York. Antheneum. 1971.

Oates, Stephen B. Let the Trumpet Sound, the Life of Martin Luther King, Jr. New York. Harper and Row. 1982.

Rovere, R.H. "Letter from Washington: Day of the March." New Yorker. September 14, 1963.

Rustin, Bayard. "From Protest to Politics - The Future of the Civil Rights Movement." Commentary. 1965.

Rustin, Bayard. Strategies for Freedom. New York. Columbia University Press, 1976.

Rustin, Bayard. "The Washington March - A Ten Year Perspective." Crisis. September, 1973.

Saunders, Doris E. The Day They Marched. Chicago, Johnson Publishing Company. 1963.

Saunders, Doris E. ed. The Kennedy Years and the Negro. Chicago. Johnson Publishing Company, Inc. 1964.

Schlesinger, Arthur J. Robert Kennedy and His Times. Boston. Houghton and Mifflin. 1978.

Schlesinger, Arthur J. A Thousand Days.
   Boston. Houghton and Mifflin. 1965.
Scoduto, Anthony. Bob Dylan. New York.
   Grosset and Dunlop. 1973.
Sellers, Cleveland w/ Robert Terrell. The River
   of No Return. New York. William Morrow and
   Company. 1973.
Sitkoff, Howard. The Struggle for Black
   Equality. New York. Hill and Wang. 1981.
Skolnick, Jerome H. The Politics of Protest.
   New York. Simon and Schuster. 1969.
Sobel, Lester A. Civil Rights 1960-1963.   New
   York. Facts on File. 1964.
Swados, Henry. "Revolution on the March."
   Nation. September, 1963.
Sorenson, Theodore C. Kennedy. New York.
   Harper and Row. 1965.
Ungar, Sanford J. FBI. Boston. Little
   Brown. 1970.
Viorst, Milton. Fire in the Streets - America
   in   the   60´s.   New   York.   Simon and
   Schuster. 1979.
Walker, Alice. "Staying Home in Mississippi."
   New York Times Magazine. August 26, 1973.
Waskow, Arthur J. From Race Riot to Sit In,
   1919 and the 1960´s.   Garden City, New
   York. 1966.
Westin, Alan F. Freedom Now - The Civil Rights
   Struggle in America. New York. Bosie Books
   Inc. 1964.
Wilkins, Roy with Tom Mathews. Standing Fast.
   New York. Viking. 1982.
Wilhoit, Francis M. The Politics of Massive
   Resistance. New York. Braziller. 1973.
Wolford, Harris. Of Kennedy and Kings: Making
   Sense of the Sixties.   New York.   Farrow
   Straus, Giroux. 1980.
Zangrando, R.L. "Direction of the March."
   Negro History Bulletin. December, 1963.
                    V.   NEWSPAPERS

The Baltimore News-American (News-Post)
The Baltimore Sun
The Cumberland (Maryland) Evening Times
The New York Times
The Salisbury (Maryland) Times
The Washington Daily News
The Washington Post
The Washington Star

VI.   PERIODICALS

America, August-September, 1963.
Business Week, July-September, 1963.
Christian Century, August--September, 1963.
Commonweal, July-November, 1963.
Congressional Quarterly, June-September, 1963.
Crisis, September 1963, September, 1973
Ebony, August-November, 1963
Esquire, December, 1963
Jet, September, 1963
Life, June-September, 1963
Look, June-September, 1963
Nation, June-October, 1963
National Review, August, 1963
New Republic, August-October, 1963
Negro History Bulletin, October-December, 1963
Newsweek, May-September, 1963
New Yorker, September, 1963
Pittsburgh Courier, January-September, 1963
Reporter, June-September, 1963
Time, May-September, 1963
U.S. News and World Report, May-September, 1963

VII.   PERSONAL INTERVIEWS

David Bogen   Seymour Posner
Patricia Ciricillo   Alan Raywid
John W. Douglas   Richard Rodes
Charlton Heston   Bayard Rustin
Thomas I. Hurlihy   Barbara Sharp
James Jost   Martha Suesse
Mary Alice Jost   Mary Travers
Jean McRea   Joseph P. Tumulty
Patrick Cardinal O'Boyle   Eleanor Whittle

VII.   MISCELLANEOUS

Transcript, CBS News, August 28, 1963 and
     September 2, 1963.
The National Leader, August 26, 1982.   "19th
     Anniversary Issue of the Historic March on
     Washington."
Transcript, Meet The Press. August 25, 1963,
     June 23, 1963, June 16, 1963, The National
     Broadcasting Company.
Letters to Author: Woody Allen, Gregory Peck,
     Seymor Posner, Kathryn Kami, Elizabeth
     Kernen, William Kahn, Joseph A. Horn,
     Morrison Bial, Sheila Michaels Kessler,
     Jessica Davidson, John Lewis, N.C. Richie,
     Lydia Heston.

ABOUT THE AUTHOR

Thomas Gentile is a Washington, D.C.
attorney and instructor at Northern Virginia
Community College, Alexandria, Virginia.